Population Registers and Privacy in Britain, 1936–1984

Kevin Manton

Population Registers and Privacy in Britain, 1936–1984

palgrave
macmillan

Kevin Manton
University of London
London, UK

ISBN 978-3-030-02752-0 ISBN 978-3-030-02753-7 (eBook)
https://doi.org/10.1007/978-3-030-02753-7

Library of Congress Control Number: 2018958723

Cover illustration: © sorbetto/Getty Images
Cover design by Thomas Howey

This Palgrave Macmillan imprint is published by the registered company Springer Nature Switzerland AG
The registered company address is: Gewerbestrasse 11, 6330 Cham, Switzerland

For Sam, Dan & Evelyn

Acknowledgements

While writing this book, I received good advice from Alex Colas, Jason Edwards, Eric Kaufmann and Ben Worthy, and it is a pleasure to be able to thank them here and to state that they are not to blame for anything that their assistance has enabled me to do.

Similarly free of blame and definitely deserving my thanks are Emily Russell, Carmel Kennedy and Oliver Dyer at Palgrave, along with their production and design team, who accepted the proposal for this book and have steered it to publication.

The research for this book was mainly done at the UK National Archive, Kew, and I owe a huge debt to the staff there for their incredible efficiency, helpfulness and unfailing good humour.

Thanks are also due to Brett, Barry, Oscar, Gabriella and Stephen for their encouragement, support and friendship.

I would also like to thank the staff at the Home Office who, while I was researching this book, turned down my freedom of information requests to see material held by their department and who, in doing so, came up with a range of excuses that would make Sir Humphrey Appleby proud and which have kept my students amused. I would also like to thank these students, not only for laughing at these tales of bureaucratic flimflam, but also for being such an enthusiastic and inspiring group of people to work with.

Contents

CHAPTER 1

Introduction

This book examines the relationship between two countervailing political forces in Britain. These are, on the one hand, the government's desire to collect, collate, and deploy data about the people and, on the other hand, the people's desire to keep their own affairs private. The interplay of these two political currents is studied from the start of preparations for domestic defence in the build-up to the Second World War, until the passage of the 1984 Data Protection Act. The first side of this political relationship, the government's data gathering, is examined through a detailed study of population registration and systems that were recognised as being de facto registers. A population register is an up to date, centralised list of everyone in the country including some of their personal information, but particularly their current address. It needs to be regularly updated to maintain this feature and it is this that differentiates it from the snap shot impression of the population given by a census (sometimes called a static register). A population register is thus, in many ways, located at the apex of government data stockpiles and can be viewed as a bellwether of government attitudes towards the people whose lives are laid bare by this information. Population registers give each citizen a unique reference (usually a number). This can provide the basis on which ID cards are issued but, more prosaically, it can also allow governments to better control the data in the myriad files it holds on any given individual because, if files held in separate departments were to contain this individual registration number, it could be used as a master key to boost the efficiency of cross referencing between these different filing systems. However, this

K. Manton, *Population Registers and Privacy in Britain, 1936–1984*,
https://doi.org/10.1007/978-3-030-02753-7_1

fillip to administration can become a real shot in the arm if the registration number becomes a common number used for indexing files across all government departments. If this happens, government data can be recast into an interconnected, if not unified, matrix allowing those at the centre to draw together the various records of an individual's relationships with separate sections of the state to form an overall picture much more easily than would otherwise be the case.

If it is quite easy to paint a picture of what a population register is and how it can advantage the work of government, defining privacy, the other force in this political relationship, can be less straightforward, but one thing is sure, the mainstream of British political culture has long been clear that privacy means the absence of population registration. The British have a history of loathing registration, condemning regimes that used it and pitying the peoples who were thus catalogued. This is something on which many historians have commented. For example, Edward Higgs writes that: "the British public associated state identification with wartime emergencies, and with the identification of the criminal, 'Johnnie Foreigner' and subject races."[1] While Jane Caplan notes that "registration and identity cards have not normally been part of the [British] apparatus of administration" and Jon Agar points out how the tensions that developed within Britain over the use of "Prussian" methods to counter Germany in the First World War were an updated version of a hostility that had traditionally focused on the bureaucratic power of the French state.[2] These continental systems were contrasted by the British, to their own predominantly localised patterns of policing and record keeping, with Agar pointing out how these local, "partial registers" were lauded for preserving "Britishness."[3] Central to this institutional framework, which acted to reflect and reinforce these attitudes and so to preserve "Britishness," was a constitutional doctrine that was crucial to the way the events studied in this book unfolded. This was the understanding that when people provided the state with information, they did so on the basis that only the department that had requested the data would have access to it and furthermore that it would only be used for the purpose for which it had been solicited. This doctrine prevented the total linking of government databases and thus prevented the introduction of a population registration system by stealth, without parliamentary authority.

What the British feared would be imposed on them, were centralised records or registration to be introduced, was encapsulated in one word:

dossiers. This term resonated with sinister implications because a dossier did not represent a benign and objective index of a citizen's rights to political participation, or to receive health and welfare benefits, but rather this heavily loaded term indicated a malign, secret file of subjective comments about the person cached alongside details of the subject's opinions and behaviour. Dossiers, it was feared, would be the inevitable outcome of any enhancement of government data gathering, and dossiers would exist for one purpose only, to intimidate people into a condition of servile conformity under the state. Thus, writers at the end of the 1960s and into the 1970s, seeking to capture the essence of dystopian visions of the near future, would be as likely to refer to "the dossier society" as to *1984* or *Brave New World*.[4] As will be seen throughout this book, British advocates of population registration regularly despaired of these attitudes, describing them as being somewhere on a spectrum that ran from a childish fear of the unknown at one end, to an almost wilfully ignorant paranoia at the other. But the fact was that this was the public attitude with which proponents of population registration would have to negotiate. Given this, it is not surprising that population registers, along with the ID cards to which they are intimately connected, have only ever been features of British life during the two world wars. Indeed the fact that the wartime National Register was abolished in 1952 is often presented as a triumph for "Britishness" allowing a return to the traditional anonymity of the British citizen: a victory for privacy.

This book will question this narrative of the post-war abolition of registration, and show how, though popular attitudes were important in this process, it was the attitude of those in the state that was pivotal to abolition. But more importantly it will reveal how, in the mid-1960s, ministers and officials planned to reintroduce population registration (or a system using the common numbering of government files that they viewed as a de facto register) and how this process drew governments into a protracted war of position with popular attitudes as these coalesced into campaigns to defend privacy. In presenting the facts of what happened around government data gathering in this period it will be shown how, in the 1960s, the intellectual milieu of government came to accept that more data about the population was needed and that this attitude transcended party political boundaries to the extent that a policy, called *People and Numbers* (a plan to introduce population registration) that had been devised by Harold Wilson's Labour government in 1969, was embraced by Edward Heath's Conservatives. Moreover, not only did governments of all political stripes plan to increase their data holdings, they commensurately resisted attempts to bolster the people's privacy against data capturing forays into their day-to-day lives. It will be argued here that this policy of endorsing the reintroduction of population registration in the 1960s and 1970s demonstrates how much had changed in this area since registration's abolition in 1952 and that the roots of this volte-face can be found in the outlook of ministers and officials who, in the 1960s and 1970s, abandoned any defence of a traditional "Britishness."

As such this book will highlight policy continuities that cut across party divides. Political histories that cover sections of the period examined here tend to focus on one government, or one party, with the result that they do not draw out these continuities. Additionally, because interest in the topics covered here: data, privacy and (in broad terms) surveillance is relatively new, these topics are not usually raised by more general political histories. Thus, the literature on the Labour governments of 1945–1951 does not mention the issue of registration and neither do works on Labour in the 1960s and 1970s. These works similarly have nothing to say about the reform of government statistical services, and if they comment about government and computerisation it is on government policy towards the production of computers, not governments' use of the technology. Political histories of the Conservative government elected in 1979, or its predecessor in the early 1970s, are similarly silent on the subjects discussed here. But having said that, the copious literature on Thatcherism and the New Right does offer conceptualisations, such as Andrew Gamble's *The Free Market and the Strong State*, which can be used to aid understanding of the attitudes and behaviour of some ministers in the 1979 government.[5]

Biographies and autobiographies written on or by the main Conservative political players in these events also invariably omit these topics with the exception of a passing mention of computerisation in Margaret Thatcher's published diaries.[6] However, the issues at the centre of this book are sometimes raised in the autobiographies, contemporaneous journalism and published works written by some of the key Labour actors. Where any of these latter works discuss these topics, as in Tony Benn's diary coverage of the debates on privacy within the government in 1969, or Peter Shore's advocacy of open government, these need to be juxtaposed to a staunch advocacy of a "bold use of data processing" on Benn's part, and a key position at the heart of the government's data-gathering operations where Shore is concerned.[7] Similarly, Harold Wilson committed some of his thoughts about data gathering to paper and by interrogating his motives, along with those of some of his ministers and key officials such as Claus Moser and Michael Reed (the chief statistical officer and the registrar general respectively), this book will highlight the certainty among progressives that increasing the flow and scope of data was in itself a laudably progressive end for government.[8] This will be contrasted to other contemporaneous views of government data in general and of population registration in particular that expressed the public's chariness about allowing increases in the government's data stockpile.

However, recent interest in data collection has produced three books edited by Jane Caplan and John Torpey, Keith Breckenridge and Simon Szreter and Ilsen About, James Brown, and Gayle Lonergan that examine population registration systems.[9] Many authors in these books point out what might be called the positive side of population registration, highlighting how registration gave people access to the political and socio-economic benefits of citizenship and further, how registers could therefore become the site of political struggles rather than simply a method of state control and surveillance. However, this book is premised on the fact that such political negotiation or struggles between the registering state and the registered people can only occur in states where registration is used. This explains why the authors in these collections have not studied Britain in this period: they have written about registration systems, and Britain did not have population registration in peacetime. So what is studied here is not a series of struggles based on a functioning registration system, rather it is the struggle of the British state to introduce a system of registration, along with the earlier struggles of some political actors within the state to keep the wartime system in place in peacetime. Despite this central difference, between Britain and other states studied in these three edited volumes, it was nonetheless the case that those who wanted to introduce peacetime registration sought to use arguments of fairness and entitlement on the occasions when they attempted to make their case for registration to the British people. However, what is overwhelmingly obvious is that these would-be registrars of the British were not successful. It is the political relationship at the heart of this British exceptionalism and the course of events that unfolded on this political terrain that will be the focus of this book.

In addition to these works on registration systems, there are also histories that examine aspects of government surveillance or data gathering in Britain and points they make will be developed here. Thus, for example, Rosemary Elliot's work on the National Register in the First World War highlights the genesis of common numbering systems for files held by the British state, and Edward Higgs shows the importance of medical research and discusses the perceived need to link files across government departments.[10] These are themes that this book will explore in depth in the post-war period.

The period covered by this book includes the time when the government's use of computers increased and, in many senses, computers provide a link between the two centrifugal forces, privacy and registration, that are the focus of this book. Jon Agar has written about government computerisation in a work that views the technology as a continuation of earlier manual and mechanical systems for manipulating data on paper and punched cards.[11] He also draws out aspects of the significance for British society of this increased pace of government data gathering through the twentieth century.

It is not the purpose here to criticise or repeat the broad thrust of Agar's work, but rather to locate it in a wider political context. It will be argued here that when looking at this period it is necessary to keep in mind the fact that, though they were seen as the future of data processing, computers were less important to government than their paper-based records. Thus when, in the late 1960s, computers came to the attention of the public in the most negative manner conceivable: seeming to be the agents of the widespread creation of dossiers, government found itself in a real bind. On the one hand, it categorically did not want the negative attention that computers were receiving, but on the other hand, it needed to prevent this privacy spotlight from falling on its plans to increase the flow of data through its paper-based records, indeed it wanted to keep public attention away from anything to do with its manual records which still held the majority of its data. Thus, working out a response to the privacy campaign's focus on computers was not easy for government and involved a lot of discussion and some setbacks. That such a policy was nevertheless produced thus speaks volumes for the attitudes across government and Whitehall towards data. The broad policy eventually produced synthesised three elements. First, the government wanted to limit the scope of any discussion to purely technical issues arising from the use of computers. Second, it sought to restrict any external oversight of government computers to the absolute minimum, and third, government fixedly pursued methods to keep its paper records completely shielded from any discussion about its computerised record keeping. The outcomes of this work framed the response to the 1972 *Report by the Younger Committee of Enquiry into Privacy*, which Wilson had been obliged to establish by parliamentary pressure, it also underpinned the two white papers on computers published in 1975 and the 1978 report of the Lindop Committee that was set up to make recommendations towards implementing Younger's conclusions. In fact this thinking was ultimately the framework of the 1984 Data Protection Act. Thus, this book will indicate how, in this period, computers were more than technological devices promising vast improvements in administrative efficiency, they were also the central objects of political struggles within which the technology was used by those who advocated an improvement in the overall flow of government data (including, of course the proponents of population registration) to deflect attention onto technical matters and away from any debate about the power inherent in all government records.

The topics that are central to this book can be placed under the broad heading of surveillance, and examinations of this topic are often undertaken at a level of some theoretical abstraction and grounded in Michel Foucault's analysis of power in modern society. There are two ways in which this understanding is relevant for the purposes of this book. The first of these is the view of how power functions that Foucault explains through his analysis of the Panopticon. The Panopticon prison was designed to encourage the prisoner to modify his own behaviour by placing him into a system within which, though he was aware that he could at any time be under surveillance, he would never know if the guards were actually monitoring him at all. The aim of the system being that the prisoners should internalise the requirements of power, modify their behaviour and thus discipline themselves.[12] The second aspect of Foucault's work that will be utilised in this book is what he sees as the purpose for which Panopticon power systems are used in the modern world, this is the exercise of what he calls biopower, or biopolitics. Foucault sees biopolitics as the sum total of attempts to exercise power not over individuals, but rather over people as a mass, in other words: the population.[13] However, this process does not focus the gaze of power onto a population that already exists, rather the exercise of this power calls the population, as it is understood through power, into being. As Bruce Curtis puts it "population is not an observable object, but a way of organizing social observations. The concept emerges out of projects that seek to configure social relations so that these may be known and mastered."[14] Achieving this, as Curtis has noted, involves the government in gaining access to the abstraction of the population through increased access to the individuals who comprise it. In other words it involves the use of political technologies such as population registration.[15] This is not to suggest that biopolitics in Britain began with wartime registration or the attempts to reintroduce population registration into Britain in the 1960s and 1970s. This political tendency clearly had deeper roots. But it is to highlight the fact that population registration clearly belongs to this categorisation of devices that seek to know and master the population by affording the government concrete and practical access to individuals. Thus, this book will demonstrate how, in the 1960s, attempts to reintroduce registration were made for reasons that fit into Foucault's analysis, principally to know the people in order to improve them as a unit through the provision of welfarist policies.

However, Breckenridge and Szreter reject this analysis arguing that Foucault's theory is no help in understanding how the history of population registration unfolded, since for all his general observations about systems for monitoring and controlling the population, Foucault "pays little attention to the actual workings of registration, in any of its forms."[16] This presents an accurate picture of the nature of Foucault's work. However, it is important to note that having described the workings of the police in France and Germany as "the concrete form of this new political rationality," Foucault added "I think the meaning of the English word 'police' is something very different," and that elsewhere he was at pains to contrast the system he described and analysed on mainland Europe to "a much looser Anglicized system."[17] Indeed Edward Higgs has shown how the British General Register Office carried out its work in very different ways to its continental counterparts because it existed to provide data for different reasons: in Britain the office focused on providing data that would guarantee the rights of inheritance of legitimate heirs.[18] So while he might be criticised for not detailing the (for example) French registration system, Foucault cannot be taken to task for ignoring Britain since he had acknowledged that Britain was governed by a slacker system that was considerably different to the type he analysed in continental Europe.

Moreover, the best theoretical works on governments' relationship with data accept the limitations inherent in their more ahistorical work. Thus, though Bruce Curtis has written that: "national systems of civil registration ... developed unevenly internationally" and even though his work is premised on the idea that "there is a close formal connection between liberal democratic political forms, state administration, and statistical knowledge of the population," he nevertheless acknowledges that this can only be seen in "real social struggles that need to be examined empirically."[19] Additionally, Nikolas Rose is clear that understanding how the system he conceptualises actually unfolded, "would be a matter for a certain type of empirical investigation," one that examined the complexities, contingencies, local variables and illogical twists of this process.[20] This book is a work of political history that aims to present this empirical process in order to show how the efforts of British governments to both move towards a continental-style population register and to increase their use of computers played out within this comparatively "loose Anglicized system" and therefore, had to navigate a course around convoluted contingencies that were characteristically British.

Though this book's main aim is thus to chart and examine this troubled course of under-examined events, in doing so it will also draw out three interconnected reasons why Foucault's ideas can shed light onto why the complex chain of incidents presented here was initiated in the first place and how the main protagonists viewed their aims and objectives. First, because Foucault's understanding of power and how it works can give access behind the veil of scientific objectivity and a-political neutrality with which those who wanted the registration of the British sought to mask their policies. This will allow this book, following Curtis's work, to view population registration as "a political-scientific activity," an "inherently disciplinary practice [seeking]... to tie individuals to places within an administrative grid and then to hold them steady so that they may become objects of knowledge and government."[21] Second, this book will highlight the complete change of policy that occurred between the abolition of wartime registration in 1952 and its being propounded by government in the late 1960s, and in doing so it will argue that understanding both components of this contrast necessitates an examination of the thinking of the ministers and officials who made these decisions. Foucault's conceptualisation of bio-power illuminates these thought processes and so aids this exploration. Third, because the thinking that underpinned the drive to re-introduce population registration, in the 1960s and 1970s, focused overwhelmingly on policy areas such as health, welfare and education that are central to Foucault's notion of biopolitics. Though registration would have uses for the security services, theirs were never the main reasons for the government's seeking its reintroduction. Moreover, the Wilson government's moves towards registration were immediately preceded by attempts within the medical profession to create a unified, or at least more interlinked, system of medical records. This medical data push not only reinforced the intellectual climate in favour of the construction of webs of data up to and including registration, it also provided an architecture of records that key officials such as the registrar general, Michael Reed, sought to manipulate and use as a clandestine population register in lieu of the real thing.

Welfare is central to Foucault's understanding of modern power and the way welfare functions within this framework has been analysed by Nikolas Rose and Peter Miller.[22] They argue that welfare is a composite system, made up of a variety of mechanisms and arguments, which seeks to realise its aims by creating an interconnected web of knowledge to link hitherto discreet networks. This whole is designed to bring knowledge about the people, whose lives are to be the objects of policy, from the peripheries of the state's gaze to the centre of its focus so that they can be observed and understood and thus acted upon. In order for these processes to function, the knowledge has to be transferred in a standardised format meaning that the people's lives need to be rendered into statistics. The three watchwords of the data system that Rose and Miller place at the heart of welfare are thus standardisation, centralisation and linkage, and importantly this book will determine that these were the three main data policies pursued by British governments in this period, and that these condensed into the pursuit of population registration.

Various officials, such as the registrar general and the chief statistical officer, along with other civil servants had key roles in the unfolding of the events discussed here. Thus, it will be shown how, after the Second World War, most officials across Whitehall were either happy to see the end of registration, or were indifferent to its fate, yet by the 1960s and 1970s they, or rather their descendants in office, had become ardent proponents of the same policy. Given the importance of civil servants in these events, it might be thought that this was simply an example of bureaucratic mission creep and that this serves to highlight the warnings given by Max Weber of the power of officials. For sure it is true that a re-introduced population register would give officials power, but this acknowledgement deepens rather than explains the contrast with the official enthusiasm for relinquishing this power in 1952. This volte-face thus presents a conundrum and it is one of the main arguments of this book that in attempting to explain this dramatic change in policy, it is necessary to understand why these officials and their political masters thought they needed the data that could flow from registration in the mid-1960s when they did not hold this view in the late 1940s and early 1950s. Thus, though this book is mainly concerned with examining and explaining the complexities, contingent variables and twists of the politics of population registration and privacy in this period, this must be underpinned by an understanding of why population registration resurfaced in the 1960s, and it is here that this book will seek to deploy Foucauldian conceptualisations to understand what these later politicians and officials thought they were doing.

This is not to say that Weber's understanding of the dynamics of bureaucratic expansionism is irrelevant in these processes, but in probing the thinking of ministers, such as Tony Benn and Harold Wilson, two things become obvious. First, that they shared Weber's view of the efficiency of bureaucratic administration and lauded what they portrayed as the scientific objectivity of data and its gathering through systems such as population registration, but second, that they were impervious to Weber's cautioning that the same efficiency could also lead to a loss of freedom in society. Thus, while Weber argued that bureaucratisation could result in "the parcelling out of the soul," Benn maintained that the numbering systems of government departmental files held on all individuals were "liberating factors."[23] This can be seen as exemplifying a process whereby, as Nikolas Rose puts it: "once political power takes as its objects the conduct of its subjects … and takes the well-being of these subjects as its guiding principle, it is required to rationalise itself in particular ways."[24] But how and why politicians adopted this mode of thought and how they rationalised it are both, like the political environment that conditioned the choices open to them, something that can only be studied empirically. It is, in other words, necessary to look at the courses of action they advocated, what they thought they would achieve by these attempts to tighten up the relatively loose "Anglicized" system they inherited and how British political culture constrained them. This is how this book intends to proceed.

In examining these topics this book is divided into eight chapters, these are arranged as a chronological narrative and can be viewed as pairs. The first pair examines the national registration system used in Britain in the Second World War. Chapter 2 shows how the advocates of wartime registration never wanted it to be something that would only exist for the duration of hostilities. They planned to introduce registration before the onset of war precisely so that it would become a permanent feature of British life. When this plan was thwarted and the introduction of registration was delayed until war was declared, they laboured to keep the register alive into the post-war period. This chapter also explains how registration was introduced and operated. In doing this, it focuses on the central problem faced by the authorities, namely how to ensure that people kept the register informed of any changes of address and illustrates how this end was secured by tying registration to the food rationing system. The considerable friction this produced between the register and the Ministry of Food is examined, as are contemporary criticisms of wartime registration. Chapter 3 critiques the arguments that the register was an objective, scientific instrument and analyses why the registration authorities' desire to keep their creation alive in the peace came to nothing. This explores their attitude towards both sides of the registration equation: the people who were registered and the state that registered them. It argues that the two common explanations for abolition of registration in 1952, that it fell victim to austerity, or that it was abandoned under popular pressure, cannot completely explain abolition and that a fuller explanation needs to take into account the attitudes of officials and ministers in the immediate post-war period. This chapter will detail how most civil servants and politicians did not agree that government needed the data that could flow from a population register and so were content to see the National Register abolished.

Chapters 4 and 5 study events in the 1960s. Chapter 4 charts the development of the thinking that led to the resurfacing of population registration as a government strategy under Wilson's Labour government. Here this chapter will consider the roles of key reports in highlighting the paucity of government data and weigh up the contribution made by medical researchers who were drawing the same conclusions and thus fostering a mentality that was both very different to that across government in the post-war period and, as will be seen throughout the rest of this book, very resilient in its pursuit of data. It similarly demonstrates how this thinking led Harold Wilson to set up a committee to realise his government's data ambitions and it interrogates the motives of those politicians and officials involved to establish how these ideas conformed to what Foucault described as biopolitical thinking. This committee, the Statistical Policy Committee, advocated both population registration and the common numbering of files and this chapter will determine how the committee imagined it could deal with popular hostility towards these developments. The chapter concludes by considering the role envisaged for computerisation in these plans: how the technology could increase the standardisation, centralisation and linking of data, and further considers the extent of computerisation within government at the time. The following chapter concentrates on how these government policy initiatives were brought together in a draft Green Paper called *People and Numbers*. This presented and justified government plans to introduce population registration and the common numbering of files into Britain. After surveying this plan, this chapter shows how Wilson reluctantly postponed its advance in the face of mounting public and parliamentary interest in the issue of privacy. As a result of this privacy campaign, the government was eventually backed into a corner where, in 1970, it had to set up the Younger Committee on Privacy. This chapter details how the government tried to neuter this committee and how the attitudes and plans of the Labour government were shared by its Conservative successor to such an extent that *People and Numbers* resurfaced, only to be submerged by another flare up of the agitation around privacy.

Chapters 6 and 7 investigate events around the Younger Committee and its 1972 report. Chapter 6 scrutinises the social survey undertaken by Younger, it assesses what this revealed about public attitudes and, more importantly, it establishes how these survey returns were interpreted by the committee and the government as bolstering their shared view that it was impossible to define privacy and that, therefore, a general right of privacy was a chimera. This chapter also examines the public's fearful attitude towards computerisation and how this was articulated through dystopian projections of the increased dossier-building potential these machines would offer government. These concerns are discussed in relation to people's overall fears of the government amassing data and, from the other side of the equation, to government's awareness that the people were wary not only of computers, but of all data stockpiles. This chapter thus begins this book's survey of how government worked to keep the spotlight of privacy campaigners turned away from its paper-based records. Chapter 7 builds on this by analysing the feverish efforts of a government committee that, working in parallel to Younger, set out to achieve this strategic objective. This body, the Graham-Harrison Committee, refined and condensed government policy and buttressed the political decision to exclude all the government's paper-based records from any oversight regime that might be established by Younger. These officials strained to keep the attention of privacy campaigners focused onto purely technical issues connected to computerisation, thus depoliticising the issue of government data stocks and their use. Their difficulties in achieving these ends are illustrated by the problems that flowed from an intervention by the prime minister, Edward Heath. But the resolve of data's defenders is illustrated by the effective response of officials to this setback.

The final pair of chapters follows the twists of the narrative up to the passing of the 1984 Data Protection Act. Chapter 8 begins with an appraisal of the Labour government's attempts to draft white papers on computers, a policy driven by Alex Lyon, a junior minster at the Home Office, and his advisor, Paul Sieghart. Discussion here shows how their proposals were severely diluted by the input of a Whitehall that was now solidly behind attempts to enlarge and consolidate government data and how this pressure formed the basis of the two white papers on computers produced by the government in 1975. This discussion of these white papers details the fundamental dishonesty of much of their contents and then moves to review the nature of the Lindop Committee, established in July 1976 to provide practical guidance in setting up the Data Protection Authority envisaged by Younger. This chapter explains how and why this committee suggested a form of data protection that was unacceptable to government and why the advent of Jim Callaghan as prime minister and Merlyn Rees as home secretary made its December 1978 report irrelevant. The last chapter follows the reception of the Lindop Committee's report by the Thatcher government. This government initially focused on the security implications of data protection, but quickly shifted its attention onto what it portrayed as the report's constitutional implications. Given this level of hostility, which replicated that of the preceding Labour government, this chapter asks why this government passed the 1984 Data Protection Act at all. The answer is found in the 1980 *European Convention for the Protection of Individual with Regard to the Automatic Processing of Data*, which obliged signatories, such as Britain, to take some action on data protection. However, the government's initial proposals were substantially altered by the intervention of ardent free marketers in the cabinet, the debates started by this intervention, which led to a greatly reduced role for the data registrar, are analysed here. The book concludes by demonstrating how the 1984 act protected government data by: giving ministers carte blanche to place data beyond the remit of the Date Protection Authority by defining it as pertaining to national security and, more importantly, by finally enshrining into legislation a formula that ruled out any oversight of the government's paper-based data by fixing the focus of debate firmly onto the technical issues of computerisation.

Notes

1. Edward Higgs, "Consuming Identity and Consuming the State in Britain Since c.1750," in *Identification and Registration Practices in Transnational Perspective: People, Papers and Practices*, eds. Ilsen About, James Brown, and Gayle Lonergan (Basingstoke: Palgrave, 2013), 177.
2. Jane Caplan, "'This or That Particular Person': Protocols of Identification in Nineteenth-Century Europe," in *Documenting Individual Identity: The Development of State Practices in the Modern World*, eds. Jane Caplan and John Torpey (Princeton: Princeton University Press, 2001), 64; Jon Agar, "Modern Horrors: British Identity and Identity Cards," in *Documenting Individual Identity*, eds. Jane Caplan and John Torpey, 103.
3. Jon Agar, *The Government Machine: A Revolutionary History of the Computer* (London: Massachusetts Institute of Technology Press, 2003), 137.
4. See, for example, Arthur R. Miller, *The Assault on Privacy: Computers, Data Banks, and Dossiers* (Ann Arbor: University of Michigan Press, 1971).
5. Andrew Gamble, *The Free Economy and the Strong State: The Politics of Thatcherism* (Basingstoke: Macmillan, 1988).
6. Margaret Thatcher, *The Downing Street Years* (London: HarperCollins, 1993).
7. When he was first elected and held government office Benn was known as Anthony Wedgewood Benn. For the sake of simplicity he is referred to as Tony Benn throughout the text of this book, but in endnotes where necessary, his name is given in the form of the publication. Tony Benn, *Out of the Wilderness: Diaries 1963–67* (London: Hutchinson, 1987); Anthony Wedgewood Benn, *The Regeneration of Britain* (London: Victor

Gollancz, 1965); Peter Shore, *Entitled to Know* (London: MacGibbon and Lee, 1966); TNA HN 1/60, *Data Protection in Government, Memorandum by the Minister of Technology*, 4 March 1969, 6.

8. Harold Wilson, *The New Britain: Labour's Plan Outlined by Harold Wilson* (London: Penguin, 1964); Harold Wilson, *Purpose in Politics: Selected Speeches by Rt Hon. Harold Wilson* (London: Weidenfeld and Nicolson, 1964); Harold Wilson, "Statistics and Decision-Making in Government—Bradshaw Revisited," *Journal of the Royal Statistical Society. Series A* 136 (1973): 1–20; Harold Wilson, *The Governance of Britain* (London: Sphere, 1977).
9. Caplan and Torpey, eds., *Documenting Individual Identity*; Keith Breckenridge and Simon Szreter, eds. *Registration and Recognition: Documenting the Person in World History* (Oxford: Oxford University Press, 2012); About, Brown, and Lonergan, eds. *Identification and Registration Practices.*
10. Rosemary Elliot, "An Early Experiment in National Identity Cards: The Battle Over Registration in the First World War," *Twentieth Century British History* 17 (2006): 145–76; Edward Higgs, "Medical Statistics, Patronage and the State: The Development of the MRC Statistical Unit, 1911–1948," *Medical History* 44 (2000): 323–40.
11. Agar, *The Government Machine.*
12. Michel Foucault, *Discipline and Punish: The Birth of the Prison* (London, Penguin, 1991), 201.
13. Michel Foucault, *Society Must Be Defended* (London: Penguin, 2004), 246.
14. Bruce Curtis, *The Politics of Population: State Formation, Statistics, and the Census of Canada, 1840–1875* (London: University of Toronto Press, 2001), 24.
15. Ibid., 40.
16. Ibid., 7.
17. Michel Foucault, *Power: Essential Works of Michel Foucault 1954–1984*, ed. James D. Faubion (London: Penguin, 2002), 410; Michel Foucault, *The Birth of the Clinic* (London: Routledge, 1989), 48.
18. Edward Higgs, *Life, Death and Statistics: Civil Registration, Censuses and the Work of the General Record Office, 1836–1952* (Hatfield: Local Population Studies, 2004).
19. Curtis, *The Politics of Population*, 36; Bruce Curtis, "Foucault on Governmentality and Population: The Impossible Discovery," *The Canadian Journal of Sociology* 27 (2002): 530.
20. Nikolas Rose, *Powers of Freedom: Reframing Political Thought* (Cambridge: Cambridge University Press, 1999), 19 and 210.

21. Curtis, *The Politics of Population*, 27 and 26.
22. Nikolas Rose and Peter Miller, "Political Power Beyond the State: Problematics of Government," *The British Journal of Sociology* 43 (1992): 173–203.
23. Max Weber, in David Beetham, *Max Weber and the Theory of Modern Politics* (London: Polity, 1985), 81; Benn, *The Regeneration of Britain*, 15.
24. Rose, *Powers of Freedom*, 7.

CHAPTER 2

The Wartime System of National Registration

The period covered by this book includes thirteen years when Britain had a population register. These were the years of the Second World War and the immediate post-war period, and this chapter covers the first segment of this time, up to the end of the war. The first section of this chapter details the thinking of those who designed and would run the wartime system and how, from the beginning of their planning, they wanted the register to become a permanent feature of British society. This discussion focuses on their understanding of the biggest problem they anticipated would arise in operating a population register: how to oblige British people to provide updates of their address every time they moved. Having detailed this, the section concludes by examining a Whitehall argument over control of the proposed wartime registration system.

The second section provides an overview of how the wartime system was introduced on the outbreak of hostilities and then surveys how the system worked, covering the tussles between the registration authorities and the Ministry of Food, upon whose rationing system the register depended for notifications of changes of address. This section also presents contemporary press criticisms of the National Register and how the registration authorities responded to these and concludes by showing the remarkably high level of public compliance with the demands of wartime registration.

The last section of this chapter returns to the main theme, that the authorities wanted registration to become a permanent feature of British

K. Manton, *Population Registers and Privacy in Britain, 1936–1984*,
https://doi.org/10.1007/978-3-030-02753-7_2

life, and examines how, as the war drew to a close, they thought that the people could become habituated to the strictures of permanent registration. This section concludes by showing how closely this thinking compares to that of Michel Foucault's analysis of the panoptic nature of power in modern society.

Planning to Number the People

British pre-war defence planning began in early 1936 when, as the international situation deteriorated, Parliament debated the need to have a figure to coordinate the armed services. As a result, on 13 March, the government announced the move of the attorney general, Sir Thomas Inskip, to the new post of minister for the coordination of defence. Inskip established a series of committees to plan aspects of the country's defence some of which, such as the system for food distribution and rationing, as will be seen in the next section of this chapter, barely existed even on paper when war broke out. However, the pre-war planning of national registration was a world away from this ramshackle disorder because it was marshalled by a long-established and indefatigable advocate of the cause of registration in Whitehall; this was the registrar general, Sylvanus Vivian. His would be the agency that ran the wartime system of registration, and in 1936, he wrote a lengthy memorandum that set out his thinking and raised issues that would remain central to debates about registration throughout the period covered by this book.[1] This memorandum covered four main aspects of population registration. First, Vivian presented the case for establishing registration rather than relying on any other set of records. Second, he outlined the practical and political problems inherent in doing this. Third, he suggested methods to convince a reluctant population of the benefits of registration and, perhaps mindful of the paucity of these inducements, he outlined how such a system could be enforced. Fourth, he described some of the main operational features of his proposed system. In this document, Vivian made it plain that he not only wanted this system established before the onset of war, he also wanted it to remain after the war ended. He advocated making population registration a permanent fact of life for the British people and his views will now be examined in more detail.

The first thing Vivian did was to stake out a claim on behalf of population registration in order to establish its superiority over rival systems. The National Register was to be a centralised list that would contain items of personal information, most importantly the address, of everyone in the country, which would be used to provide people with an identity card. Immigration records, the registration of births, marriages and deaths along with the military's enlistment records already covered particular aspects of population changes; thus, the "real and formidable difficulty" was how to keep track of people if they changed address.[2] Here, Vivian looked at the example of the British 1911 medical insurance scheme and the lessons he drew from this informed his own plans. This earlier system had suffered from the major shortcoming that if an insured person moved to a new area there was not any mechanism for guaranteeing that his record would move with him. He could present himself in this new district and demand benefits without his record being updated since this might never be found. Despite this, the earlier record would remain in the system even though a new one would have been started by his subsequent claim. This duplication thus led to statistical inflation within the system. This system covered about eleven million people, but what Vivian described as the "notorious" and "makeshift" system based on this insurance scheme that was introduced in the First World War had a greater coverage and so amplified this basic problem.[3] Indeed, Vivian reported a survey from that earlier period that suggested that registers were inaccurate by as much as 50%.[4] The dangers inherent in this system were that a government relying on such information might not know how many people were eligible for conscription or might be unable to find many of them.

Having thus, to his own satisfaction at least, established that his proposed system was the only one that was fit for purpose he, second, confronted the problems it might encounter. Vivian understood that during a war registration would be linked to the food rationing system since an identity card, issued by the registration authorities, would be the prerequisite for receiving rations. Thus, in addition to the wartime population's "patriotic motives," the authorities could rely on a card being "treasured" by its owner for personal and practical reasons and could therefore rely on people to notify the authorities of any change of address.[5] However, Vivian wanted the system to be introduced in peacetime and this raised the "real danger that they [identity cards] would be forgotten and neglected" or worse; if there were a long period of peace after their issue, they might be "lost or mislaid on a wholesale scale."[6] In addition to this, Vivian had to face up to a bigger problem than indifference or forgetfulness: popular opposition to registration. Like many

British advocates of registration, Vivian admired the continental registration systems that provided governments with a permanent flow of statistical information about the population. Indeed, this is exactly what he wanted, writing that if registration were established in peace "it must be regarded as a permanent peacetime institution."[7] But in 1936, he admitted that such a system of registration "would not meet with much popular welcome" in Britain where registration was "not a common and regular feature of administration."[8] A year later he chaired the Subcommittee on National Registration, reporting ultimately to the Committee of Imperial Defence (CID), and wrote in his report "of the risk of passive resistance or organised obstruction arising out of political hostility to a measure of peacetime National Registration."[9] This potential hostility towards peacetime registration meant that the system would need to insinuate itself into existing social, political and economic relations and institutions in order to derive what Vivian termed a "parasitic vitality" from them.[10] This would be necessary because, with the population permanently in flux, public compliance was essential if the register was to be a live record. The authorities would need the people to notify them of any change in their address, and this cooperation could not be taken for granted in Britain the way it might in much of the rest of Europe where people were already conditioned to conformity with the constraints of registration.

Given his understanding of this latent opposition, Vivian went on to describe the carrots and sticks that could be applied to the British people to encourage them to fall in line behind the system. The first aspect, its positive side, has been highlighted by many of the authors in the three books edited by Jane Caplan and John Torpey, Keith Breckenridge and Simon Szreter, and Ilsen About, James Brown and Gayle Lonergan.[11] These works highlight how registration gave people access to the political and socio-economic benefits of citizenship and further, how registration could therefore become the means of political struggle, rather than simply a method of state control and domination. Though David Lyon cautions against overstating this case, it must be accepted that registration systems were, at least potentially, a double-edged sword for the authorities.[12] But political negotiation or struggles between the registering state and the registered people can only exist where registration is in place. Indeed, not only can positive benefits be attained only through a registration system that actually exists, the British case also highlights how difficult it was to imagine what these benefits might be before the system was up and running. Thus, even Vivian could not see much that could be described as a positive benefit, for the ordinary British person, of the system he wanted to introduce in Britain.

In trying to come up with positive aspects of registration, Vivian mentioned a point studied by Jon Agar: the "curious" and often-noted fact that registration would virtually eradicate bigamy.[13] However, true as this might be, he also discounted it, writing that this could hardly be used as the sole justification for registration. He also discarded the fact that registration would provide data about the population to the government as something that would make the system appeal to the people, since it was precisely the thought that this flow of information might increase, to the extent that it would allow government to compile dossiers on individuals, that worried the British. Once these had been discounted, Vivian was left with only four things he could offer that might favourably dispose the public towards a permanent system. The first of these was that that it would facilitate coordination between different branches of the social services. But whether the British would actually appreciate this increased coordination was surely a moot point since it would have depended entirely on how the outcome of this improved efficiency impacted on the individual concerned. His other three positive benefits to this system were all, even in his own words, rather vague and had, at best, only a tenuous relationship to individual citizens. They were: first that pension and annuity paying bodies might get notice of the death of their customers, second that the register might protect the Post Office Savings Bank from some forms of fraud and last that it "might provide a usefully framed identity document for other questions of identity and proof of age [that are] perpetually arising."[14]

It is thus immediately obvious that even as staunch an advocate of registration as Vivian could not produce a list of positive features of the system to endear it to the people: a problem that would arise again and again as discussions around registration resurfaced in the post-war period. This meant that in order to get the system he wanted in peacetime, Vivian had to focus his attention on ways to cajole or coerce people into using the register. Here, he met the fundamental challenges head on. The problems, whether rooted in the people's slipshod attitude towards notifying the authorities of a change of address, or in a principled opposition to registration, would have to be tackled. Thus, if the register were "strengthened by supplementary measures and stringently enforced in practice … the people might become so educated into the habit of notifying changes of address that the difficulties and dangers of incomplete maintenance might largely disappear." Anything less than this stringent enforcement could, he argued, be disastrous because: "if the problem of maintenance is tackled in a half-hearted way … without that obligation being effectively reinforced by other measures, and if the penalisation of non-compliance is shirked for political or other reasons … the register would become … ineffective for its primary war purpose."[15]

By "supplementary measures" Vivian meant encouraging or obliging the use of registration documents in a wide variety of interactions to further increase the system's parasitic vitality. In this pre-war period, Vivian was at pains to point out that the system would work better if the obligation to oversee its use by ordinary people were placed on the more responsible sections of society. Here, he repeated arguments that Margaret Elliot shows he had used during the First World War, advocating again that all employers be obliged to record the registration numbers of their staff and requiring landlords, letting agents and people taking in lodgers to act similarly with their tenants.[16] Additionally, Vivian suggested that all educational establishments and banks do likewise with their pupils, students or customers. Furthermore, the granting of licences, the registration of businesses or of professional status, claims for public assistance and the registration of births, marriages and deaths should also, Vivian suggested, be made conditional on production of national registration details.[17] The purpose of this was twofold. First, to encourage people to use the system and second, by doing so to make them aware that any change of address would be noticed, and thus had they not already reported it, that their recalcitrance would come to the attention of the registration authorities. He also suggested that the register could be updated annually were it to be combined with the electoral roll. This would necessitate a modification of the electoral roll survey to include everyone over sixteen and to show whether residents had changed address in the previous year. This latter feature of this trawl would be another way of netting those who had not notified the National Register of a change of address. Vivian maintained that people caught like this should be subject to "exemplary punishment" and here, in his desire for stringent enforcement, he certainly could never be accused of tackling the issue in a half-hearted way since he went so far as to suggest that such people could be disenfranchised.[18]

However, just as in his view, the people needed to be educated or disciplined into fulfilling their part in the registration schema, so the authorities had a duty to devise a system that worked. Where people were caught by registration spot checks, such as his envisioned electoral roll updates, they could be fairly blamed for not notifying the authorities and penalised for non-compliance, but unless the system actually moved records from office to office after receiving a notification of a change of address, blame could not be fairly placed on the individual concerned. Vivian wrote that in theory, it would be relatively easy to deny access to services to people who had failed to notify the registrar of a change of address. But though possible in theory, in practice it would be impossible to refuse people their rights. Indeed, if a man presented himself for military service, it would be utterly self-defeating to turn him away simply because his registration details had not been updated, particularly since this may not even be his fault. It was thus clearly incumbent on those designing a registration system to make sure that it worked and that receipt of a notification of a change of address would lead to the relevant records also being moved.[19]

Vivian was very clear about what his proposed system would look like and the fourth element of his memorandum provided an outline of some of its more important operational design features. Here, he stressed two fundamental points. First, this was to be national scheme, and as such, every aspect of the process was to be designed and run from the centre. As Vivian put it: "it is impossible to administer a system of National Registration on the lines of issuing general instructions to be interpreted by local agents."[20] The register would be administered through local offices, and Vivian was adamant that these needed to be set up before the war even if registration did not start until war broke out. But once they were open, these offices were to have no autonomy whatsoever and were to carry out, to the letter, the instructions of the central authority. For this reason, though the office might be housed in local authority buildings, it was to be institutionally distinct from the local authority itself. Second, the system would identify individuals by a number. Vivian insisted that this was the only failsafe way to find a particular person. Names were ruled out because, apart from the fact that many people had the same name, variations in spelling, ordering and usage rendered them unreliable. Dates of birth were equally unreliable as they could be forgotten, and many people were sensitive about revealing their age and so might not give a real date. Occupations, which were recorded in the First World War system, were open to a wide variety of descriptions and so were not precise enough, and in any case were subject to change, so under Vivian's plan, the British were to be numbered.

But Vivian's was not the only plan for national registration to be brought forward in the build up to war. The Ministry of Labour suggested that it, not the registrar general, should organise and run the system. The ministry's argument did not engage with the minutiae of how its proposal would work because it was largely one of administrative expediency, and thus the focus was on the organisational arrangements of registration. It was maintained that the register could be organised through the existing network of employment exchanges and "that Managers would be able to re-adjust their organisation on well established and well recognised lines with a minimum of delay and dislocation."[21] This was because employment exchanges were used to dealing with sudden influxes of people and also to recording changes in people's circumstances. Moreover, the Ministry of Labour then went on to flatly contradict one of Vivian's most important tenets by stating: "it would be an easy matter for the exchanges to record any changes which occurred in the addresses, or occupations, or other circumstances, of the people."[22]

The eventual decision about the form of registration to be used was taken in a subcommittee set up under the Subcommittee on Manpower of the CID. Vivian chaired this registration committee and its 1937 report bore the hallmarks of his thinking and repeated verbatim sections of his memorandum of the previous year.[23] There was, however, one major difference between this report and Vivian's earlier writings: the report ruled out the introduction of registration in peacetime.

The committee recommended that registration only be introduced when war began because, it concluded, without the stimulus provided by food rationing, there was no way to make the public notify the authorities of a change of address. The report examined all Vivian's previous suggestions that people such as landlords and employers could enforce the system, and though it agreed these could provide an incentive to the public, it nonetheless concluded that they alone would not be sufficient to ensure active and universal compliance. Moreover, since the initial phase of registration was to be for men of military age, without rationing in place the whole process would be seen for what it was: an arm of conscription, and this "would be politically impossible."[24]

However, this did not mean that Vivian abandoned his desire to see registration permanently established in Britain. Far from it, as far as he was concerned all that the report did was to move the introduction of this system to the outbreak of war on the assumption that "a universal system of National Registration … though designed for war purposes is expected to remain in being for an indefinite period of time."[25] Vivian understood that during the war, the register would derive most of its parasitic vitality from food rationing, but, he reasoned, it would be better if it could also be used for the other purposes he had listed. This was the case because when the war ended and rationing was abolished, registration would need to be associated with some other services that the public would find agreeable, or at least useful, and "the greater the justification which can be found on account of wartime purposes other than conscription, the more acceptable and workable a peacetime National Register would prove."[26] Though, in 1937, Vivian could not yet locate compelling replacements for rationing's role as the anchor of registration, it was clear that he was keen to find them, because as far as he was concerned, once it was introduced registration was going to become a fact of life and the British would have to be conditioned to accept it.

A Numbered and Conscripted People

National registration was announced in Parliament on 1 December 1938. But after this, the government kept publicity to a minimum; for example, it went ahead with recruiting enumerators but did so under the pretext that these were to be working for a forthcoming census.[27] However, this surreptitiousness was abandoned three weeks after war was declared when Walter Elliot, who as minister of health was responsible for Vivian's work, broadcast to prepare the country for the initial registration survey, "a roll-call of the whole nation," which was due to start the following week on Friday 29 September 1939.[28] Elliot stressed that it would be in people's self-interest to take this seriously as it would form the basis of the subsequent issue of ration books. He told listeners that they should have received their registration forms through the post by 28 September, when there would be another broadcast to help them complete these, and that on that day the enumerators would start their rounds of every house in the country. The forms were delivered with a leaflet that was laid out as a series of questions and answers to help people understand what the process was for, emphasising how the rationing system would depend on their compliance in this registration process and telling people how to complete the form and so do their bit towards compiling "Britain's new Doomsday Book."[29] The follow-up broadcast was made by Vivian. He took people through the form step by step and urged them to invite the enumerator into their homes to complete their identity cards at a table, rather than leave him standing outside in the darkness of the blackout. He ended by emphasising in the strongest possible terms that the onus was on his listeners to complete the forms and to notify the authorities of any subsequent change of address. Ration books, he told the listeners, would be sent out to the address they had given the register, and they could not expect these books to "follow you about like a pet lamb."[30]

By 5 October, the Ministry of Health could proudly claim that nearly all the forty four million people in the country had received their identity cards and Vivian followed this up with more information telling people what to do with these cards. Vivian had concluded his report to the CID by suggesting that the government should be circumspect in the information it gave to the public "about the ultimate conscription purposes of the scheme."[31] But now, in October 1939, perhaps because the system had plainly secured the mass cooperation of the people, or perhaps because war had begun and patriotic motives could be relied on, this new piece of public information did not attempt to secure compliance by stressing rationing. Thus, Vivian was altogether more frank and began by showing how the system represented the people's involvement in the war "just as the soldier has his identification number, so each member of the civil population now has an identification number. It is the thing which links you to the whole system and the services which it affords."[32] Then he showed how, given the grim realities of total war, the system could benefit his listeners. Thus, he urged people to keep note of the registration numbers of members of their family as these could be used to reunite people separated during future evacuations, just as they were already being used to put parents in contact with children who had been evacuated. Then, with a clear nod to the widely anticipated mass casualties from aerial bombing, he wrote that if people wore their identity number on a disc, their body could be identified should the worst happen.[33]

Once national registration was fully operational, it encountered two main problems. The first of these was the fraught relationship between the register and the food rationing authorities. Vivian was well aware that registration relied upon the rationing system, but unfortunately for the register, the rationing authorities proved themselves to be very unreliable. William Hancock and Margaret Gowing, in their volume on the war economy in the civil service history of the Second World War, disagreed with this view concluding that "preparations for food control had been carried a long distance" by the start of the war; however, it has been shown that this conclusion is not supported by the evidence.[34] For example, in April 1939, the man in charge of the Food (Defence Plans) Department (F(DP)D), Sir Henry French, addressing a conference of divisional food officers stated that "there is still a great deal … to be done."[35] The important point here is that, contrary to the impression given by Hancock and Gowing, this laxity was obvious at the time, perhaps particularly to Vivian. Indeed, a year before French made this admission, Vivian wrote to him three times asking for information about what was happening at F(DP)D and his frustration is palpable, a letter of April 1938 for example, ended "regarding your plans … all I want is to know what they are."[36]

The issue inherent in this relationship for the registration authorities was that though the register needed food rationing, it was widely believed in government in general, and the Ministry of Food in particular, that food rationing did not need the register. This illustrates how Jon Agar's general point that various sections of the state "moved in different directions" was certainly the case at this point; indeed, the registration authorities had fundamental disagreements with the Ministry of Food until these were resolved in early 1943.[37] Agar is one of the only recent authors on registration to focus on the British case, but when he presents the link between the wartime register and the Ministry of Food, he does not study the hostility between the two.[38]

In reality, Vivian's frustration with the F(DP)D, which bordered on animosity, was reciprocated and relationships did not improve when the F(DP)D became the Ministry of Food on the outbreak of war. Vivian's response to French's delay in getting plans for rationing in place highlights how the underlying reason for this fraught relationship was a mixture of his bureaucratic desire to control the processes and a genuine concern to see that important work was done properly. From the F(DP)P's perspective, officials saw the register as taking over the enumeration of the population on which food rationing would depend, but assumed that the register's officials would prioritise the register over rationing leaving the wartime Ministry of Food dependent on staff that it could not control. As one official put it at the start of 1939, "our loss may be the Registrar General's gain … is it too late for this Department to withdraw from this alliance?"[39]

But there was more to the Ministry of Food's attitude than its simply defending its bureaucratic turf. The ministry did not want to be tainted in the public's mind through association with the register because it assumed the register would be seen as an imposition designed to dragoon people into conscription.[40] Richard Hammond, the author of the official history of the Ministry of Food, noted that the rationing administrators saw that their duty was "to feed the people, not to provide a means to control civilian life in war," and further how they worried that their rationing system might seem to be "starving the people into submission" with the demands of the register and conscription.[41]

Equally, there were strong concerns within the registrar's office about the impact that too close a relationship with rationing would have on the register. Vivian, as has been seen, had wanted the register introduced in peacetime because he thought this would better equip it to become a permanent feature of British life. By 1942, he was openly attempting to subsume many of the functions of the electoral roll within the remit of the register and describing the register's potential to become "a common service instrument": the central supplier of data and information across Whitehall.[42] To achieve this, he reasoned, the register needed to broaden the range of departments it worked with rather than deepen its relationship with rationing.[43] This was the case not only because rationing could never be seen as permanent, but also because the register needed to maintain its independent records. This in turn was necessary because these "infallible" records were far superior to those of the rationing system and might be diluted by too close a union.[44]

In the end though, over the winter of 1942–1943 the two organisations were fused, with registration staff usually moving into the local food administration's offices. The aims of this "common sense" process were to save manpower by amalgamating certain functions of both organisations, to free up office space and to make life a bit easier for the public by bringing both services together.[45] However, even though the two were to share office space, Vivian remained firm that none of this should impinge on his ability to discharge his statutory responsibilities; in other words, an independent register would still exist.[46] He also sent out instructions to local food administrators that they were make sure that registration files were under the care of people who knew their value and how to use them. The announcement of the fusion of these offices in February 1943 was made by Lord Woolton, the food minister, and drew a warm response from the press.[47] However, the register did not always receive such favourable coverage in the papers, the criticism it received from this quarter was the second of the storms the system had to weather.

Thus, in 1941 sections of the press lambasted the register. However, this was not a case of the press giving voice to popular opposition against the register's oppressive disciplining of the public, rather it was maintained that the register was not stringent enough. The *Daily Sketch* argued that identity cards: did not provide sufficient information, should bear photographs and were seldom subject to wholesale inspections.[48] Where the first two of these arguments were concerned, Vivian had rehearsed all his replies the year before and gave four reasons why putting a photograph on the identity card would not strengthen the system. First, there were two practical points: that it was virtually impossible to get everyone in the country to provide a photograph and, second, that even if they did, these photographs would need to be endorsed somehow to prove that they were of the person named on the identity card, this being a process which would itself necessitate identifying the person doing the endorsing. Third, he maintained that photographs would not increase security because a traitor or fifth columnist would have a photograph-bearing identity card just like everyone else. Fourth, he turned the argument about photographic identity cards back on its proponents by insisting that placing a photograph on a card would lend a spurious authenticity to stolen or forged cards: it would in other words be "a free gift to the fifth column."[49]

More importantly, Vivian insisted that this whole discussion was fundamentally muddle-headed since it confused two different things: a pass and the National Register. A pass was a document that authorised a particular individual to enter a restricted area: it conferred a privilege that could be withdrawn, or expire. A pass thus gave a judgement about a person, whereas an identity document from the register gave facts.[50] Vivian accepted that passes were necessary, but added that they could only be issued to people who could confirm their identity in the first place. In other words, these documents were dependent upon a registration scheme and the precise form they took was outside his remit since they would be designed to fit only one particular purpose.[51]

Moreover, Vivian insisted that the National Register provided a means of checking that the person presenting an identity card was actually the person named on it. When people were first entered into the register and given an identity card, they provided the enumerator with personal details that were recorded in the system, but not written on the identity card, most notably their date of birth. Thus, if a police officer had reason to suspect that a card was stolen, all that was necessary was to detain the bearer, ask them their date of birth and check that this was accurate with the registration office. The chance of someone guessing the correct date was obviously remote and though this process might take longer (though Vivian maintained this could be done quite quickly) than looking at a photograph it offered, given the drawbacks of photograph-bearing identity cards, "a good deal more service than" its much-touted rival system.[52]

If the first element of the press criticism of the register concerned its design, the second element of this criticism was that registration was not enforced with sufficient vigour. Vivian agreed, as has been seen, that the more times the public were required to produce their card, the greater their compliance with the system was likely to be. But he also knew that the legal requirement to notify the authorities of a change of address, linked as it was to the rationing system, provided another method of achieving the same compliance. Additionally, this method had the advantage of proceeding more "unobtrusively" and it could be very effective.[53] Looking back over the history of the register from the vantage point of 1952, the General Register Office noted how registration contributed to the war effort by "securing the registration of over 100,000 men ... and of well over 500,000 women" who had not complied with requirements to register for national service or employment.[54] By June 1940, compliance had improved considerably from the opening months of the war with Vivian reporting that notices of change of address from one area to another alone were running at two hundred thousand per week. But when the numbers moving within an area were taken into consideration, Vivian calculated that the register would handle fifteen million notifications per year. This proved to be an overestimate, but even so, the register handled over one hundred million changes of address in its lifetime, with the peak period being the first four weeks of the German V rocket attacks in the summer of 1944, when the register dealt with one and a quarter million notifications.[55]

But even so, there was still a place in the system for random trawls of the people by the authorities. There were two types of these, the first of which was targeted at men of military age. After the war, it was noted that: "during the last war it was the practice for the police to round up young men occasionally ... and bring to notice those who had shirked their national service obligations. This, though having no appreciable effect on manpower, was a salutary procedure from the psychological point of view and added to the difficulties of the shirkers."[56] The second type of trawling exercise imposed a blanket check on everyone. These, contrary to the view of the critical sections of the press, certainly occurred and when they did it was noted that on follow-up checks, a week or so later, a higher percentage of people were found to be carrying their cards. In other words, the checks were effective at reinforcing compliance. But the level of compliance even at the first wave of checks would seem to belie the fuss made in the press. Thus, in 1941 the Security Executive received a report detailing compliance with the system. Checks made in Canterbury, stopped 9626 people of whom only 3% (299) were not carrying their cards, in York the figures showed that 5% (811) people out of 17,646 who were stopped, were not carrying theirs. In Brighton, only 0.5% of 23,160 people did not have their card with them when stopped (perhaps because security was more stringent in coastal areas) and in an exercise conducted by South-Eastern Command, only ten out of 2184 people who were challenged could not produce theirs.[57] *The Daily Telegraph* cavilled that when people could not produce a card "all the police can do is order such persons to produce their cards at a police station within 48 hours."[58] But the evidence is that overwhelmingly people did just that. Thus, of the 299 people who did not produce a card in Canterbury, only ten did not subsequently appear with it at a police station. People in York behaved likewise with seven hundred of those who had not had their card with them when challenged attending a police station within forty-eight hours, and the rest soon afterwards.[59] Thus, the figures would seem to show that most people, though they might not have liked registration, complied with its demands.[60] However, the real question for the register was to what extent was this compliance a product of the patriotic motives of wartime, or of self-interest generated by the food rationing system, in other words, would Vivian be able to get what he had always wanted, and would he be able to impose a peacetime register on the British?

Planning for a Register in Peacetime

In September 1944, Vivian was asked by the Treasury to produce a memorandum outlining his views of the future of the register. In this lengthy document, he listed all the administrative advantages that could be obtained from keeping the register in peacetime.[61] These would become the backbone of the defence of registration in the years leading up to its eventual abolition in 1952 and so will be reviewed in the next chapter. But this document also gave remarkable insights into what might be called Vivian's strategic thinking about the place of the register in post-war Britain and these will be the focus of this section. The key word that Vivian used here was "habit." He wanted now, as the war entered its final phase, what he had written about in 1936: he wanted the people to become habituated to the register. Given that he was, as has been shown, fully aware of the hostility of the British towards registration, this might seem overly ambitious if not foolishly optimistic, but Vivian saw "an object lesson" from which he drew hope. This was the registration of births. This had been introduced over a century before the war and like the National Register it imposed "duties of a detailed and extensive kind closely touching the personal concern and personal responsibility of individual citizens."[62] Nevertheless, he noted that even before full enforcement systems were introduced by an act of 1874, compliance was at a level that he himself would have been proud of. Moreover, "at the present time birth registration is wholly taken for granted. The prevailing public attitude is mainly a matter of habit."[63]

Insofar as Vivian was attempting to make people internalise the functions of registration, just as they had internalised the registration of their children's births, it is clear that he had in mind the type of system described by Michel Foucault through the metaphor of the Panopticon. In the Panopticon prison, designed by Jeremy Bentham, the object was not to punish the prisoner's body, but rather to encourage him to internalise the disciplinary requirements of the system and so to modify his own behaviour. Thus, the system's success would be measured by how little force was ultimately needed to ensure compliance; by how well oriented the subject became to the new patterns of thought and behaviour. This was to be achieved by placing the prisoner in a situation where he was fully aware that at any point of the day he could come under surveillance without knowing that he was being watched "a state of conscious and permanent visibility that assures the automatic functioning of power."[64] Bentham's prison was thus, in Vivian's terms, to be habit forming.

Additionally, there are two main ways in which the detail of Vivian's view of registration can be seen to exemplify Foucault's view of the panoptic power system. First, in that Vivian clearly anticipated that it would be necessary to apply "supplementary measures" to the population to press them into habituating themselves to registration. The measures that Vivian suggested or implemented before and during the war focused on rationing and have been detailed above, but in 1944, he extended this. He wrote that conscription in peacetime would not only be the raison d'être of the register, it would also be one of the main replacements for rationing, becoming a means for the continuation of registration. Conscription would fulfil this function in two ways. First, by providing a vital service from which the register could continue to draw succour. Second, by establishing a fertile environment for the inculcation of habits of personal discipline that could only be to the advantage of registration. Moreover, these advantages would be magnified were the state to introduce some kind of military reserve so that men would be liable for call-up as reservists after completing their basic stint in uniform and therefore, be obliged to notify the register of a change of address throughout a big part of their lifetime.[65]

The second echo of Foucault that is clear in Vivian's thinking comes from the fact that Foucault described how the Panopticon forms the behaviour not only of the prisoner, but also of the guard and Vivian paid a lot of attention to how a permanent register would impact those who used it, namely government departments. Vivian contended that a peacetime register would benefit all government departments, with any individual department deriving benefits in excess of the effort demanded by its contribution. But all departments would have to contribute. Thus, if one were informed of a person's change of address, this information would be passed onto the register to keep it updated and live, ready to be used by all. A rational awareness of this self-interest would, Vivian maintained "dispose them to cooperate in the maintenance of a level of efficiency … The consideration essential to ensure the necessary degree of cooperation is merely that the quid pro quo should be reckoned on a broad basis and not in relation to each isolated branch of administration."[66] Thus, the fact was that for the registration system to work without rationing it would need both the people and the bureaucrats to internalise its requirements and modify their attitudes and behaviour accordingly: the governed and the governors would all have to become habituated to the system.

It is certainly true that the number of government departments and agencies using the register increased as the war progressed. In fact though the act of 1939, that established the register, gave the system three functions: conscription, rationing and national security, by 1950 the register was being used by thirty-nine government departments.[67] But this did not mean that they were contributing to it. Notifications of changes of address still came to the register through rationing. Consequently, it is clear that what Vivian regarded as "merely" a strategic reckoning of self-interest by any given department, would in fact involve a considerable modification of procedures, in fact more than this it would necessitate the adoption of what Nikolas Rose calls a new "intellectual technology."[68] Similarly, the fact that people were required to use their registration number in a wide variety of transactions with state bodies did not mean that they, any more than the bureaucrats within these departments, had become habituated to the system. Vivian undoubtedly thought along lines similar to those Foucault saw as the foundation of the panoptic system of modern disciplinary power, but there is a very important caveat to this comparison. Foucault himself noted that the continental systems, so admired by Vivian, were different to what he called "a much looser, Anglicized system."[69] In other words, the fact that Vivian had to make a case for registration was highly indicative of a British political culture, both in the country at large and inside government departments, that was not, and did not want to become habituated to it. Vivian retired in 1945 and after the war those who argued for the continuation of the register in peacetime would find themselves on the defensive.

Notes

1. TNA, RG 28/27, *Note by the Registrar-General*, n.d., ca. early 1936, 2.
2. Ibid.
3. Ibid., 4; TNA, RG 28/27, from S. P. V., 12 June 1936, 1.
4. *Note by the Registrar-General*, 4.
5. Ibid., 3 and 10.
6. Ibid., 3.
7. Ibid., 4.
8. Ibid., 3 and 17.
9. TNA, CAB 57/21, *Report of the National Registration Sub-committee*, 11 March 1937, 3.
10. *Note by the Registrar-General*, 5.
11. Jane Caplan and John Torpey, eds. *Documenting Individual Identity: The Development of State Practices in the Modern World* (Princeton: Princeton University Press, 2001); Keith Breckenridge and Simon Szreter, eds.

Registration and Recognition: Documenting the Person in World History (Oxford: Oxford University Press, 2012); Ilsen About, James Brown, and Gayle Lonergan, eds. *Identification and Registration Practices in Transnational Perspective: People, Papers and Practices* (Basingstoke: Palgrave, 2013).
12. David Lyon, *The Electronic Eye: The Rise of Surveillance Society* (London: Polity, 1994), 32.
13. Jon Agar, "Modern Horrors: British Identity and Identity Cards," in *Documenting Individual Identity*, eds. Jane Caplan and John Torpey, 115–20; Note by the Registrar-General, 4.
14. *Note by the Registrar-General*, 4.
15. Ibid., 11 and 12.
16. Rosemary Elliot, "An Early Experiment in National Identity Cards: The Battle Over Registration in the First World War," *Twentieth Century British History* 17 (2006): 157.
17. TNA, RG 28/27, *Possible Provisions for Making the Identity Document a Live and Necessary Thing and/or Securing Collateral Records of Identity Number for Purposes of Replacement Upon Loss*, n.d., ca. 1936, 1–4.
18. *Note by the Registrar-General*, 14.
19. Ibid., 6.
20. Ibid., 7.
21. TNA, RG 28/29, *Proposal for a Scheme of National Registration*, June 1936, 6.
22. Ibid., 5.
23. *Report of the National Registration Sub-committee.*
24. Ibid., 5.
25. Ibid., 8.
26. Ibid., 10.
27. TNA, MAF 99/1243, *Report of the Sub-committee on Personal Identification in Time of War*, 17 December 1952, 9.
28. TNA, MH 55/978, Ministry of Information, *No 16*, 22 September 1939, 1.
29. TNA, MH 55/978, Ministry of Health, *National Registration Guide for Heads of Households*, September 1939, 4.
30. TNA, MH 55/978, Ministry of Health, *National Registration*, 29 September 1939, 6.
31. *Report of the National Registration Sub-committee*, 11.
32. TNA, MH 55/978, Ministry of Health, *What to Do with Your Identity Card*, 5 October 1939, 1.
33. Uri Bailer, *The Shadow of the Bomber: The Fear of Air Attack and British Politics, 1932–1939* (London: Royal Historical Society, 1980), 2 and 3; G. C. Peden, *Arms, Economics and British Strategy: From Dreadnoughts to Hydrogen Bombs* (Cambridge: Cambridge University Press, 2007), 108.

34. W. K. Hancock and M. M. Gowing, *British War Economy* (London: H.M.S.O., 1949), 51; Kevin Manton, "Sir William Beveridge, The British Government and Plans for Food Control in Time of War, c.1916–1941," *Contemporary British History* 23 (2009): 363–385.
35. TNA, MAF 72/524, *Conference of Divisional Food Officers*, 27 April 1939, 1.
36. TNA, RG 28/27, Vivian to French, 8 April 1938, 2.
37. Agar, "Modern Horrors," 119.
38. Ibid., 107–8.
39. TNA, MAF 72/627, from A. H., 6 January 1939, 2.
40. Ibid.
41. R. J. Hammond, *Food: Vol. 2: Studies in Administration and Control* (London: H.M.S.O. and Longmans, Green, 1956), 463, 466, and 492.
42. TNA, RG 28/106, *Proposed Unification of NR and Food Offices*, 25 August 1942, 6 and 1.
43. TNA, RG 28/106, Vivian to Roseveare, 29 September 1942, 3.
44. *Proposed Unification of NR and Food Offices*, 5.
45. TNA, RG 28/106, *Notes for Divisional Food Officers*, n.d., ca. February 1943, 2; TNA, RG 28/105, *Fusion of National Registration and Food Offices*, 22 December 1942, 1 and 2.
46. TNA, RG 28/105, *Fusion*, n.d., ca. January 1943, 1.
47. TNA, RG 28/105, Press cuttings.
48. TNA, CAB 114/2, "Identity Cards," *Daily Sketch*, 22 October 1941.
49. TNA, CAB 114/2, S. P. V., *Preparations now Being Made for the Issue of Documents of the "Pass" Type*, 24 June 1940, 1.
50. Ibid., 3.
51. Ibid., 2.
52. TNA, CAB 114/2, Vivian, Annex to Memorandum, *Alternative Provision in Place of Photograph-Bearing Identity Card*, n.d., ca. June 1940, 1.
53. Ibid., 3.
54. TNA, MH 55/978, General Register Office, *History of National Registration, How Identity Cards Have Been Used*, 21 February 1952, 1.
55. Ibid., 2.
56. TNA, LAB 25/209, *Note by the Ministry of Labour and National Service*, 2 September 1952, 3.
57. TNA, CAB 114/3, Security Executive, *National Registration Identity Cards*, 24 October 1941, 1–2.
58. TNA, CAB 114/2, "Identity Cards Check Up," *Daily Telegraph*, 1 September 1941.
59. Security Executive, *National Registration Identity Cards*, 1–2.
60. TNA, MH 78/119, The Registrar General, 6 August 1942, 1–5.

61. TNA, HO 45/25014, Vivian, *The Future of National Registration*, September 1944, 25.
62. Ibid., 19.
63. Ibid.
64. Michel Foucault, *Discipline and Punish: The Birth of the Prison* (London: Penguin, 1991), 201.
65. Vivian, *The Future of National Registration*, 19–20.
66. Ibid., 21.
67. Agar, “Modern Horrors,” 114.
68. Nikolas Rose, *Powers of Freedom: Reframing Political Thought* (Cambridge: Cambridge University Press, 1999), 27.
69. Michel Foucault, *The Birth of the Clinic* (London: Routledge, 2003), 48.

CHAPTER 3

The Abolition of National Registration

The previous chapter established that the registration authorities wanted their system to become a permanent feature of British life. This chapter analyses their efforts to bring this about and keep the National Register alive after the war. The first section observes how in their campaign to achieve this, they concentrated all their efforts on attempts to win over a reluctant officialdom. It critiques their arguments that the register was an objective and scientific instrument and shows how the use of the register as a common numbering system emerged for the first time in these post-war years as part of their defensive struggles.

The second section follows the campaign waged by the register's backers as it proceeded through the chain of Whitehall and government committees that eventually recommended its abolition. In doing so, this section explains how the common explanations for abolition fall short because they do not take into account the attitudes towards the register of the officials and politicians on these committees, most of whom could not see a real need for it in peacetime. This view, the received wisdom within government, is contrasted to that of George North, the registrar general, (he replaced Sylvanus Vivian and served from 1945 to 1958) who developed and propounded a host of ways in which the register could enhance public administration up to, and including, a redrawing of all government files through a common numbering system based on the register. However, North lost the argument in the post-war period and what is drawn out of this failure is that there was a considerable difference between official attitudes towards population registration in this

K. Manton, *Population Registers and Privacy in Britain, 1936–1984*,
https://doi.org/10.1007/978-3-030-02753-7_3

period and the later periods studied in subsequent chapters: North's views were ahead of their time in the late 1940s, but they would be mainstream twenty years later as biopolitical thinking assumed greater importance in government circles.

The last section looks at the process of abolition and its immediate aftermath when the military made plain their attachment to national registration. This highlights the discrepancy between on the one hand, the view of the register's backers that the system could be inserted into many aspects of British life and, on the other hand, the reality that the wartime system had been introduced to meet the needs of the mass mobilisation of labour and once this wartime need had passed, was unwanted not only by the people but, more importantly, by ministers and the bulk of officialdom alike.

A "Common Service Instrument"?

Those who wanted the register to be a permanent fixture of British life after the war followed Sylvanus Vivian, the wartime registrar general, in seeing that both the people and the state would need some prompting if they were to become habituated to this development. This section will review their very different attitudes towards these two groups starting with their view of the public. In 1936, Vivian had perceptively commented that registration would not be popular in Britain. He was right, and despite wartime compliance, this essential opposition to registration did not fade away and the British did not become accustomed to registration. Indeed he obviously understood this too, since he began his 1944 memoranda to the Treasury by noting: "it is, of course, clear that ... prejudice and reaction from war controls will influence public opinion."[1] In fact even before the war ended *The Daily Mirror* was reporting bitterly that registration might "go on and on after the war to the delight of Whitehall and the annoyance of everyone else," while from Liverpool the press reported that: "a good deal of feeling is being aroused by the rumour that the identity card system is to be retained after the war." For its part, *The Evening News* reported that it had uncovered Whitehall studies of foreign registration arrangements and suggested that these systems were being examined with a view to adapting them for peacetime use in Britain, adding that though these alterations may produce a system that was less onerous than its continental templates, "difference in degree is not difference in essence."[2]

Vivian retired in 1945, but the following year he published his views of the opposition to peacetime registration. He began with a rhetorical question: "is there any logical ground for this hostility?" Unsurprisingly, his answer was a resounding "no," and he sought to establish this thesis by listing all the ways that the register had benefitted the public. Thus, he stated, it had allowed an election to be held at a time when without registration there would not have been an electoral roll, it ensured fairness in the implementation of conscription, it underpinned rationing, it allowed families split up by evacuation to be reunited and it allowed "the health services to maintain their unsleeping watch over the well-being of the community under the strain of war."[3] Given this evidence of the beneficial effects of the register he maintained that opposition to it was irrational. In fact, he likened hostility towards registration to the "taboos" of "primitive tribesmen" against having their photographs taken lest the camera remove their soul. It was a manifestation of a "deep-seated," "primitive" and "vestigial," instinct: a throwback to "the pit whence we were digged" which somehow lived on in a few people.[4]

His successors at the registry were more temperate in their language, but made the same basic point, that there was nothing rational to fear in registration, by asking their own version of Vivian's rhetorical question: "who can justifiably object to holding a card and producing it when required when the purposes are beneficial to the owner or afford his protection against fraud?"[5] Addressing the argument that the register was in some way alien to the English way of life they asked: "what is the English way of life?" In reply they listed all the ways in which this had changed since the 1834 Poor Law up to and including the creation of the National Health Service (NHS): making the unspoken case that registration was just another incremental development that would soon become part and parcel of Englishness.[6] One element of the view that registration was un-English, and which needed to be tackled more thoroughly however, was its association with an overweening state. Traditionally, the British may have associated this with Catholic continental Europe, or more recently with "Prussianism," but by the mid-twentieth century this meant totalitarianism.[7]

Attending to the view that the register was innately totalitarian "all that need be said on this score" was, according to the registration authorities in 1950, that while the register would indeed make it easy for a government to find any individual, it could never be used to track down whole classes of the population such as Jews, Catholic priests or the bourgeoisie.[8] Similarly it was claimed that the register could never be used to turn Britain into a police state. Two, additional and related arguments against the register were that, first, it might be used to the detriment of individuals under even a democratic government. Here the reply was that experience showed that this had not happened. The government had, for example, resisted pressure to make the register's records available for debt collecting.[9] Second, it was sometimes asserted that the register turned "the citizen from a human being into a mere cypher in the eyes of the government."[10] This view echoed Weber's notion that organisational efficiency and personal dossiers would lead to the "parcelling out of the soul" under the control of the "bureaucratic ideal of life."[11] But the registration authorities insisted that if these attitudes were prevalent it was not the register that was at fault because it was an apolitical scientific instrument. Such behaviour and thinking came from the government departments that used the register in their dealings with the public and so could not reasonably be used as a justification for criticising the register as such.

Bruce Curtis has written about the Canadian census and in doing so has explicitly addressed the claim made in defence of the register that it was a rational and objective instrument. He argues that "census making is a political-scientific activity" that is designed to open up the lives of individuals to scrutiny and discipline.[12] Nikolas Rose has further pointed out that protestations of the objectivity of statistics (and this can be applied to Vivian's defence of the National Register) "produce a public rhetoric of disinterest in situations of contestation."[13] Similarly, William Alonso and Paul Starr have shown how "political judgements are implicit in the choice of what to measure, how to measure it, how often to measure it, and how to present and interpret the results."[14] To which it should be added that when the choice is made to measure everyone in the country, by compulsion and on a permanent basis, as was the case with the National Register, then it is surely all the more political. This political nature of registration will be clarified when the thinking behind the use of registration is examined in the next chapter. But even without this, it is plain that there was a very political campaign waged by the registrar to keep the register alive after the war.

Public opinion was important in these debates. For example, the registration authorities argued that it would be wrong to keep the register only as an arm of post-war conscription and therefore that those who thought this was the sole operational reason for continental registration systems were wrong. In fact, they maintained, these registration "systems are of use for some public purpose of obvious benefit to the registered individuals as well as being of use for the purpose of National Service."[15] In order to be accepted, the register therefore needed to be of some benefit to the people as a whole and as a corollary of this it also needed to be universal and not simply target a section of the population such as men of conscription age. However, even though the attitude of the public was accepted as fact of political life during all considerations about registration in the post-war period, it is notable that neither Vivian nor his successor, George North, made any serious attempt to change the public's perception. Instead they lambasted the people for their irrationality and focused their efforts on the other group that needed to become habituated to permanent registration: the government and the civil service. These attempts can be divided into two broad types: those that sought to portray the register's macro advantages, detailing what it could offer to government administration as a whole, and those that emphasised ways in which the register could be of use in particular settings.

The first of these portrayals of the register's usefulness clearly embodies Vivian's desire to see the register as a common service instrument. This would mean that the register would not simply improve the efficiency of existing departmental systems; rather it would transform them into one unified matrix of information that could all be accessed from any departmental node, producing a web of information that was greater than the sum of its parts. This would be achieved by the register's serving as a universal, or a common numbering system for all public administration. This, it was proposed, would overcome something that advocates of registration would consistently portray as a structural problem in British public administration, namely that within the state, departments filed their data in different ways thus hindering inter-departmental cooperation. Vivian had touched on this subject in his 1944 memorandum where he had highlighted suggestions for how the registration number could facilitate medical research by drawing together disparate medical records. He extrapolated from this example the possibility that registration numbers could be used to link together various data sets, but went no further than suggesting that this might be useful for compiling statistical data.

It was the post-war registrar, George North, who developed the idea of the register as a common numbering system in this period. North recognised the same reality that Weber had noted, and described it as a fact of contemporary life that people needed numbers to identify themselves, but added that this could be made more acceptable, or at least less onerous, if people used one number for all purposes. He suggested: "combining the medical card and the identity card in a single card which might be called a social register card and bear a single number" that could be used in place of all existing numbers. This "would then be the key to social benefits and to corresponding social obligations."[16] Meetings held under the auspices of the Treasury, in December 1948, concluded that such a common numbering system would have four advantages. First, it would benefit the public by streamlining administration, improving efficiency and therefore reducing costs. Tellingly however, and clearly keeping a weather eye on public attitudes, the meeting thought that this increase in efficiency "should not be over emphasised."[17] Second, it could assist the process, already underway, of connecting records. The meeting heard that several different data sets were already connected by an ad hoc use of registration numbers, which were used, for example, to expedite claims for family allowances. Third, this system could verify claims made on state bodies and so prevent duplicate claims being made. Fourth, such a system would be adaptable: it could be used to file new sets of records. An example of this was seen in the way in which the Dental Estimates Board used the National Register to number its files.[18] Clearly, with this last point, the advocates of the register as a common numbering system saw room for this to expand as government needs for data grew.

Moreover, were the government to decide to rationalise its administration by adopting a common numbering system, it was concluded that "the odds are heavily weighted on the side of the National Registration number" being used for this purpose.[19] This was because the only alternative, the National Insurance (NI) system would, it was maintained, "before long ... be faced with a very big problem in trying to keep straight a 26 million entry alphabetical record."[20] The insurance authorities had to process half a million name changes annually, whereas the register used numbers that, once issued, never changed, and were already committed to memory by a large number of people. Indeed the advantages were so overwhelming that the discussion moved onto how the insurance system could itself be redesigned to use the registration numbers.

Whereas this macro view saw the register providing a common numbering system that could allow the register to become a spine running through all government administration, the other argument in favour of maintaining the register in peacetime sought to bolster its connections with other data sets, even though these might continue to be catalogued separately. Here the aim was to use other departments to provide the data on which the register existed and which it currently drew from rationing. Just as in 1944 Vivian had expected that the rational self-interest of administrators would predispose them to assist the register so, in 1949, the registration authorities claimed that "it is reasonable to expect that any government service which has the right type of counter contact with the public should contribute to the National Register for the purpose of maintaining its most valuable feature i.e. knowledge of current address."[21] For example, it was argued that a member of the public consulting any section of the NHS should be asked to produce an identity card. If a discrepancy were noted between the person's recorded personal details and those given to the NHS staff, then "various steps might be taken with the object of getting the card and the National Registration records brought up to date, e.g. making the correction of the card a condition of rendering the service, impounding the card … warning the holder of his duty to have the card corrected or notifying the National Registration authorities, who would then communicate with the holder."[22] Clearly compliance was going to be enforced.

Though the registration authorities saw this level of cooperation between other arms of the state and themselves as being in the rational self-interest of all concerned, they still had to make a case for how this would benefit the other state actors. A case in point is the NHS, where the register's backers expended a good deal of effort in presenting their view of how it could provide administrative benefits. This focused on how doctors were paid. Doctors were not salaried but received a capitation fee based on the number of patients enrolled with them. Therefore, if a patient changed address and registered at a new surgery but forgot to de-register at their former doctor's, two doctors would be paid for the same individual. In 1950, it was calculated that doctors' lists covered a number of people equal to about 98% of the population, but that only 92% of people were actually registered with doctors. The difference between the two figures, 6%, represented the inflation caused by this lack of notification of change of address. This cost the system one million two hundred thousand pounds p.a. Purging these lists was thus an urgent priority and the best way of doing so, according to the registration authorities, was by cross-referencing doctors' lists to the

National Register, a process that, though it would cost about five hundred thousand pounds, would produce a substantial saving which would almost offset the total the annual running costs of the register.[23]

The Post Office Savings Bank had already used the register to streamline its records and thus reduce its administrative costs and in addition to this, and solving problems for the NHS, the register's backers determined that it could make a contribution to a wide range of other state activities. The NI system would benefit by a similar cooperation with the register, as would local authorities and schools.[24] However, these efforts to override the objections of the people and shift the perceptions of government departments to either wholeheartedly embrace registration, or at least to carry on using it, came to nothing because registration was abolished after the war. The next section will examine the procedures that led to this decision and will question the two usually accepted explanations for this outcome.

Rejecting Registration

The fact that war can have profound and lasting effects on the shape of society is a point that has been made often. For example, Nikolas Rose has shown how new political technologies can be "conjured up" by the demands of total warfare that require "the invention of new practices of government."[25] There cannot be any doubt that this is so, indeed the arrival of the National Register in 1939 is a case in point. However, this example should also draw attention to the fact that these changes, ushered in to meet the demands of war, were not necessarily all destined to survive as permanent features of society since on 21 February 1952 the National Register was abolished. This section will analyse the reasons for this abolition and the Whitehall process that implemented this thinking.

Two years before the announcement of the end of the register the Committee on National Registration, under its chairman Sir Nicolas de Villiers issued its report. The committee's terms of reference instructed it to examine the future of registration from the standpoint of practical registration.[26] Given this remit the committee looked at how abolition would effect the departments that used the register which meant that it did not examine North's schemes to turn the register into a common numbering instrument for all government administration. The committee accepted that the police benefitted from the register. However, it described other departments as falling into one of two groups.

The first were those such as the NHS where the register was used in lieu of something that the health service could probably produce for itself, in other words the NHS used the register simply because it was there, not because it needed the register as such. The second group comprised departments such as the Ministry of Food that neither needed, nor wanted it. The committee considered all the methods that had been presented (above) for maintaining the vitality of the register in the absence of rationing but rejected all of them. In doing so, the committee reported that it was reflecting the attitude of the public. People turning up to transact some business with a state agency, such as a hospital or school, would be fully aware that any check of their identity cards "was made largely for administrative purposes and rarely for the immediate benefit of the applicant." Moreover, the ill will this produced would be magnified were they turned away for not having the card with them. More fundamentally, this hypothetical situation would be built on the reality of a public that accepted registration, but only as a wartime measure, and would find its permanent continuation unacceptable regardless of how this were to be administered. This was the "overriding objection to the registrar's proposals."[27]

After the de Villiers Report was issued the registry was on the defensive a fact that was demonstrated by the manner in which it ramped up its rhetoric. Thus, after this publication the General Register Office (GRO) described the inflation in doctors' surgery lists as "evil."[28] Additionally, it was at this point that the registration authorities advanced their denials of the register's totalitarian propensities (above), a process which involved a very substantial rewriting of an earlier draft of this document where they had admitted that the claim that the register was totalitarian was in fact "a very real objection."[29] That those who wanted to end registration were gaining the upper hand in the debates is also clear from the fact that security and law enforcement, both issues that had rarely been discussed as reasons for keeping the register after the war, were also brought forward. Thus, it was stated first, that MI5 wanted to keep the register open because the only other national set of records, those of the NI system, did not contain any information about at least 25% of the people they were interested in.[30] Second, the registration authorities also showed how the register had assisted the police in catching two murderers. In the first of these cases, the register tracked the killer down even though only the initials of his name were known. In the other case, the police asked all men in an area to come forward for fingerprinting, and the register was used to find the only man who did not volunteer.[31]

The de Villiers Report came out just as the Attlee government was re-elected, and the following year the Government Organisation Committee considered its findings. Here it was stated that when de Villers had looked at the issue it had seemed as though the writing was on the wall for rationing but now, in the summer of 1951, rationing looked "likely to continue indefinitely."[32] However, this was not necessarily a lifeline for the register, because weighing on the other side of the scales were two factors. The first of these was the "strong political objections to it," while the second was the commitment of the government to an austerity drive that wanted to cut "all activities which were not strictly necessary."[33] The key point here was that this committee agreed with de Villiers that though some users found the register to be convenient that was all it was: a convenience because it was not strictly necessary.

Thus, the committee's work did not stall over an issue of principle: whether to keep or abolish the register, but rather only over the more practical point of whether to recommend that preparations to end registration should begin immediately, or whether to postpone the final decision to abolish registration for at least a year, during which time detailed plans for substituting the register's functions might be prepared. The committee had thus reached its crucial decision regarding the fate of the National Register, however, given its indecision over the practicalities of realising this abolition, it recommended that the issue should be passed to the Lord President's Committee where the options for the timing of abolition could be weighed up.

The Lord President's Committee met to discuss registration in August 1951, and like the Government Organisation Committee before it, was split over how to proceed but this time the division was overshadowed by the judicial decision in the case Willcock v. Muckle. Clarence Willcock was a staunch liberal who, in December 1950, was stopped while driving by PC Harold Muckle. The officer asked to see Willcock's identity card but Willcock refused to show it on the grounds that cards had been brought in only as a wartime measure. The case worked its way up through the courts with the eventual decision being in Willcock's favour. This decision highlighted what the Lord President's Committee called "an important political issue" concerning the maintenance of the register in peacetime: that it had been introduced as a wartime security measure.[34]

The case of Willcock v. Muckle brought to a head the simmering popular discontent with the maintenance of wartime measures into the peace and is often presented as the reason for the abolition of registration. For example, Benjamin Goold and Daniel Neyland have written of the "successful 1952 challenge to abandon the use of wartime identity cards in the UK" and David Lyon has written that the abolition came "in response to complaints about police abuse of the system."[35] Given this, it is hardly surprising to find that Clarence Willcock is sometimes described as a "hero" and cast in the role of an unlikely David standing up to the Goliath of the registering state.[36] There can be no doubt that there was very considerable opposition to registration after the war, this had been accepted by the de Villiers committee and even acknowledged by the register's strongest advocates. However, Willcock's principled stand cannot provide an adequate explanation of the abolition of the register in 1952, because it must be remembered that the de Villiers Report was published in February 1950, in other words the process of dismantling registration was in train ten months before Willcock's car was stopped by PC Muckle.

This forces attention onto those who proposed the abolition of registration. Jon Agar has noted that the judicial decision in Willcock v. Muckle was delivered "much to the frustration of Whitehall" and that registration was abolished in the aftermath of this decision "despite pleas within Whitehall" to continue.[37] But the point is that all the pleading came from the GRO and the registrar general, there was not a general clamour within the state to keep the register, in fact the absence of any pan-departmental backing for registration is clearly evidenced by the extent to which the register had to attempt to convince other departments of its usefulness. Moreover, this absence of support is thrown into stark relief when events in the 1960s and 1970s are examined. Here, as will be seen in subsequent chapters, governments of both parties, along with officials across Whitehall, were very well aware of public hostility to anything that smacked of dossier-building and identity checking. However, they went ahead and developed plans to register the population through either overt or covert systems regardless of this understanding because they saw the advantages of registration. But in the immediate post-war period, when the register was already in existence, the bulk of their predecessors did not even want to keep it.

It is certainly true that an important element in the post-war opposition to the register was the fact that registration had been introduced (against Vivian's wishes) only as a wartime measure and that therefore its continuation would have been unpopular and politically difficult for any government. But this public hostility towards registration was a constant facet of British political culture and so would also be faced by later governments, yet these would wholly endorse plans to introduce registration. Thus, it is possible to see that the difference between the two periods is to be found less in the nature of popular opposition, focused on the fact that registration had been introduced only as a wartime expediency, and more in the attitude of the much of the state itself. For example, even the post-war home secretary, James Chuter-Ede, described the National Register "something alien to the English way of life." Adding that "I am one of those who hope that the existence of the National Register and the identity card is a purely temporary phase of our existence in this country,"[38] similarly the civil servants on the de Villiers Committee seemed to want the register to justify its pestering and cajoling of the people. However, in the 1960s and 1970s the occupants of similar positions regularly listed the advantages of registration, and in doing so brought forward arguments that, to all intents and purposes, repeated those used by Vivian and North in this earlier period. This clear contrast between this abolitionist view in the post-war period and the view of many later ministers and officials, under both Labour and Conservative administrations, is even more starkly drawn when the same person underwent a Paulian conversion on this issue. Thus, in November 1951, Tony Benn asked questions of the Conservative government that were clearly critical of the Post Office's demands that people produce identity cards, yet in the 1960s, he would champion increased government data flows and the use of de facto population registration schemes.[39]

Under these later governments, ministers and civil servants would seek to introduce some kind of registration in order to mine it for statistical information about the population, arguing that they needed this data in order to plan extensive social and economic policies. However, in the immediate post-war period, such needs were not recognised, and neither was the statistical thinking that would underpin them. George North marshalled every argument he could think of in defence of the register, yet he never really emphasised the role of the register as a provider of statistics until he knew he was fighting a rearguard action against the register's opponents and even then he only mentioned statistics about manpower, which could have been provided by the Ministry of

Labour. This would seem to suggest that even for the register itself such a role was of secondary importance. As has been shown, the de Villiers Committee did not examine the register's scheme to redraw all government filing systems through common numbering and neither did they see any real need at all for a pan-departmental register. That the representatives of various Whitehall departments, who made up this committee, placed a low value on detailed statistics about the population can be seen in their conclusion that these could be obtained "if need be" from the census and electoral register.[40]

Another factor that is used to explain the abolition of registration is that it fell victim to post-war austerity. This is one of the reasons given for abolition by Edward Higgs (he also lists popular opposition) and is also cited by Walter Pratt's 1979 survey of *Privacy in Britain*.[41] As with popular opposition, there is no doubt that austerity was a factor at play during these events. But most of the arguments made against the register were not connected to its cost. Indeed the register could prove that it could virtually pay for itself by sorting out the issues of doctors' pay for the NHS. Moreover, a focus on austerity alone ignores why the register was seen as "non-essential." Focusing on this highlights the fact that the register could not mobilise a coalition of like-minded groups. There were two reasons for this. First, it had been introduced for the purposes of wartime conscription and labour mobilisation. Therefore, though the GRO would attempt to redefine its basic remit, it was nonetheless a fact that many in government found themselves on the same side of the argument as Willcock. Second, and more importantly, because its ambitious schemes for redrawing government administration were far beyond the perceptions of many, if not most, in government: in other words, North was a man of ideas before their time. This is why the register was deemed to be nothing but a convenience by the Government Organisation Committee and this is why it was categorised as "non essential" and put on the block beneath the axe of austerity.

None of this, however, meant that the registration authorities were going to capitulate. In fact they reacted strongly against the judicial decision in Willcock v. Muckle, and they were adamant that the judges had misinterpreted the purpose of registration. In making this claim they offered four possible interpretations of the purpose of national registration. First, they maintained that the system had not been introduced for security reasons. Rather it had been drawn up to provide the government with an accurate understanding of the manpower resources at its disposal. In other words, it was designed to provide some statistical information about Britain. Second, it had supplementary uses, which had been outlined in the parliamentary debates around its introduction, such as reuniting families separated during evacuations. Third, quite soon after its introduction, registration had been used for purposes other than security, such as updating the electoral roll. Fourth, there was a broader view which maintained that the register's purpose was to help the government manage anything that arose from the wartime emergency. If this emergency were broadly conceived to cover not only the actual hostilities but also the economic aspects of total war, then practically all the uses of the register could be legitimised.[42] They needed to make this case because, as they also admitted, "it would be a bold Government that would follow the direction of the judges' interpretation and introduce a Bill at the present juncture to make National Registration permanent."[43] The problem for the register became even more acute because the Lord President's Committee ignored all these attempts to redefine the purpose of registration and declined to challenge the courts, opting instead to follow the lead of the committees that had reviewed registration before it. Thus, the recommendation was that ministers should discuss whether they were prepared to take just such a "bold" measure and introduce legislation in Parliament to make the register permanent.[44] In other words, this final committee agreed that registration had been introduced for wartime purposes only. As will be seen in the next section of this chapter, the opinions of the military carried great weight in this period, and thus the fact that the continuation of conscription after the war was not enough to justify the continuation of registration meant that the other reasons brought forward by the registration authorities were never going to win the day. However, the ministers that would have to make any decision would be those of the Conservative government that came into office two months later.

"Setting the People Free"

This Conservative government made its agenda plain less than one month after the election when Lord Salisbury said "some restrictions are absolutely vital in the modern world. But I maintain that looked at from the point of view of a parliamentary democracy. They are not a good thing in themselves, because they tend, however one may wish to avoid it, to take power from Parliament and put it in the hands of the

Executive … To my mind, the best thing one can do in the circumstance is, to … reduce the scope and number of these regulations as much as is practicably possible."[45] The National Register was clearly one of these regulations and it is equally clear that, at least where this was concerned, the government wanted to reap the plaudits for being the people's liberator. Thus, the financial secretary to the Treasury, John Boyd-Carpenter wrote to the minister of health, Harry Crookshank about abolition saying "let us have the credit for 'setting the people free' in one small respect."[46] However, this abolition could not just be implemented without addressing its consequences. These consequences were listed by the registrar in the middle of December 1951, and included the immediate mechanics of ending registration, how those that used the register should plan for its abolition and how the military should plan for what was euphemistically termed "a future emergency."[47]

The announcement of the end of registration came in a reply given by the minister of health to a parliamentary question on 21 February 1951. The government wanted the whole process brought to a conclusion even earlier but George North, who wrote the minister's reply, could not move more quickly as arrangements had to be put in place at departments that used the register, most notably the NHS. Additionally, he had to make arrangements with the Post Office to instruct its staff to deliver identity cards that were to be posted back for recycling (it was calculated that this would produce between 200 and 250 tons of good quality manila).[48] However, this was later abandoned and the public were instructed to hand cards into their local food office.

The announcement that registration was being abolished, instructed people to make a note of their number because this would become their NHS number. This meant, as North wrote to Crookshank, that the announcement of abolition should not sound too jubilant about the ending of the British identity card in case NHS numbers became as tainted in the eyes of the public as the register and identity cards.[49] In fact, after the register's numbers became NHS numbers, the registrar general continued to operate the NHS register because the 1939 act, that had established the National Register, did not permit the transfer of information collected by the register to any other department.[50] At the time of the announcement ending registration, North also noted that all the other users of the register would have to rely on records that were "as is fully recognised, inferior to the service now given" but accepted that in peacetime this situation was probably "not intolerable."[51] However, there was one department that did not find the situation tolerable, and this was the Ministry of Defence. In the last ditch defence of registration in 1951 North claimed that registration served and indeed had been introduced to serve, a wide variety of purposes above and beyond the needs of conscription. But the attitude of the military towards registration after abolition illuminates the intimate connection between registration and conscription, since in 1952 the military were agitated about the introduction of registration for a future war.

This anxiety was noted at the second meeting of the Defence (Transition) Committee in April 1952 where it was agreed that a subcommittee would examine the question in detail. North was at this April meeting and afterwards he wrote to the cabinet secretary, Norman Brook, asking Brook to do what he could to steer the subcommittee in the right direction. This, of course, would be to suggest that in a future war the recently abandoned system of national registration should be revived and that future conscription should not have to rely on "some make-do arrangements" based on the "not really tried and tested" NI records.[52] Before the war the Ministry of Labour had contested Vivian's control of the National Register. But in 1952 the Ministry of Labour and National Service completely agreed with North's view and made this clear in its submissions to the subcommittee, a process that also laid bare the reality of the link between registration and conscription.

The military argued that only a system of national registration would enable it to fully conscript the population in a future war. The records of the NI system were not up to this task since these did not receive prompt notification of changes of address. Summing up its view the Ministry of Defence said that it "would welcome the re-establishment of the National Register."[53]

The (Maxwell) Subcommittee on Personal Identification in War, where North and his allies in the Ministry of Labour and National Service made their case reported in December 1952. This report began by pointing out that it accepted the view of the de Villiers Report that registration was not necessary in peacetime. But it then went on to show how it would be vital in a future war since all the alternatives were inadequate. The records of the NHS covered 95% of the population and those of the NI system 45%, but the two systems could not be combined because of their different filing systems.[54] Nonetheless, it recommended that a future register enumerate the population using the numbering system of the NI system and gave three reasons for this. First, it felt that this system was more likely to be permanent than that of the NHS. Second, it covered all parts of the UK with one system. Third, that "the trend will be for the National Insurance records, rather than those of the National Health, to be developed for use by other Departments."[55]

This last comment by the Maxwell Subcommittee, along with its recognition of the problem caused by the incompatibility of different sets of records, shows that it seemed to envision a time in the relatively near future when the records of various government departments would be connected. This ran counter to the view of the de Villiers Committee that, as has been seen, had refused to examine common numbering despite its having been raised by North as a good reason for keeping the register. In this the Maxell Committee may be credited with, if not actual prescience, then at least an understanding of the ways in which Whitehall might go about remedying problems arising from its record systems. This solution, the use of a common numbering system, would remain below the surface of British politics for the next decade, but it would re-emerge in the early 1960s through the demands of medical researchers. Shortly after this, a common numbering system and indeed a population register itself would be championed not only by those who would run such a system, but also by some of the most powerful voices at the centre of the government.

Notes

1. TNA, HO 45/25014, Vivian, *The Future of National Registration*, September 1944, 1.
2. TNA, HO 45/25014, "We May Still Have Identity Cards in 1960," *Daily Mirror*, n.d., ca. early 1945; TNA, HO 45/25014, "Danger in Numbers," *Liverpool Post*, 13 April 1945; TNA, HO 45/25014, "Whitehall Examines Peace Identity Cards," *Evening News*, 5 April 1945.
3. S. P. Vivian, "Identity Cards and Liberty," *National Review*, August 1946, 143.
4. Ibid., 143–48.
5. TNA, RG 28/300, E. H., *The National Register and the Identity Card*, 21 July 1950, 3.
6. Ibid., 1; see also, Jane Caplan, "'This or That Particular Person': Protocols of Identification in Nineteenth-Century Europe," in *Documenting Individual Identity: The Development of State Practices in the Modern World*, eds. Jane Caplan and John Torpey (Princeton: Princeton University Press, 2001), 64.

7. See, Jon Agar, "Modern Horrors: British Identity and Identity Cards," in *Documenting Individual Identity*, eds. Jane Caplan and John Torpey, 115–20.
8. TNA, RG 28/300, *The Future of National Registration*, n.d., ca. 1950, 10.
9. Ibid.
10. Ibid.
11. Max Weber, *Max Weber and the Theory of Modern Politics*, ed. David Beetham (London: Polity, 1985), 81.
12. Bruce Curtis, *The Politics of Population: State Formation, Statistics, and the Census of Canada, 1840–1875* (London: University of Toronto Press, 2001), 27 and 26.
13. Nikolas Rose, *Powers of Freedom: Reframing Political Thought* (Cambridge: Cambridge University Press, 1999), 208.
14. William Alonso and Paul Starr, "Introduction," in *The Politics of Numbers*, eds. William Alonso and Paul Starr (New York: Russell Sage Foundation, 1987), 3.
15. TNA, RG 28/149, J. M. R., *National Registration for Conscription Purposes Only*, 24 November 1949, 1.
16. TNA, T 222/436, George North, *National Registration*, 19 April 1951, 2.
17. TNA, T 222/435, John Foster and H. O. Dovey, *Common Numbering System for Government Records*, 17 December 1948, 1.
18. Ibid., 2–3.
19. TNA, T 222/435, John Foster, *National Registration and National Insurance*, n.d., ca. December 1948, 2.
20. Ibid., 1.
21. TNA, RG 28/280, E. Horn, *Appendix*, 6 October 1949, 1.
22. TNA, WO 32/21649, *Report of the Committee on National Registration*, February 1950, 6.
23. TNA, T 227/336, *National Registration*, n.d., ca. 1950, 2; TNA, T 222/436, *Note of a Meeting at the Treasury on 22 May 1950 to Discuss the Effect Upon the NHS of the Proposal to Discontinue National Registration*, 1; *The Future of National Registration*, 2.
24. E. Horn, *Appendix*, 1–4.
25. Nikolas Rose, "Governing by Numbers: Figuring Out Democracy," *Accounting, Organizations and Society* 16 (1991): 689; Nikolas Rose and Peter Miller, "Political Power Beyond the State: Problematics of Government," *The British Journal of Sociology* 43 (1992): 178; see also, Jon Agar, *The Government Machine: A Revolutionary History of the Computer* (London: Massachusetts Institute of Technology Press, 2003), 134.
26. *Report of the Committee on National Registration*, 1.
27. Ibid., 6.
28. TNA, RG 28/279, J. M. Ross, *What the Nation Will Lose If the Committee's Proposals Are Adopted*, 28 February 1950, 2.

29. TNA, RG 28/149, *Skeleton Outline of Pros and Cons*, n.d., ca. 1949, 2.
30. TNA, T 222/436, Government Organisation Committee, *National Registration, a Note by the Registrar General*, 19 April 1951, 2.
31. TNA, RG 28/300, E. H., *The National Register and the Identity Card*, 21 July 1950, 4.
32. TNA, HO 45/25015, *Extracts from the Minutes of a Meeting of the G.O.C., 24 July 1951*, 2.
33. Ibid.
34. TNA, CAB 21/3476, Lord President's Committee, *National Registration*, August 1951, 7.
35. Benjamin J. Goold and Daniel Neyland, "Introduction: Where Next for Surveillance Studies," in *New Directions in Surveillance and Privacy*, eds. Benjamin J. Goold and Daniel Neyland (Uffculme: Willan, 2009), xix; David Lyon, *The Electronic Eye: The Rise of Surveillance Society* (London: Polity, 1994), 105.
36. BBC News Channel, accessed 23 February 2017, http://news.bbc.co.uk/1/hi/magazine/3129302.stm; Mark Egan, "Harry Willcock the Forgotten Champion of Liberalism," *Journal of Liberal Democrat History* 17 (1997–1998): 16.
37. Agar, "Modern Horrors," 110 and 111.
38. Quoted in, E. H., *The National Register and the Identity Card*, 1.
39. When he was first elected and held government office Benn was known as Anthony Wedgewood Benn. For the sake of simplicity he is referred to as Tony Benn throughout the text of this book, but where necessary in endnotes, his name is given in the form of the publication. TNA, RG 28/201, *National Registration, Proceedings in Parliament 31 October 1951–7 December 1951*, 2.
40. *Report of the Committee on National Registration*, 4
41. Edward Higgs, *Life, Death and Statistics: Civil Registration, Censuses and the Work of the General Record Office, 1836–1952* (Hatfield: Local Population Studies, 2004), 100; Walter F. Pratt, *Privacy in Britain* (Lewisburg: Bucknell University Press, 1979), 100.
42. TNA, RG 28/92, J. M. R., *Memoranda*, 4 July 1951, 3.
43. Ibid., 2.
44. TNA, CAB 21/3476, Lord President's Committee, *National Registration*, August 1951, 7.
45. TNA, MH 55/978, Lord Salisbury, 20 November 1951, quoted in, *Guidance for the Press Office*, n.d., ca. February 1952, 1.
46. TNA, CAB 21/3476, Boyd-Carpenter to Crookshank, 13 February 1952, 1.
47. TNA, RG 28/201, *National Registration, Notes for Agenda*, 14 December 1951, 1.

48. TNA, MH 55/978, *Guidance for Press Office*, n.d., ca. February 1952, 3.
49. TNA, RG 28/201, North to Crookshank, 19 December 1951, 1.
50. David H. Flaherty, *Privacy and Government Data Banks: An International Perspective* (London: Mansell, 1979), 33.
51. North to Crookshank, 1.
52. TNA, RG 28/201, North to Brook, 30 April 1952, 1.
53. TNA, LAB 25/209, *Note by the Ministry of Labour and National Service*, 2 September 1952, 3.
54. TNA, MAF 99/1243, *Report of the Sub-committee on Personal Identification in Time of War*, 17 December 1952, 5–7.
55. Ibid., 8.

CHAPTER 4

Data for "Day-to-Day Intervention"

The previous two chapters showed how, despite their developing plans to use it to improve, if not revolutionise, government administration, the advocates of peacetime population registration were thwarted in the immediate post-war period as national registration was abolished because ministers and most officials could not see a need for it. This chapter presents and examines a volte-face in these official attitudes and sets out the development of an official mindset that would be a constant feature of government for the rest of the period covered by this book: one that, through its biopolitical planning and policies, clamoured to get the data that could flow from a population register.

The first section explores how this mentality was reflected and reinforced by key government reports, which argued that government administration needed a radical programme of modernisation, and also shows how these had antecedents in the attempts of medical researchers to further their work by devising and building a network of interconnected medical data. This study of the intellectual background to the events studied here will use Foucault's ideas since these can aid an understanding of the thinking that occasioned this government focus on population registration in the 1960s.

The second section looks at the genesis of the Statistical Policy Committee, the body set up under Harold Wilson, to give form to the data-gathering zeitgeist. This section analyses how key members of this committee embraced the reform of government administrative and policy-making processes and how this can best be understood by using a

K. Manton, *Population Registers and Privacy in Britain, 1936–1984*,
https://doi.org/10.1007/978-3-030-02753-7_4

conceptualisation of welfare drawn from the work of Nikolas Rose and by contextualising the actions of government within the progressive thought of the period.

The third section demonstrates how this thinking led to the advocacy of population registration and the common numbering of all government files and how, unlike their predecessors in the immediate post-war period, these politicians and officials were swimming with the tide since their radical ideas were willingly embraced throughout Whitehall and government. However, the government was well aware that the public would not welcome these proposals, and this section therefore weighs up how they planned to deal with a public backlash to such policies.

The fourth section connects this thinking to the computerisation that was taking tentative first steps at this time. It considers the state of computerisation within government and shows how it was argued that the technology could facilitate the standardisation, centralisation and linking of data. This section thus initiates a discussion that will run through the remainder of this book concerning the politics of the relationship between paper-based and computerised files in this period.

Moving on from "12 Wasted Years"

In a speech made in January 1964, ten months before the Labour Party was elected, Harold Wilson said: "as a nation, we have missed many of the opportunities offered to us by the scientific revolution … many of our institutions and our processes … for decision-making are clumsy, amateurish, ineffective, and out-of-date."[1] Wilson was a statistician who, as he phrased it, "spent more time with statisticians and statistics than with journalists and the public opinion polls."[2] So it was hardly surprising that once in power one of the elements of the government's decision-making processes he sought to make slick, professional, effective and up to date was the provision of statistical information. In fact, it was only a little more than six weeks after the election that he received a report on *Economic and Social Intelligence*.[3] This report was the first sign that, within a short space of time, the government would take steps that would lead it to draw up plans for population registration. During this process, it would revisit and revitalise many of the ideas that had been brought up in the immediate post-war period. This time though, these ideas would not be associated with conscription, but would be seen as part and parcel of policies that were widely accepted across government as beneficial, necessary and progressive. This section will outline these ideas, the role of this report, the influence of the later Heyworth Report and the antecedents of these ideas in medical research.

Wilson would later give the credit for initiating the reform of government data gathering to the "historic" *Fourth Report of the Estimates Committee* of December 1966.[4] The importance of this report lay in its permitting reform to go ahead, but, despite its length, this said little that had not already been highlighted by the *Economic and Social Intelligence* report two years earlier. This clearly set out the government's analysis of its problems identifying three main shortcomings of the systems that supplied the government with such intelligence. First, this supply was slow, for example the report agreed with another assessment that even three years after it had been taken, analysis of the 1961 census was still only "waddling along."[5] Second, in some important fields there was little or no data at all, and if data did exist, it could be, third, contradictory and was often inaccurate. The report explained these shortcomings by saying that the central statistical apparatus of government was far too poorly organised to perform the functions increasingly required of it. Government departments each had their own statisticians who, in most cases, were isolated from the rest of the department. The Central Statistical Office (CSO) was powerless to enforce a uniformity of standards that would help in remedying the situation, and the General Register Office (GRO) was, at best, badly connected to other departments that could have used its outputs. Statisticians were the Cinderellas of the civil service. They were poorly paid, rarely promoted and often found that non-statisticians ran sections, such as the Census Office, which ought to have been a statistician's fiefdom. All of this meant that the government's statistical information was unfit for the purposes required by a Labour government wanting to "formulate day-to-day policies of intervention."[6]

This report drew most of its examples from the economy, but it indicated, both in its title and in its mentions of aspects of government work, such as housing, that its findings should apply to interventions in not only the British economy, but also the day-to-day lives of British people. In this, it was part of a broader trend that would see the Home Affairs Committee stating, in 1968, that the radical changes proposed by the government (outlined below) were necessary to provide "the kind of cross-analyses needed as a background to more sophisticated social security schemes, education, health, housing and transport policy and planning generally."[7] This trend was both reflected and reinforced by another report issued in the middle of 1965.

This was the *Report of the Committee on Social Studies* (the Heyworth Report).[8] This listed all the government policies that would benefit from the input of social scientists. These included education, welfare, health, delinquency and immigration, but only two areas-economic growth and industrial efficiency-were economic in nature. Clearly, the idea of planning for day-to-day interventions was spreading to encompass, if not indeed to focus on, the day-to-day lives of the British people. This would necessitate the increased use of cutting-edge sociometric techniques to make more data about those lives available to the planners; however, there was a lot of work to be done before this position could be reached.[9] Thus, the report stated that there was "emphatic" evidence "that much still remains to be done in respect of the provision, coordination and publication of social statistics which involves relationships both among Government departments and between departments and social scientists in universities and other research establishments."[10] To achieve this, Heyworth made recommendations that were similar to those of the report of the previous autumn. He sought the centralisation at the heart of the government machine of all those statistical operations that were fragmented in far-flung corners of Whitehall.

The Heyworth Report sought to inculcate modern thinking, principally the methods of the social sciences, into the practices of government. Michel Foucault has described the social sciences as an intrinsic part of what he calls a "new political rationality" that began to emerge in Europe in the late eighteenth century.[11] This new formulation of power, which he terms "biopolitics," was an attempt to rule not just individuals but people as a mass: "a global mass that is affected by overall processes characteristic of birth, death, production, illness and so on," in other words, the population.[12] The population thus became both the object of political action and the reason for it. Foucault's ideas have resonance for the object of this study because he argues that "the mechanisms introduced by biopolitics include forecasts, statistical estimates, and overall measures,"[13] in other words that population registration is an integral part of this mode of thought. This reveals the political content of statistics (see Chapter 3) and so shows that population registers became important when it was necessary to know the population in order to act upon it.[14] This is not to suggest that this mode of thinking and its associated political technologies began in Britain with the events examined here. Rather, it is to point out that this political rationality along with the systems and policies it promoted (and which in turn acted reciprocally to promote the mode of thought) extended both the depth and breadth of their penetration into the mindset of British governments in this period.

Foucault shows that while biopolitical mechanisms were created and implemented in Europe, Britain remained accustomed to "a much looser, Anglicized system."[15] Popular attachment to this looser style of political relations had been a factor in the post-war abolition of national registration; however, this did not prevent plans to register the British from being drawn up subsequently, and an examination of these plans will show the relevance of Foucault's analysis to understanding why government saw registration as necessary in the 1960s when it had been willing to abolish the National Register in 1952. This is the case because Foucault's work turns attention to the thinking that underpinned this change of heart, and so for all that it does not examine the detail of registration, it nevertheless encourages an examination of why registration had been adopted in Europe and, by extension, why it was increasingly advocated in Britain. Wilson may have written that the report from the Estimates Committee had got these processes moving, but it is clear that he and others had wanted this process to begin virtually as soon as Labour took power. Thus, the interconnections between Foucault's understanding of biopolitics and the drive for data in 1960s Britain can be distinguished by looking at the policies and disciplines that were central to these developments. Foucault's understanding of biopolitics focuses on the policy areas where British governments sought to use registration such as welfare, immigration, health and education. More importantly, medicine occupies a crucial space in Foucault's analysis because it acts on both the individual body and the body politic, the population, and in 1960s Britain, medical research was a discipline that increasingly pursued and used augmented flows of data about people.[16] Though this medical desire for data could work in tandem with the government, it existed independently of it and predates the Wilson government's plans. Thus, the Heyworth Report made clear that it was not the initiator of the wave of social data it promoted, but was rather trying to channel an already-rising tide into government service. For example, when it noted the necessity of placing the social survey at the heart of government planning, it wrote that: "in recent years the demands made upon it have increased very considerably both in scope and magnitude."[17]

Medical research was an integral part of this data-hungry zeitgeist within which it consumed data in pursuit of biopolitical ends, chivvied government to provide it with access to more and established its own systems that would have important ramifications for how the government pursued its own data collection and registration plans. In 1963, medical researchers in the Oxford area led by Donald Acheson (he would be UK chief medical officer, 1983–1991) began an experiment that centred on reorganising all medical records to find out whether they could create “a single integrated file of health data for a community.”[18] In other words, the purpose of the study was to link together discreet sets of medical records. Acheson became a leading advocate of this method of epidemiological research and presented a long memoranda based on this study to the Medical Research Council’s (MRC) Committee on General Epidemiology, in September 1964. This memorandum was influential in the drafting of the committee’s August 1965 report examining proposals for a national system of linked medical records.[19]

Acheson saw that the root of the problem faced by medical researchers lay in the departmentalisation of medical records, which divided data on one person into many different sets of files that were incapable of communicating with each other. He wanted to replace this division with integration: with one unified set of records for each person structured to also permit cross-referencing to blood relatives. Data collection was expensive, he said, and it would therefore be prudent to use to the full all the data that had been collected. This was not currently possible, but there were two factors at work that ought, he thought, to encourage this. The first of these was computerisation. This could speed up the whole process of retrieving data and also reduce the space required for its storage. Second was the fact that since the creation of the National Health Service (NHS), the vast bulk of the country’s health data was in the hands of one institution. But, he suggested that two key things would be required to accelerate the changes heralded by these developments and make this system work to its full potential. First, all health data would need to be recorded in a standardised format. Second, but far more importantly, this system would also need people to have a number.[20]

People already had a number: their NHS number, but Acheson pointed out that this was underused. It was not, for example, recorded on death certificates, only seldom noted on a patient’s hospital records and equally rarely recorded on local morbidity records. He did not suggest that all files be re-catalogued using the NHS number, but rather that all files contain this information to permit the creation of a de facto single entity that would facilitate cross-referencing. His problem was, of course, the same one that had confronted Sylvanus Vivian and George North with the wartime and post-war National Register, how to increase the use of the NHS number, and like them, he confronted the problem in both the institutions he wanted to use and the public he wanted to monitor. Thus, he first recommended that local medical institutions should be told what to do and instructed by the central authorities to change their administrative practices. Second, just as North had suggested the creation of what he had called "a social register card" to guide the public towards new patterns of day-to-day behaviour, so Acheson suggested that people would be more likely to remember or use their NHS number if it were incorporated into a "personal health card." This could be made more popular with the public if it also recorded the individual's immunisation record and any "drug idiosyncrasies."[21]

Both Acheson and the MRC were at pains to point out that the data linked by this system would not be shared outside the health services and that this use of the NHS number would be confined only to health records.[22] However, their proposals were very warmly welcomed by the registrar general's office. In 1944, Vivian had tentatively suggested that the National Register could facilitate medical research. But here, in the mid-1960s, the GRO saw how these linked medical records could expedite their own plans. The MRC's plans were seen as an opportunity "to carry our own thinking on record linkage a good deal further than we have been able."[23] Exactly how far they wanted to carry their own ideas was made plain when the GRO noted that if these proposals from the MRC were "successfully adopted" they would offer an opportunity for "the restoration of national registration with at least the degree of completeness which was obtained during the last war and up to 1952."[24] The GRO had been discussing a roll-out of a series of ad hoc registration schemes, to record things such as name changes, divorces and the particulars of immigrants. Furthermore, the GRO was already using the NHS register alongside its other databases for a variety of functions but had found that "the usefulness of the [NHS] register for these purposes falls far short of what would be expected from a complete national register."[25] But now the MRC's new proposals seemed to be holding out something that was altogether different: the prospect of what was, in all but name, a total population register.

When the MRC's proposals arrived at the GRO, there was a discussion about who would administer this system and the problems that might arise in using it. One of these potential pitfalls was "the political objections to it." One member of GRO staff thought that "we need not spend much time on" these, since they were "not very real," but elsewhere in the GRO, others were well aware of the political implications of these proposals.[26] The use of the NHS register by the GRO had not "been made the subject of particular public announcement" but was nonetheless going ahead. As a result, it was noted, "there is a body of opinion within the Ministry of Health which is already seriously concerned about a possible allegation that we are running national registration under the counter."[27] It is important to recognise that this "body of opinion" was not hostile to using the NHS database as a de facto population register, but rather argued that it was time that ministers were made aware of what was happening and asked to specifically approve it.

However, elsewhere Michael Reed, the registrar general, made it clear that he knew that there could well be a lot of public hostility towards this development from a population as yet unhabituated to registration. He was present at a meeting in June 1966 with the MRC and others to discuss its proposals. He pointed out that the costs of the new system could be reduced if it were to completely replace the existing NHS register. However, he went on to note that "an important point was that the apparently de novo establishment of a national register might have political repercussions, the strength of which should not be underestimated."[28]

These discussions in June 1966 concluded that: "a strong case had been made in principle for the eventual establishment of record linkage on a national scale."[29] Additionally, this meeting also made two other things plain. First, that links across records would not be built into the system. Permanent links would not be practicable, as Reed told the MRC, however, the system could, and would be designed to allow the creation of ad hoc links according to the needs of particular research projects. Second, that this system must remain a medical filing system. Access by other departments to this databank (the police and the Ministry of Pensions and National Insurance were used as examples) should not be permitted.[30] Later, in its 1972 report, the Younger Committee on Privacy (see Chapters 5–7) would maintain that strong medical ethics protected the patient's privacy and on this basis it would condone the linkage of medical records.[31] However, as has been seen, while the GRO was running these records, they were accused of using them as a de facto National Register. Perhaps, technically, this was not giving an unauthorised body access to NHS data, since the GRO was supposed to be running the system inside the Ministry of Health, but at the same time, the system was clearly, in some minds, being run for purposes that were beyond those for which it had been established. Moreover, the notion that all medical personnel wanted to adhere to the highest standards of patient record confidentiality is misleading.

John Edwards, a leading medical geneticist, wrote the report for the MRC on the use of record linkage in genetic studies.[32] He saw that the linking of medical records would give his field of research a huge fillip. Genetic studies had always been limited to studying rare conditions precisely because all the research had to be undertaken by personal interviews with patients, so a connected web of primary medical data would open up a whole new realm of possibilities for the discipline. However, he also showed that were these medical records, as a matter of policy, linked to other official records, then the value of the combined record system would be far greater than the value of any of these sets on its own. This linkage would allow for more detailed research into features such as morbidity and blood groups, and it would have an immediate practical value in, for example, allocating expectant woman to appropriate obstetric centres. But he also maintained that the benefits of these linked records could and should be spread even wider. Clearly echoing Acheson's ideas, he stated that data was expensive to collect but relatively cheap to share, and that therefore sharing data that had already been collected was both rational and prudent. This report thus recommended that NHS data be shared with the welfare and education services. It is worth pointing out that these plans did not come to fruition: this pan-departmental data web was not created here. But equally it needs to be noted that influential voices were openly calling for its establishment while the GRO was simultaneously being accused of covertly operating a nascent version of such a system. Moreover, all these developments predate the December 1966 report of the Estimates Committee that Wilson would later claim initiated the drive to create data fit for day-to-day intervention. Therefore, it is clear that the drive for standardised, centralised and linked data had roots in 1960s Britain that were both deeper and wider than simply the government. Consequently, if these developments are to be understood, it is necessary to look not only at government policy, but also at the mindset within which the government worked.

So far as the ordinary member of the public was concerned, the government's day-to-day interventions were to be transmitted through the conduit of welfare-type policies. Building on Foucault's work, welfare has been characterised by Nikolas Rose and Peter Miller as "the assembling of diverse mechanisms and arguments through which political forces seek to secure social and economic objectives by linking up a plethora of networks with aspirations to know, programme and transform the social field."[33] They show how the government's desire to know the people involves a huge effort to transform individuals into information, and how in order that this information can be collated, it needs to be presented in a standardised format, in other words as statistics, and that these must flow to the centre to be processed so that events that occur at a distance can be absorbed into the grid of knowledge.[34] It is clear that the Labour government that came to power in 1964 was not alone in operating within this milieu: having this desire to know the population through centralised and standardised data, or wanting to act on the population by using this information. But the government could not govern the people through the MRC. To achieve its aims, it needed new nodes of power at the centre to design, direct and deploy a data matrix of its own.

Building the New "Command Structure"

The report on *Economic and Social Intelligence* that Wilson received in November 1964 had recommended the total reconditioning of the government's statistical apparatus to create a new "command structure" capable of delivering and directing the increased data flows that ought to underpin modern government. This new structure was inaugurated, after the Estimates Committee reported in December 1966, and began its work in April 1967. This was the Statistical Policy Committee. This committee began work on social statistics that had such "vast potential for public administration and social conscience" that Wilson did not hesitate to describe its work as "revolutionary," "a great leap forward" and the "great charter of statistical reform."[35] This section will look at the establishment of this committee and will interrogate the fundamental views of some of its key members.

Following the advice of the *Economic and Social Intelligence* report, Wilson chaired the committee's first meeting in order, as he put it later, "to show that I meant business," and he also made himself available to chair subsequent meetings if there were inter-departmental disagreements to resolve, or if Claus Moser (director of the CSO) and the statisticians needed heavyweight political back up.[36] However, this committee was normally to be run by specially selected, numerate, junior ministers, and its first chair was Peter Shore. Shore was an economist who, having only been elected in 1964, was enjoying a meteoric rise that would see him installed as secretary of state at the Department for Economic Affairs (DEA) at the end of August 1967. He was an ideal choice to spearhead an overhaul of government statistics because he understood that this was an urgent task. Indeed, a few months before this appointment he had written of "the lack of research centres or policy planning units in the Ministries," noting that: "even at the lowest level of information, there is quite inadequate feedback arrangements through which departments can evaluate the effects of their own actions."[37]

But as well as coming into this post as a new broom, right from his arrival in Parliament, Shore also had the reputation of being a committed advocate of open government.[38] Moreover, he was not alone in this because Shirley Williams was also a member of the committee. She would later champion the right of privacy by standing up for doctors in Oxford who refused to participate in creating "a nationally-linked system of medical records … without any question of the consent of the patients being sought." In other words a system from the same mould as Acheson's programme, and one which she described as a "disturbing" system of power over individuals.[39] Notwithstanding these positions championing the people against the data-gathering state, Shore's committee would regard the confidentiality of records and the privacy of the individual as something that should be dealt with on an ad hoc basis rather than as a matter of principle.[40] Furthermore, this committee would pursue policies (discussed below) that were designed to follow the pattern already laid out by the MRC and the GRO and which would disturb Williams so much. Thus, how Shore and Williams could work on this project is something that clearly merits examination.

Along with Wilson and probably a big majority of the British people, both Shore and Williams believed that the aims they pursued, for example better health and welfare policies, were innately progressive, but the welfarist purpose of policy is not the issue here, rather the focus is on the mechanism chosen to deliver it: a method which Shore and Wilson (and usually Williams), unlike many British people, also saw as progressive. The *Heyworth Report* concurred with this and concluded: "the government has a duty to encourage the most progressive techniques of management."[41] These progressive techniques were described two years later as being centred on a rational analysis of the whole process to provide management with a clear picture of the inter-relationship between discreet elements in order to eliminate anything that was superfluous. This analysis, it was maintained, should be in a quantified form because this standardised form of data would allow for greater linkage between elements of the process concerned.[42] Standardisation, centralisation, and linkage of data were thus the watchwords of progressive administration.

That this data was quantitative is important because, as Nikolas Rose has pointed out, this meant that it would be "guided by expertise" and "would not be arbitrary but scientific."[43] Rose sees this as productive of a "new form of government of the economic, social and personal lives of citizens."[44] This new political rationality would operate to shape the conditions under which free citizens would live their lives and make their own choices in fact its aim was to increase the range of their choices and the reach of their decisions. Thus, its advocates, such as Shore and Williams, could legitimately maintain that it was democratic in nature.[45] However, the unfolding of this new governmental mode was an empirical matter, in other words, it was rooted in its time and place and consequently what it meant to be progressive in 1960s Britain can best be understood in the terms of those progressives themselves.[46] One way to access this is by looking at the forces to which they juxtaposed their progressivism. Wilson was very clear about what a reactionary Britain meant. It meant a Britain that was "nostalgic and backward looking," run by "vested interests" based in "institutions of a dead past" and peppered with "upper-class accents," all of which was encapsulated in the term the "old-boy network."[47] Alain Desrosières argues that the period 1950–1975 saw an effort made to "unify the economic and social debate around a common language," namely that of statistical thinking.[48] It is certainly possible to locate Wilson within this conceptualisation as a representative of a trend that Patrick Joyce (following Foucault) sees as originating in the nineteenth century, one that sought to make a world fit for modern systems of government by rendering people into an abstract, standardised statistical form, a process within which "judgements of quality were taken away from those who did the measuring."[49]

Rose has noted that "experts were vital relays for social government, linking political objectives and personal conduct,"[50] and Labour's drive to gather data to rationalise and expand the provision of policies was all of a piece with Wilson's trenchant critique of the prevailing ethos of the civil service and commensurately promoted the role of the expert. As early as 1959 the prevailing Whitehall culture had come under withering attack from Thomas Balogh who categorised it as *The Apotheosis of the Dilettante*. A 1964 Fabian report agreed with his conclusions and in the campaign for the election of that year, Wilson remarked "we are living in the jet age but we are governed by an Edwardian establishment mentality," and lambasting the "social prejudices and anti-scientific bias of the old boy network," the party's manifesto promised to "make government … more efficient" by introducing "new kinds of skill and experience."[51] This may serve to show how the party had a firm belief in what Max Weber characterised as the efficiency and rationality of administration based on modern models, but understanding this also makes it possible to see how statistical data and population registration could be accepted as an inherently progressive tool of government because first, it was objective and equalising and second, because it was produced by scientists, people who possessed qualifications rather than connections: new brooms rather than old boys.

Some members of the government, such as Shirley Williams, may have been ambivalent about some of the effects of some of these methods (though the minutes of all the meetings she attended do not record any opposition and she would go on to chair the committee in 1978) or may have been wary of a hostile public opinion. However, these concerns would be balanced against a political trajectory that increasingly became accepted wisdom within government circles in the period studied here: a view that overwhelmingly saw these techniques as progressive in nature. In fact, Claus Moser went so far as to describe the linking of data, such as later horrified Williams, as a contribution to "enlightened and efficient government," whilst others described it as being "in the interests of progressive administration."[52] Tony Benn wrote that it was an inevitable feature of modern life that people were known as numbers. But whereas Max Weber saw these as de-humanising (see Chapter 3) Benn described them as "liberating factors that simplify the handling of my business by the agencies with which I deal." What he found "terrifying" about this enumeration was that "the agencies that deal with us and our problems are too often concerned only with the narrow sector of our lives which touch their particular field." This established process of taking "a narrow view of human beings" was, he continued, "both destructive of the individual personality and also unscientific."[53] Bearing this in mind, it is unsurprising that a briefing from the CSO, received by Peter Shore in 1968, examining proposals for a population register and common numbering system should have described Britain's lack of progress towards these ends as "embarrassing."[54]

The origin of this embarrassment could well have lain in international comparisons with states that were seen as generally progressive and which had a far greater degree of linked data than Britain. The chief comparators here were Sweden and Israel both of which had full population registers. One academic author made a comparison between British and Swedish record keeping and noted that "incredible as it might seem to most people," British government departments did not link their records and so lagged lamentably far behind Sweden.[55] This was also felt across government, thus *Proposals for a Population Register System in Great Britain* was the title of a paper written from the GRO in October 1967.[56] The author had been a member of the British delegation to a symposium on population registration in Jerusalem and the paper was written as a direct result of how impressed the British had been by what they learned about the Israeli and Swedish registration systems.[57]

In the summer of 1967, as result of the work of Shore's committee, Wilson was told that "there is now widespread recognition by departments of the need for greater centralisation of statistical work and for strengthening the role of the Central Statistical Office."[58] The committee further noted that though the provision of economic statistics was poor, the supply of social data was "deficient."[59] As a result, Shore wrote to Wilson asking for clarification about what the committee should examine and in October Edmund Dell, Shore's successor as chair of the committee, got the reply he wanted when Wilson told him that the committee could broaden its remit to look at social policy statistics.[60] In principle, this meant that the day-to-day lives of the British were now going to be subjected to day-to-day intervention, but this general, macro-level thinking left open the issue of how this was going to be achieved. The "command structure" would soon produce its answers to this question.

"Radical Change": Population Registration and a Common Numbering System

In July 1967 the Statistical Policy Committee agreed that there was a "need for radical and urgent change."[61] The following month, in his interim report to Wilson, Shore noted how the government's statistical service had grown up in a piecemeal fashion as a series of ad hoc responses to an assortment of needs. But the increased sense in government of the need for policy to be built on data meant that this established provision was not only antiquated, it was also inadequate. Government departments each maintained their separate files, moreover, even within one department there could be fragmentation of data with some files, such as those of driving licences, being maintained locally.[62] As a result, communication even within a department could be difficult, whilst cross-departmental coordination might be all but impossible. Thus, there was a need for a far greater degree of centralisation and in order to achieve this, the committee, along with the CSO and GRO, forwarded two interconnected policies: they pursued a population register and a common numbering system.[63] This section will examine what these systems meant to their advocates and then how these proposals received wholehearted endorsements as they passed upwards through the government. It will then move on to look at the vexed question of popular opposition and the proposals made for outmanoeuvring this countervailing political force.

In October 1967 the registrar issued a paper outlining the potential for population registration, and the following month a paper jointly authored by both registrars (Scotland had a separate official) and the CSO examined population registration and common numbering.[64] These papers formed the basis of meetings of the Statistical Policy Committee where population registration was discussed in terms that were identical to those used by Vivian during the Second World War. Thus, both papers defined a population register as being exactly the same as the wartime National Register: a list of peoples' names, addresses and certain other personal details such as date of birth and marital status. Another similarity with the wartime register was that a degree of coercion was seen as essential to make a population register work. People would have to inform the authorities of any change in address (it was noted that in Sweden there was a statutory penalty for people who did not notify the authorities of a new address), and government departments would have to pass on any changes in the status of an individual that came to their attention. However, unlike much that was written by defenders of the wartime system the whole thrust of these papers clearly indicated that none of their authors thought that there would be any need to press government departments into carrying out their side of the process. In the 1960s, these officials saw themselves as driving a process whose time had come, not driving recalcitrant colleagues forwards.

However, though registration's advocates were swimming with the administrative and intellectual tide, they still had to win the political arguments. Precisely because existing records were inadequate, creating a register would need a special enumeration exercise along the lines of that carried out in 1939 and this would be expensive. However, this expense could be justified because the register would: eliminate inflation in NHS statistics, maintain accurate records across the whole health system, provide detailed and permanent information about population migration, compile the electoral roll and allow the more efficient compilation and maintenance of all large files by bodies such as the Post Office. Additionally, it would be available for any future needs that arose and stimulate the processes of computerisation. In other words, it would be the central nervous system of day-to-day intervention.

For its part, a common numbering system promised a step-change in the ways government utilised the vast amount of data it had at its disposal by making it possible to link information across departmental divides. It would thus herald an era of simplification, rationalisation and effectiveness in the storage and use of data, and so meet the evident and increasing demands from all layers of government and universities. Broadly speaking, pressures for the information that could flow from the record linkage produced by common numbering came from two directions. The first of these was the desire to know about events, such as health matters, that occurred at different times in an individual's life, whilst the second was the wish to be able to relate certain contemporaneous characteristics of a given individual, such as educational qualifications and occupation, to each other.

As far as the authors of these 1967 papers were concerned then, both the need for registration in some form and the recognition of that need already existed, thus their real problem was how to meet this need and implement these radical changes, in other words the technical feasibility of registration. Whereas a full register would need an expensive initial enumeration, a common numbering system could be introduced gradually by changing the method of birth registration. This would have the advantage of avoiding upheavals in filing, but would have the disadvantage of taking upwards of seventy or eighty years to cover only about 90% of the population. For a group of radical reformers who saw their mission as urgent, this was clearly neither fast nor thorough enough and it was dismissed as an option. What they labelled an intermediate scheme would have involved extending the coverage of a number that already existed. Here the numbers that could be used were the existing National Insurance (NI) and NHS numbers, or the proposed joint number for these systems. The existing system of NI numbers would have the disadvantage of not encompassing children and so would not meet the needs of the education system. But this problem could be solved if an NI number were given to all school pupils and anyone else who did not have one, whilst people born after a certain date would be issued one of the new-style numbers, which could thus be phased in. With all these variables in play, the authors decided that what was needed was a feasibility study. This would look at the whole gamut of issues raised including: the needs of various local and national bodies, the methods of establishing and maintaining a register (particularly how to record addresses), the best form for a common number, the costs and savings incurred and accrued by any such system, the timing of the introduction of these changes and any necessary legislative aspects.

However, before this feasibility study could be undertaken the Statistical Policy Committee needed to make its case to and get endorsement from, the Home Affairs Committee. This higher-level body willingly embraced these ideas. In fact, it noted that, in addition to the plans being pursued by the MRC, there were already several ad hoc record linkage schemes in the pipeline that were being held back in the knowledge that this broader programme was being developed. The Department for Education and Science was reconfiguring its records to link them across the stages of a pupil's life, the Ministry of Transport was designing a new number to link driving licences and vehicle registration and there had already had been studies of how one number could be used across the NI and NHS systems.[65] These latter studies had found that it would be practicable to make the change, but this had been put on hold once the scale of the demand for a more generalised common numbering system became apparent. This was the demand that the Statistical Policy Committee and its allies in the GRO and CSO were aiming to meet and the Home Affairs Committee was thus of one mind with these radical reformers. Agreeing that this mission was "urgent," it endorsed the proposals for a feasibility study and passed its views to the minister at the Home Office along with a briefing that stated: "the advantages claimed for the two projects are unquestionable."[66] This draws out a marked contrast between events in 1952 when government had been content to abolish the National Register, and the period of Wilson's government when there was unequivocal support for these attempts to get it reintroduced. Clearly, by the late 1960s, data had become the lingua franca of government.

These discussions of these two policies highlight the fact that their backers saw them as connected. Thus, in July 1968 Claus Moser and Michael Reed, the registrar general, described a full population register as "a logical development" of a common numbering system. But then added that the two did not necessarily stand or fall together, so if a "full register were either not feasible or politically unacceptable, it might still be possible to make a case for the common number."[67] It is thus clear that two of the foremost advocates of population registration in the late 1960s, like Sylvanus Vivian and George North in the war and post-war period, saw a common numbering system as an acceptable alternative to registration. Moreover, just as the GRO had seen the MRC's proposals for the linkage of medical records as producing something tantamount to the wartime system of registration, so the generalised common number could be the gateway to the full register. Thus, the Statistical Policy Committee's July 1968 recommendation to examine whether a common numbering system should be expanded into a full population register was built on the understanding that it could be expanded in this manner.[68] A similar understanding of the relationship between the two systems can be seen in the findings of the Home Affairs Committee which noted that a full population register was "a natural and logical development from" a common numbering system adding that the two could be investigated "as a single operation."[69] This committee also showed how, as well as being connected to each other, a common numbering system and register could in turn be linked to something else: "a population register would very probably entail a personal identity card."[70]

When the Statistical Policy Committee decided to focus on the technical feasibility of registration or common numbering it did not examine the constitutional or political feasibility of either scheme. The constitutional position on data held by the government had been laid out in 1966 by the lord chancellor, Lord Gardiner: "for over 100 years Parliament has said – with, I should have thought, the general consent of the people as a whole – that it is all right for the state to force the taxpayer to tell it exactly what his income is, but that this information will not be disclosed to other people."[71] As far as this doctrine was usually understood in Whitehall, the phrase "other people," did not mean only other members of the public, but also clearly indicated other government departments.[72] Moser was well aware of this and wrote in 1968 that while data collected under the terms of compulsory powers could be shared across departments, data supplied voluntarily could not, thus he concluded that some new legislation would be required.[73]

Reed's awareness of a potential public backlash to the creation of linked medical records has already been mentioned and this awareness also influenced these wider proposals. In thinking about the political feasibility of population registration and common numbering, Moser and Reed saw that the public's reaction to the introduction of registration would be coloured by their experiences of national registration in the war "and its association with identity cards, food rationing, mobilisation, direction of labour, control of movements and so on."[74] A year later Moser repeated this point adding that it was nonetheless irrational for the public to fear the introduction of a common number since they already had a multiplicity of numbers, and all the proposal was aiming to do was replace these with one single number.[75] But, as the Home Affairs Committee concluded, that was precisely the nub of the problem: the public, unhabituated to registration, were irrational. Logical arguments would not reach them because they were obsessed with the fear that any improvements in the efficiency of government administration would be used to build personal dossiers. These might lead to aspects of their past, for example illegitimate children or a prison sentence, which they had long lived down, coming back to sully their reputations, or people feared dossiers might be used in some other, indefinable yet sinister way to control their lives: what was once described as "fears of 1984."[76] The British, it was asserted, thus preferred anarchy to efficiency and their unenlightened senselessness left them prey to the misrepresentations of the government's intentions by the sensationalist press.[77]

The continuity with Vivian's view of the unreasonableness of the public in the post-war period (see Chapter 3) is clear in all this. But the political situation was very different. In 1946 Britain had a system of national registration so Vivian and registration's other defenders did not have to overly concern themselves with persuading the public to accept it, what they had to do was convince the state to keep it. However, in the late 1960s the state's position had, in general, changed to one of accepting or wanting registration, but this meant that these backers of registration had to confront the question of how to deal with a hostile public opinion. Broadly speaking three solutions were brought forward. The first of these suggested that since the public feared that centralised or co-ordinated files could be used to build personal dossiers, the way to alleviate their concerns was to allow people access to their own files.[78] However, this was presented as a highly hypothetical suggestion and even then it was made only once. Clearly for a period in which people were not allowed to see even their own medical records this suggestion was too radical to contemplate.

The second solution to the issue of the public's opposition was a careful presentation of the facts of the matter. Thus, when the Home Affairs Committee was discussing the feasibility study for population registration and common numbering, it was keen to test parliamentary opinion before committing to the study and suggested that a private member's motion might provide a useful sounding board. There was also a concern to stress to the public that the feasibility study would also look at ways in which the privacy of the individual could be safeguarded were the new systems to be adopted. But where the public were concerned the proposers of these innovations were keen to avoid using phrases that would create "alarm and despondency" such as "population register" and "common numbering system." Instead they advanced a strategy of dissimulation and recommended that these developments should be linked with more positive features of the state that were already familiar such as the NHS or NI numbers, the census, or the electoral roll.[79] Moser and Reed's aim was to convince the public that what was happening was nothing new, merely "a natural extension of national insurance and birth registration schemes."[80] But this did not get around the central problem of the public's mistrust because the government could not justify these changes on the grounds of increased efficiency, for fear of exacerbating anxieties about a dossier-compiling, totalitarian big brother. The government needed to be able to tell the public how these changes would directly benefit them, but the problem it encountered here was that the only thing that the radical reformers could offer the public was "a reduction in the calls on individual members of the public to provide information."[81] Though this lack of something to offer as an inducement was one that had plagued the advocates of registration both before and after the war, at these times the problem had not been felt so acutely since, before the war, planners have assumed people's patriotic motives would encourage them to accept registration, while after the war, as registration already existed, public opinion could be largely ignored. However, in the 1960s this lack of something tangible to offer people, coupled with an awareness of the public's opposition, led to the third solution to the problem of a public who were at best dubious about, and at worse hostile towards registration.

This solution to the people's obduracy began by accepting that this intransigence was a fact of British political life but noted that this need not stand in the way of the introduction of a common numbering scheme, since this "could be introduced administratively without publicity by extending the use of some existing number system."[82] Secrecy was thus seen as acceptable in the pursuit of these progressive ends. It is therefore not surprising that while the Home Affairs Committee agreed that the feasibility study should go ahead, it also agreed with another point made by the Statistical Policy Committee that: "it was important not to allow the proposals to become public prematurely," since "unprepared disclosure of the projects might well be fatal for their whole future."[83] The results of this drift of policy towards deception and, what had earlier been called, "under the counter tactics" will be examined in the next chapter.

Computerisation

In addition to the creation of a new "command structure" the *Economic and Social Intelligence* report that Wilson received at the end of November 1964, had also advocated computerisation as a solution to the paucity of the data available for day-to-day interventions. This section reviews the extent of computerisation at the time, analyses what its advocates thought the process could deliver and then begins the discussion of what its opponents feared it might impose.

It is important to note that computerisation was envisaged as a process: one of introducing computers into an administrative system that, generally speaking, did not have them. This meant that throughout the period discussed in this book, computers existed side by side with paper-based or manual systems of record keeping and that these remained the main method of storing and manipulating data. Indeed, in November 1968 a report that looked ahead at the use of computers in central government over the following ten years concluded that wholesale computerisation was not possible even in the medium term. According to these authors, engineers and technicians who claimed that it could be achieved much more quickly were wrong because they did not factor in the lack of technically qualified staff. Moreover, even if it were attained it would turn Whitehall upside down and impose an unacceptable degree of central control on departmental activities.[84]

This is not to say that computerisation was non-existent. Clearly, the use of this technology in the country in general and the government in particular increased in this period. For example, the police national computer (developed as a result of projects set in train by Roy Jenkins[85]) began operating in 1974. More generally, while there were 160 computer-based tasks planned or operational in central government in 1972, this figure had increased to two hundred by 1975.[86] Throughout the whole of the public sector, there were 1870 computer systems in 1971 and 3255 in 1975, whilst the figures for the country as a whole for the same period showed an increase from 6075 systems to 13,263.[87] These were obviously noteworthy increases, but the total scale of computer use within government was dwarfed by the use of paper records. In September 1971 a government committee examined twelve departmental record systems and found that none of them were completely computerised.[88] Moreover, there were also significant gaps in the spread of the technology in this period. Even in 1983, towards the end of the period covered here, the only material held on computer at 10 Downing Street was a list of names and addresses of the prime minister's correspondents, along with microfilmed copies of their letters.[89]

Thus, computerisation was a process the results of which were more anticipated than realised in this period. In 1969 a Home Office meeting looked forward to an increase in the overall efficiency of computer-operated databases which, it claimed, was already high when compared to manual systems and which would deliver a "vast increase in statistical information which … would bring much greater efficiency in formulating and executing government policy."[90] It was widely seen that computerisation would deliver this by permitting an increase in the depth and breadth of the factors that Rose (above) described as the foundation of welfarism: the standardisation, centralisation and linkage of records. These three dimensions of computerisation will now be examined.

In January 1967, Tony Benn, who had recently become minister of technology, received a lengthy briefing on computer policy. This noted that one key factor in increasing the scope of computerisation was the standardisation of the data.[91] When this was considered it was noted that the prerequisite of the most effective use of computers was that the data should already be in a standardised format.[92] It has already been seen how one justification for a population register was that it would facilitate computerisation, and the same reasoning was also applied to common numbering. As Moser wrote "the use of a common number of standard format would greatly facilitate the general trend toward computerisation in record-keeping and the extraction of statistics from records particularly in respect of records of individuals."[93] Thus, in this period when computers were being introduced to government administration, the anticipation of wider computerisation, perhaps somewhat paradoxically, became another reason for increasing the efficiency of paper-based files by standardising and linking them through common numbering. Shore recognised this in his interim report from the Statistical Policy Committee in August 1967 writing that before computers could be successfully used to buoy policy "information must move freely across Departmental boundaries and its organisation, storage and collection must be increasingly centralised."[94] Additionally, it needs to be borne in mind that computerisation was not even the main factor pushing forward the processes of standardisation, because computers did not create the data. Thus, at the MRC, Donald Acheson was a staunch advocate of linked medical data and also of computerisation, but he acknowledged that the primary force behind the standardisation, centralisation and linking of medical data was the creation of a unified NHS which brought all medical data into one institution and so created the potential for unified records.[95]

This standardisation of data would also be a powerful tool in creating the second of Rose's factors at the core of welfarism, namely centralisation. Rose has written of how numbers and statistics can function as what he calls "fidelity techniques" for ensuring that the centre can maintain a hold over those who are on the periphery of the grid of power.[96] This can be seen in the relations between central and local government in Britain in this period. Thus, in December 1968 the Ministry of Technology held a meeting about data processing in public administration which discussed at some length the issue of whether computerised data should be stored centrally or locally. The meeting did not reach any firm conclusions, but it was noted that existing problems in the distribution of power through the government machine were likely to be exacerbated by computerisation.[97]

The third of these features was the linking of data. Moser sat on the Advisory Committee on Computers, the terms of reference for which stated that it was to comment on "the desirability of facilitating the interchange of data between machines."[98] When the committee reported, in January 1968, it clearly saw this as a highly desirable outcome. The 1969 Home Office meeting (referred to above) heard that "more important than the sheer mass of information which could be kept available was the possibility of inter-linkage between different systems. While computers were still in their infancy, the time could be foreseen when all the information recorded about an individual in all his dealings could be made available through one computer network."[99] This increased linking of computers (see Chapter 7), with departmental terminals being used to dip into a commonly held pool of data, would further promote efficiency by eliminating the need for data to be held in multiple sites. Additionally, it would necessitate, and so boost, the standardisation of the shared data.

Therefore, as Richard Coopey has pointed out, it is the case that for those who agreed with it, computerisation was unambiguously "positive and unproblematic."[100] It could hardly be otherwise when computers promised to deliver the standardised, centralised and linked data that government was pursuing through paper files. Speaking at Labour's 1963 conference in Scarborough, Wilson stated: "there is no room for Luddites in the Socialist Party,"[101] and one member of his government who definitely was not a Luddite where computers were concerned was the minister for technology, Frank Cousins, who regarded computers as "the hottest invention of recent times."[102] In July 1966 he was succeeded in this post by Tony Benn who, the previous February, had visited the Post Office Saving Bank headquarters where he saw that "a complete computerisation programme had been set in hand," this was, he recorded in his diary, "a fantastic sight."[103] In May 1968 he said: "the pressures for changes along these lines are as inevitable as was the incoming tide that ultimately engulfed King Canute."[104] But Benn did not just watch the tide, he did everything he could to assist it. Thus the following year, in a memorandum on the topic of data processing in government, he wrote of how "the possibilities presented by the bold use of data processing" should be at the heart of all major policy decisions.[105]

This advocacy of computerisation seems, from the vantage point of the twenty-first century, to be nothing but common sense. Thus, Edward Higgs has noted: "the 1960s saw the beginnings of the replacement of punched-card technology with electronic computers … [which] speeded up the processes involved in manipulating information by reducing mechanical operations."[106] However, it needs to be stressed that this was, as Higgs says, "the beginnings" of this process, and though computerisation's leading advocates shared Benn's view of the practicality and precision of computers, others were aware that there was still a lot of work to be done before this potential could be realised across all government operations. In 1973 even a committed technophile like Wilson reported that he still used a slide rule and could "wins hands down" with it against colleagues who used "one of those pocket electric calculators."[107] More importantly, even the registrar general, Michael Reed, a staunch advocate of linking records, expressed reservations about the practicalities of computerisation given the extent of the technology at the time. In 1966 when discussing the linking of medical records, he noted that the Ministry of Pensions used a computer to cover its target population of 20 million people, but found that the machines were only quicker and cheaper to use on the very simple and non-urgent elements of the work. The existing manual systems were preferred for anything more complex. Since the linking of NHS records, would involve processing a greater depth and breadth of data, he questioned whether automatic data processing was the best course to adopt.[108] Those such as Donald Acheson, who argued for the immediate and complete computerisation of this project, were, according to Reed's staff, full of "unrealistic zeal."[109] Similarly, looking back at these early days of computerisation, Moser wrote that, in this initial phase of their use, computers actually complicated and slowed down the flow of government statistics.[110] He noted that by the time of his writing, in 1977, these teething troubles had been overcome, but the point remains that whilst he and Reed were great proponents of standardised, centralised and linked, data, in the 1960s and 1970s computers were not necessarily the best means for achieving these ends.

Despite these evident technical shortcomings, and indeed despite the fact that the most important thrusts of policy on data flows were directed at paper-based records, computers came to assume a special place in public fears about overweening power. In 1967, the computer division of the Ministry of Technology presented Benn with a long paper on computer policy. This concluded by drawing attention to the social consequences of computerisation. These included the concentration in government computers of records about an individual's health, education, taxation and misdemeanours along with the concentration of financial records in various separate but inter-linked systems. Put together these two facets of the process gave "much greater possibilities … for government surveillance of the individual."[111] But two years later this acknowledgement of the potentially dystopian outcomes of computerisation was side-lined by Benn who wrote that it was necessary to "ventilate and deal with the problem" of public criticism of computerisation before "irrational fears inhibit the development of computer systems which are in themselves desirable."[112]

Benn wrote this in 1969 as a response to a pamphlet called *Computers and Freedom* that had been issued by the Society of Conservative Lawyers.[113] This work crystallised fears about the new technology by highlighting practices in the USA, which it claimed would inevitably arrive in Britain. It argued that there needed to be an open and frank discussion about the correct balance to be struck between the need to improve the efficiency of public administration and the desire to preserve traditional British liberal values. The place of this pamphlet in the British opposition to computerisation, and the nature of that opposition, will be examined in the next chapter where it will be seen that computers became the predominant focus of those who wanted to check the increase of government data powers. But while computers loomed in the public mind, the government was planning to improve the efficiency of its predominantly paper-based records as the Statistical Policy Committee began to move ahead with its feasibility study of population registration and the common numbering of files.

Notes

1. Harold Wilson, *The New Britain: Labour's Plan Outlined by Harold Wilson* (London: Penguin, 1964), 11.
2. Harold Wilson, "Statistics and Decision-Making in Government—Bradshaw Revisited," *Journal of the Royal Statistical Society. Series A* 136 (1973): 4.
3. TNA, PREM 13/1432, T. B., *Economic and Social Intelligence*, 30 November 1964.
4. Wilson, "Statistics and Decision-Making in Government", 8.
5. TNA, PREM 13/1432, T. Balogh to Prime Minister, *Statistics*, 6 March 1967, 2.
6. T. B., *Economic and Social Intelligence*, 3.
7. TNA, CAB 134/2861, Home Affairs Committee, *A Population Register and Common Numbering System for Great Britain*, 11 October 1968, 6.
8. *Report of the Committee on Social Studies*, Cmnd. 2660 (June 1965).
9. *Fourth Report from the Estimates Committee, Session 1966–67, Government Statistical Services*, December 1966, 104, xl.
10. *Report of the Committee on Social Studies*, 43.

11. Michel Foucault, *Power: Essential Works of Michel Foucault 1954–1984*, ed. James D. Faubion (London: Penguin, 2002), 417.
12. Michel Foucault, *Society Must Be Defended* (London: Penguin, 2004), 242–43.
13. Ibid., 246.
14. Bruce Curtis, *The Politics of Population: State Formation, Statistics, and the Census of Canada, 1840–1875* (London: University of Toronto Press, 2001), 26–27; William Alonso and Paul Starr, "Introduction," in *The Politics of Numbers*, eds. William Alonso and Paul Starr (New York: Russell Sage Foundation, 1987), 3.
15. Michel Foucault, *The Birth of the Clinic* (London: Routledge, 2003), 48.
16. See Edward Higgs, "Medical Statistics, Patronage and the State: The Development of the MRC Statistical Unit, 1911–1948," *Medical History* 44 (2000): 323–40; Foucault, *Society Must Be Defended*, 252–53.
17. *Report of the Committee on Social Studies*, 43.
18. E. D. Acheson and J. G. Evans, "The Oxford Record Linkage Study: A Review of the Method with Some Preliminary Results," *Proceedings of the Royal Society of Medicine* 57 (1964): 11.
19. TNA, RG 48/3149, E. D. Acheson, *Proposals for the Reorganisation and Integration of Medical Information into a Single National System*, 14 September 1964; TNA, FD 1/8310, Medical Research Council, Committee on General Epidemiology, Subcommittee on Record Linkage, *Proposals for a National System of Linked Medical Records*, August 1965.
20. E. D. Acheson, *Proposals for the Reorganisation and Integration of Medical Information into a Single National System*, 1, 4 and 9.
21. Ibid., 4 and 5.
22. Medical Research Council, Committee on General Epidemiology, Subcommittee on Record Linkage, *Proposals for a National System of Linked Medical Records*, 6.
23. TNA, RG 48/3149, R.G.O., *Record Linkage*, 13 August 1965, 1.
24. TNA, RG 28/306, *Note from Mr. West*, 18 May 1966, 1.
25. Ibid., 2.
26. R.G.O., *Record Linkage*, 1 and 2.
27. *Note from Mr. West*, 2.
28. TNA, FD 1/8310, Medical Research Council, *Informal Meeting of Departmental Representatives to Discuss Proposals for a National System of Linked Medical Records*, 15 June 1966, 2.
29. Ibid., 4.
30. Ibid., 2 and 3.
31. David H. Flaherty, *Privacy and Government Data Banks: An International Perspective* (London: Mansell, 1979), 73.

32. TNA, FD 1/8305, J. H. Edwards, Medical Research Council Subcommittee on Record Linkage, *The Use of Record Linking for Genetic Studies*, n.d., ca. February 1965.
33. Nikolas Rose and Peter Miller, "Political Power Beyond the State: Problematics of Government," *The British Journal of Sociology* 43 (1992): 178.
34. Ibid., 185; Nikolas Rose, *Powers of Freedom: Reframing Political Thought* (Cambridge: Cambridge University Press, 1999), 211.
35. Wilson, "Statistics and Decision-Making in Government", 9, 10 and 4.
36. T. B., *Economic and Social Intelligence*, 4 and 5; Harold Wilson, *The Governance of Britain* (London: Sphere, 1977), 90; Wilson, "Statistics and Decision-Making in Government", 6–7.
37. Peter Shore, *Entitled to Know* (London: MacGibbon and Lee, 1966), 154–55.
38. Martin Crick, "Peter Shore," in *Oxford Dictionary of National Biography* (Oxford: Oxford University Press, 2004).
39. *Parliamentary Debates*, Commons, 13 July 1973, Vol. 859, col. 1980.
40. TNA, CAB 134/3274, Statistical Policy Committee, *Minutes, 13 July 1967*, 3–4.
41. *Report of the Committee on Social Studies*, 42.
42. TNA, BA 17/44, M. Spiers, *A Note on the Machinery of Government and the Electronic Computer*, December 1967, 1–18.
43. Rose, *Powers of Freedom*, 229.
44. Rose and Miller, "Political Power Beyond the State", 191.
45. Rose, *Powers of Freedom*, 229.
46. Ibid., 201.
47. Wilson, *The New Britain*, 12, 13 and 15.
48. Alain Desrosières, *The Politics of Large Numbers: A History of Statistical Reasoning* (London: Harvard University Press, 1998), 333.
49. Patrick Joyce, *The Rule of Freedom: Liberalism and the Modern City* (London: Verso, 2003), 13–14 and 25.
50. Rose, *Powers of Freedom*, 149.
51. Kevin Theakston, *The Labour Party and Whitehall* (London: Routledge, 1992), 115–20.
52. Claus Moser, "The Role of the Central Statistical Office in Assisting Public Policy Makers," *The American Statistician* 30 (1976): 59; TNA, HO 411/1, *Code of Conduct for Government Computers*, 4 March 1970, 3.
53. When he was first elected and held government office Benn was known as Anthony Wedgewood Benn. For the sake of simplicity he is referred to as Tony Benn throughout the text of this book, but where necessary in endnotes, his name is given in the form of the publication. Anthony Wedgewood Benn, *The Regeneration of Britain* (London: Victor Gollancz, 1965), 15.

54. TNA, BT 70/750, C. S. O., *A Population Register and Common Numbering System for Great Britain*, 22 October 1968, 2.
55. Peter Hall, "Computer Privacy," *New Society*, 31 July 1969, 163.
56. TNA, RG 28/306, *Proposals for a Population Register System in Great Britain*, 3 October 1967, 1.
57. TNA, RG 28/306, MacLeod to Rooke-Matthews, 3 October 1967, 1.
58. TNA, CAB 139/566, to Prime Minister, n.d., ca. August/September 1967, 1.
59. Statistical Policy Committee, *Minutes, Meeting 13 July 1967*, 2.
60. TNA, PREM 13/1432, Shore to Prime Minister, 18 August 1967, 1; TNA, PREM 13/1432, Wilson to Dell, 26 October 1967, 1.
61. Statistical Policy Committee, *Minutes, Meeting 13 July 1967*, 4.
62. TNA, CAB 139/562, Ministry of Transport, *Centralisation of Issue of Driving Licences*, 3 May 1967, 1.
63. TNA, CAB 139/567, *Interim Report by the Chairman of the Statistical Policy Committee, Reorganisation of the Government's Statistical Services*, 11 August 1967.
64. *Proposals for a Population Register System in Great Britain*; TNA, CAB 139/562, Chief Statistical Officer and Registrar Generals, *A Population Register and Common Numbering System for Great Britain*, 14 November 1967.
65. TNA, CAB 139/563, Home Affairs Committee, *A Population Register and Common Numbering System for Great Britain, Brief for the Minister of State*, n.d., ca. 1968, 2.
66. Home Affairs Committee, *A Population Register and Common Numbering System for Great Britain*, 11 October 1968, 1.
67. TNA, BT 70/750, Director Central Statistical Office and Registrar Generals, Statistical Policy Committee, *A Population Register and Common Numbering System for Great Britain*, 18 July 1968, 1.
68. TNA, CAB 134/3276, Statistical Policy Committee, *Minutes, 23 July 1968*, 5.
69. Home Affairs Committee, *A Population Register and Common Numbering System for Great Britain*, 11 October 1968, 1 and 3.
70. TNA, CAB 134/2861, Home Affairs Committee, *A Population Register and Common Numbering System for Great Britain*, 23 October 1968, 3.
71. TNA, CAB 164/829, Lord Gardiner, 24 May 1966, quoted in, The Inland Revenue, *Questionnaire—Computers and Privacy, Commentary on Protection of Confidentiality*, n.d., ca. 1970, 1.
72. Ibid.
73. TNA, CAB 139/568, Director of Central Statistical Office, *Confidentiality of Statistical Information in the Economic Field*, n.d., ca. 1968, 6; TNA, BT 70/750, Director of Central Statistical Office,

Statistical Policy Committee, *A Common Numbering System for Individuals*, 19 July 1968, 7.
74. Chief Statistical Officer and Registrar Generals, *A Population Register and Common Numbering System for Great Britain*, 11.
75. Director of Central Statistical Office, Statistical Policy Committee, *A Common Numbering System for Individuals*, 7.
76. Home Affairs Committee, *A Population Register and Common Numbering System for Great Britain*, 23 October 1968, 3; TNA, BT 70/750, A. G. Carruthers, *A Population Register and Common Numbering System for Great Britain*, 17 October 1968, 1.
77. Home Affairs Committee, *A Population Register and Common Numbering System for Great Britain, Brief for the Minister of State*, 5.
78. Statistical Policy Committee, *Minutes, Meeting 23 July 1968*, 6.
79. Home Affairs Committee, *A Population Register and Common Numbering System for Great Britain*, 23 October 1968, 4–5.
80. Chief Statistical Officer and Registrar Generals, *A Population Register and Common Numbering System for Great Britain*, 12.
81. Ibid., 7.
82. Statistical Policy Committee, *Minutes, Meeting 23 July 1968*, 6.
83. Ibid., 7; Home Affairs Committee, *A Population Register and Common Numbering System for Great Britain*, 23 October 1968, 4.
84. TNA, HN 1/22, *Computers in Central Government—Ten Years Ahead—Report of the Review Team*, 28 November 1969, 1.
85. Philip Allen, "A Young Home Secretary," in *Roy Jenkins: A Retrospective*, eds. Andrew Adonis and Keith Thomas (Oxford: Oxford University Press, 2004), 66.
86. TNA, HO 411/18, *Government Computers and Privacy, Draft Report to Ministers (2), Note by the Secretary, iii Survey of Personal Information Held in Government Computers*, n.d., ca. January 1972, 1; *Computers: Safeguards for Privacy*, Cmnd. 6354 (16 December 1975), 4.
87. *Computers: Safeguards for Privacy*, Cmnd. 6354, 38; *Report of the Committee on Privacy*, Cmnd. 5102 (July 1972), 178; *Computers: Safeguards for Privacy*, Cmnd. 6354, 34.
88. TNA, HO 411/17, *A Report by C.S.D. on some Manual Systems of Personal Information*, September 1971, 14.2.
89. TNA, PREM 19/2219, Butler to Patten, 10 February 1983, 1.
90. TNA, HO 411/1, *Lord Windlesham's Motion, Note of Meeting 21 November 1969*, 3.
91. TNA, FV 49/2, *Minister's Meeting on Computer Policy, 19 January 1967*, 8.
92. TNA, BA 17/44, *Meeting to Discuss Civil Service Records and A.D.P., Minutes, 19 July 1966*, 1.

93. Director of Central Statistical Office, Statistical Policy Committee, *A Common Numbering System for Individuals*, 3.
94. *Interim Report by the Chairman of the Statistical Policy Committee, Reorganisation of the Government's Statistical Services*, 2.
95. Medical Research Council, Committee on General Epidemiology, Subcommittee on Record Linkage, *Proposals for a National System of Linked Medical Records*, 2.
96. Rose, *Powers of Freedom*, 212.
97. TNA, HN 1/60, Ministry of Technology, *Data Processing and Public Administration*, 29 January 1969, 2–3.
98. TNA, BA 17/44, Advisory Committee on Computers, *Interim Report*, January 1968, 1.
99. *Lord Windlesham's Motion, Note of Meeting, 21 November 1969*, 2.
100. Richard Coopey, "Industrial Policy in the White Heat of the Scientific Revolution," in *The Wilson Governments 1964–1970*, eds. R. Coopey, S. Fielding, and N. Tiratsoo (London: Pinter, 1993), 112.
101. Harold Wilson, *Purpose in Politics: Selected Speeches by Rt Hon. Harold Wilson* (London: Weidenfeld and Nicolson, 1964), 15–16.
102. Frank Cousins quoted in, Jim Tomlinson, *The Labour Governments 1964–70: Volume 3, Economic Policy* (Manchester: Manchester University Press, 2004), 104.
103. Tony Benn, *Out of the Wilderness: Diaries 1963–67* (London: Hutchinson, 1987), 216.
104. Tony Benn quoted in, Antony Thompson, *Big Brother in Britain Today* (London: Michael Joseph, 1970), 50.
105. TNA, HN 1/60, Minister of Technology, *Data Processing in Government*, 4 March 1969, 6.
106. Edward Higgs, *The Information State in England: The Central Collection of Information on Citizens Since 1500* (Basingstoke: Palgrave Macmillan, 2004), 169.
107. Wilson, "Statistics and Decision-Making in Government," 3.
108. TNA, FD 1/8310, *Informal Meeting to Discuss Proposals for a National System of Linked Medical Records, Extract from Registrar General's Letter of 1st February Addressed to Dr Faulkner*, June 1966, 3.
109. TNA, RG 48/149, *Record Linkage*, 24 June 1966, 2.
110. C. A. Moser, "The Future Role of the Central Statistical Office," *Statistical News* 38 (1977): 1.2.
111. TNA, FV 49/2, *Minister's Meeting on Computer Policy, 19 January 1967*, 23.
112. Minister of Technology, *Data Processing in Government*, 5.
113. Society of Conservative Lawyers, *Computers and Freedom* (London: Conservative Research Department, 1968).

CHAPTER 5

People and Numbers

The attitudes and ideas within the Wilson government that were examined in the previous chapter coalesced into a draft green paper called *People and Numbers* which made the case for the introduction of population registration and/or the pan-departmental common numbering of files. The first section of this chapter examines the paper's proposals and how those who were driving these plans forward aimed to deal with the hostile public reception that they anticipated would greet their ideas.

The fact that this green paper was never issued was not down to a change of heart within government, but to the wholly contingent arrival of privacy as a political issue. The second section of this chapter explores the impact of this privacy campaigning on the government and how it backed ministers into a corner where they were obliged to establish the Younger Committee on Privacy. This parliamentary agitation was the background to Wilson's decision to halt work on *People and Numbers*, but it also saw the government honing the arguments and tactics that would be used in defence of its data-gathering operations throughout the rest of the period studied in this book.

The third section of this chapter focuses on the Younger Committee and reveals how this body was set up to be a paper tiger in order to reach decisions that would not threaten the government. This section surveys how this was achieved through handpicking the chair and secretary of the committee and giving the committee terms of reference that barred it from examining the actions of any government bodies. It further

K. Manton, *Population Registers and Privacy in Britain, 1936–1984*,
https://doi.org/10.1007/978-3-030-02753-7_5

details how both the Labour government that had set up Younger, and its Conservative successor held fast to these restrictive terms of reference.

The last section of this chapter develops this commonality between Labour and Conservative governments and establishes that the biopolitical thinking that had produced *People and Numbers* was not confined to the Labour Party. It does this by analysing the many plans laid under the Conservatives to standardise, centralise and link databases. Indeed this section observes how *People and Numbers* itself was almost resurrected under this government, only being halted by another contingent flare-up of privacy agitation.

People and Numbers

When the Statistical Policy Committee approved a feasibility study of population registration and common numbering, it was agreed that this would not begin until after a green paper had been published to explain these proposals to the country. How the government could head off the anticipated public hostility to its plans was discussed at the Home Publicity Committee in the Treasury in July 1969. Here the members had to try to plot a course between two obstacles. To one side lay the threat of "emotional opposition" that might be aroused if the paper were published before the government were in a position to explain fully the safeguards it planned to install to protect people's confidentiality.[1] This might seem to indicate that moving ahead without publicity could be the best option. However, here lay the other problem: an "adverse public reaction," that might prematurely close down the government's options, "could also happen if it became publicly known that the Government were studying the matters in question without having taken the public into their confidence."[2] In the end, this committee decided that publishing the green paper was the safest course, even though it recognised that explaining these matters without causing popular outrage would be a difficult task. Consequently, the green paper was duly drafted. It was called *People and Numbers* and this chapter will begin by examining its contents and how the government envisaged presenting its plans to the public.

In fact, the problem of presentation was recognised as so acute that two different drafts of *People and Numbers* were prepared for publication, each designed to target a different audience: "a quality one and a popular one."[3] This spoke very clearly of the continuation in government circles of the belief that the irrationality of many, if not most, of the people prevented them from hearing what the government said it when it spoke about data gathering. These two papers shared core elements that described the advantages of population registration and common numbering systems. Where they differed was that the "quality" paper discussed the issue of confidentiality, along with the more technical aspects of the schemes, while these topics were not mentioned by the other edition, making the "quality" version the longer by six pages. These papers condensed and refined the thinking on population registration and common numbering that had been going on in the Medical Research Council, the General Register Office, the Central Statistical Office (MRC, GRO, CSO) and the Statistical Policy Committee. Central to both versions was a presentation of why the government needed population registration and common numbering and therefore, why they wanted to go ahead with a feasibility study.

The previous chapter showed how the intellectual underpinning for this data drive was drawn from the well of biopolitical thinking and here, as these ideas cohered into policy, it is possible to see that when the government categorised the people as a population, it simultaneously required that individuals be subject to control. Thus, somewhat paradoxically, the notion of population involved, as Bruce Curtis writes, "both a greater degree of abstraction in the conceptualisation of human beings and more concrete and practical points of access for the arts of government."[4] Thus, *People and Numbers* claimed that most people would probably not object to the government having anonymous statistical data about the population, nor to this data being linked, as long as it was all kept within the department that had commissioned it.[5] However, the papers explained, the government needed more than that. It needed information about individual people and families, because these were the constituents of the aggregate. Thus, in order to know the population, government needed to know the people.

The government's problem was, as *People and Numbers* explained, that it could not obtain this access to individuals through their names. One-eighth of the people shared twenty surnames and about half a million people had a full name that was not unique, there were for example, seven thousand people called John Smith and five thousand called Thomas Jones. Thus, the only way to identify individuals was by giving them a unique number. The government did not want the information that would flow from a register in order to pry into "the personal affairs of every man, woman and child in the country," rather this data was needed for the same reason that every darts team, bank, angling club or local council needed information: to identify and locate the people it worked for.[6] Government worked to manage the economy, to target social services, to control the use of natural resources and to direct investment, and for all of these tasks it required knowledge of the people to "form the foundation of sensible decisions in public policy."[7] Existing sets of government data could not provide this. The census was a snapshot impression of the population at one moment, so it could not provide an image of how the population grew and moved, making it, in the words of Claus Moser (the chief statistical officer), a "rather clumsy instrument for policy making."[8]

The government's presentation of registration and common numbering in these two papers stressed four things. First, it presented these innovations as incremental and evolutionary developments of existing systems that had long been universally accepted and recognised as beneficial. Thus, despite their having been conceived as radical reforms, these plans were presented as being similar to the "valuable" and "indispensible" systems used in medical research.[9] The papers made the case that a common numbering system would really do little more than replace, with one number, the chaotic plethora of numbers that were already used to identify a particular John, or Jane, Smith. Second, it was shown how a register could be produced from a process that could be tied to the annual updating of the electoral roll.[10] It was thus not the case that it would be necessary for people to report a change of address to a central authority, because this information could be obtained "with little or no more trouble to the public than they are already put to."[11] Third, an increasingly efficient use of the data that the government already held could mean that people would need to supply information to the government less often than they already did.[12] Fourth, *People and Numbers* maintained that, far from being a 1984-style threat to the individual, common numbering would enhance what was later described as the "British citizen's traditional anonymity."[13] As things stood, with departmental numbering systems being incompatible, data transfers between departments could only be achieved by using people's names. Thus, a common number would increase the anonymity and protect the confidentiality of data by rendering it all into statistical form. These systems were thus by their nature safe, moreover their implementation would make the data in the government's hands even safer because they would not be introduced until additional protections had been designed along the lines of those that already protected medical records.

It was noted in the previous chapter that one solution brought forward as a possible strategy to circumvent popular opposition to data linkage was to use administrative means, in other words to introduce it without telling anyone. By drafting these green papers, the government obviously did not intend to adopt this strategy, and yet what it proposed was based on a considerable degree of dissimulation. This is made plain by the repeated references to medical research in these papers. *People and Numbers* argued that because medical researchers were already linking records, the system had already proven that it was safe and "there is no new principle involved here": government proposals were presented as a difference of degree, not a new departure.[14] The first thing to notice here is that this medical record linkage had been undertaken without any prior public consultation. Thus, the fact that it had occurred could hardly be taken as an endorsement of the practice. In fact far from being acceptable, the linking of records by medical researchers was increasingly attracting hostile attention. In December 1970, Enoch Powell attracted press attention for a campaign against the National Morbidity Survey and two months later Shirley Williams would make public her opposition to the Oxford study (see Chapter 4).[15] Second, the presentation in *People and Numbers* stated that the government would like to conduct studies into the linkage of medical records independent of those looking at the creation of a population register and the common numbering of government data. In fact, as was shown in the previous chapter, these linkages had already been trialled. Furthermore, the notion that medical records could be treated independently from other data sets: that they alone might be linked and that this newly linked medical entity would remain sealed from both other sets of records and non-medical personnel, thus guarding the confidentiality of medical data, flies in the face of all the evidence that has shown (see Chapter 4) that such links with medical records were already being made by the GRO, which had declared that fully linked medical records were, to all intents and purposes, a population register. Thus similarly, when the papers stressed that though they could be linked, population registration and common numbering were separate things, they were saying something to the public, which Moser and Michael Reed, the registrar general, had previously stated was not the case at all.

Even so and despite these embellishments, when the official *People and Numbers* group had their inaugural meeting, on the day the draft green papers were issued, they thought that the papers were so dangerously candid that they risked alarming the public by raising the issues of confidentiality.[16] What the group thus proposed was a considerable downgrading of both the quality and the quantity of the publicity to be given to population registration and common numbering by the green papers. Moser was a member of the *People and Numbers* group, he was at this meeting and this had always been his view. The previous September he had written to Reed counselling against raising the issue of confidentiality at all and arguing that since the risks to privacy from statistical data were not real "it would be a great mistake to fall over backwards in exposing the possible threats."[17] Thus, the group concluded that, an even better course of action than reserving a discussion of confidentiality for the select readership of the "quality" version of the papers, would be to admit that confidentiality and the right of privacy were issues that concerned people, and to suggest that they be examined separately from the core issues of population registration and common numbering.

This would have three useful outcomes. First, this separation would allow the feasibility study to go ahead unhindered by association with what was already a growing public concern with privacy. Second, it would not commit the government to doing anything about privacy and third, once hived off from the feasibility study, any work on this topic would succeed or fail on its own merits independent of the feasibility study. Moser was even cautiously optimistic that there might be, what he saw as, a positive outcome from an enquiry into confidentiality since it might relax controls and so open up the possibility of yet greater access to data through increased linkage.[18] More importantly, the feasibility study could also be expedited if the government had the courage of its own convictions and just stated that it was going to go ahead with it, rather than seeking approval for this course of action. Thus, the meeting concluded that the proposals in the green papers were "too tentative and the Government should be less defensive about the questions raised and display more confidence in their right to conduct the proposed feasibility study."[19] In fact, the government should, it concluded, stop talking about "studies" of feasibility and confidentiality altogether, as this might encourage people to ask for the findings to be made public rather than allowing the government to just state its conclusions. The government should, in other words, have the courage of its own convictions.

This meeting referred to growing public and international concern over the issue of privacy. That this was mounting by the time these green papers were drafted is shown by the publication, in December 1968, of the pamphlet *Computers and Freedom* which was followed, in February 1969, by a National Council for Civil Liberties (NCCL) campaign for the "right to be let alone." In fact, as early as March 1969 Moser made it explicit that he was aware of how the political climate was changing and urged the Statistical Policy Committee to adopt "a piecemeal movement towards a freer flow of statistical information," even with fairly non-controversial industrial data, "rather than a sudden radical change."[20] Thus, the green papers were drafted at an inopportune time, which may go some way to explaining the aggressive nature of their defence at the *People and Numbers* group meeting. However, the political circumstances would get more problematic for the government's data enthusiasts, because, in addition to this extra-parliamentary campaigning, within three months important government ministers mobilised around the issue of a right of privacy.

This temporarily fractured the unity of the government behind the radical increase in its data harvesting operations. However, though political differences would still emerge between politicians in central government, and between central and local government, and though differences would also sometimes be apparent between politicians and officials, it is nonetheless the case that from this period on, the attitudes across Whitehall to data gathering came together to form an increasingly stable, pan-departmental mindset to defend, if not to increase, the government's data holdings. There would not be any repeat of the wartime Ministry of Food's principled opposition to registration. In fact, in this period, Whitehall and government increasingly packed into a phalanx that was very different to the formation adopted by their predecessors in 1952 when abolition of the National Register had been accepted. This newer formation would, moreover, be all the more necessary given the mounting pressure of the privacy campaign. This agitation was the backdrop to Wilson's decision to "stand down" the *People and Numbers* project for a year, that is to say until after the coming general election.[21] The next section will examine this political campaign for privacy and how the government responded to it.

The Politicians, the People and Privacy

Though it is possible, and indeed useful, to map out the thinking behind the drive for the data required to power day-to-day interventions, this understanding cannot explain what actually happened when the government attempted to turn its ideas into reality. Where the actual interplay of political forces is concerned it is necessary to look at what Nikolas Rose terms the complexities, contingencies, variables and twists of how events played out.[22] One of the most important twists in the course of the events studied here was the advent of privacy as a political issue in Britain. This was triggered by political developments in the USA, where a congressional Sub Committee on Privacy was established in 1964. Over the following years, this body's hearings came to focus on federal government plans to computerise its records and set up a national databank. This databank, proposed by the Social Science Research Council of the American Economic Association, was to hold only purely statistical information on an aggregate basis, thus it was not to maintain files on individual citizens and therefore, it could not and would not become a surveillance centre. Despite these assurances and denials, the databank became a lightning rod for discontent and disquiet about government records in general and computerisation in particular. In fact, the agitation was so great that it threatened to engulf traditional US data-gathering operations such as the census.[23] The reason this concern had to spread to Britain from the USA, rather than being generated domestically, was revealed in Home Office discussions in September 1971: "at the time of the public hearings in the USA, in 1966 and 1967, there was little reaction in the UK because the use of computers by government was not publicised."[24] In the USA, the committee's 1968 report forestalled plans for the databank, moreover even before this date, the shock waves of the dissent that it had produced had (contrary to the Home Office's recollections) already reached Britain.

It was against this background that on 18 February 1967 Alex Lyon introduced a Right of Privacy Bill into Parliament and two days later Peter Bessell similarly introduced a bill on telephone tapping, though neither piece of legislation made any further progress. The British cabinet first considered the issue of privacy at a meeting on 28 September where ministers looked at a proposal that a select committee should discuss whether there was a need for a statutory restraint on the invasion of privacy. The lord president, Richard Crossman, suggested this and nearly two weeks later he received a letter from the home secretary, Roy Jenkins, who had been mulling over the discussion in the meantime. Jenkins wrote that he now felt that such a committee would inevitably seek to broaden its remit and that this would lead it into sensitive areas, namely "telephone tapping and other forms of eavesdropping and interception of communications." Moreover, a committee would be unlikely to confine its enquiries to the use of such practices by private detectives, but would want to extend its coverage to include "official methods of interception," an area where he "should be most reluctant to see interest ... being stimulated," adding that this was the reason why he had stymied a suggestion earlier in 1967 by Lord Gardiner, the Lord Chancellor, to pass the whole issue of privacy to the Law Commission.[25]

Crossman replied to Jenkins's objections by expressing incredulity that they had not been raised in cabinet and informing the home secretary that, in the time that had elapsed since the cabinet, he (Crossman) had discussed with Gardiner the best ways to proceed on this issue.[26] Gardiner gave Crossman strong support and his office wrote to Jenkins overruling the Home Office's objections by insisting that "sooner or later" this "legitimate demand" was going to become irresistible and that, in the Lord Chancellor's opinion, it would be possible to set up a select committee with terms of reference that explicitly ruled out any oversight of security issues.[27] This propelled the Home Office into a state of uproar. Their reply stated that the committee's terms of reference could not exclude state interceptions of communications, because this would be a de facto admission that such activities occurred and these involved "breaches of the law."[28] Such a select committee would therefore inevitably hamstring the vital activities of the security services. Despite this, Crossman told a meeting of the parliamentary Labour Party on 1 November 1967 that a select committee was going to discuss the topic of privacy. As soon as this news reached the cabinet office, officials there "had a word with the Lord President's Office (on an idiot boy basis) to find where matters stood." They were clear that Crossman had "gone off the rails" and recommended that the prime minister's office apply itself to sorting this mess out as a matter of urgency.[29]

At a subsequent meeting Wilson, Jenkins and Burke Trend, the cabinet secretary, met with leading officials from the Lord Chancellor and lord president's offices. At this meeting, terms of reference for a select committee were drawn up to exclude oversight of activities by state servants along with the employees of both nationalised industries and local authorities. These blanket exclusions were, it was maintained, justified because the activities of these people were governed by statute and hence subject to parliamentary scrutiny.[30] However, two months after the meeting, Burke Trend discussed the matter further with Wilson and they agreed that though they might be able to win over Gardiner, they were very unlikely to be so successful with Crossman. Additionally, the government was more than halfway through its term of office, there was very little clamour for action on the issue of privacy, and Crossman himself had stated in cabinet that the pressures on Labour MPs and the parliamentary timetable were great and increasing. They therefore concluded that the best policy was "to let sleeping dogs lie and see if they would continue to slumber."[31] However, within a few days a "considerable cat" was "among the pigeons" as Gardiner produced his own terms of reference for a committee. Wilson's office decided at this point, 2 February 1968, that the next cabinet meeting should be used to "sweep the 'privacy' enquiry … back under the carpet for the time being."[32] It is interesting to note that Crossman's diary contains a version of events that is completely at odds with the official correspondence that led up to this cabinet meeting. Here Crossman wrote that he had not really been in favour of the privacy enquiry, that he preferred that any new committee should examine the role of PR firms working for foreign governments and that he scuppered a "good deal of support for" the privacy enquiry that built up in discussion.[33]

This remarkable volte-face might have been caused by Crossman's officials letting him know of Wilson and the Home Office's strength of feeling about his "idiot boy"-style behaviour. But whatever the cause, it left Gardiner isolated. This did not immediately end the division at the highest strata of the government over the countervailing issues of data and privacy, but later in the year, on 22 October 1968, Gardiner wrote to Wilson saying: "I have been converted." He now recognised that a select committee was likely to trespass into sensitive territory and that a departmental committee, which "having no powers, can easily be kept within their terms of reference," would be preferable.[34] Moreover, he agreed that any such committee should examine specific breaches of privacy, rather than the general concept, a course of action that would allow its work to be channelled towards discreet changes in the law rather than towards a general right of privacy.

By the following spring, the government was again concerned about these issues. It was in the process of steering a Post Office bill through Parliament and was trying to smuggle through in this legislation, "in suitably colourless language," a clause that would protect the right of the government to intercept communications.[35] The needs of the security services received the full support of both the Foreign Office and the home secretary, Jim Callaghan (he had replaced Jenkins on 30 November 1967 and served until Labour lost the election of June 1970).[36] However, the government's potential problems in Parliament on this delicate matter were exacerbated by events outside, because on 19 February 1969 the NCCL launched its national privacy campaign. Burke Trend, along with Michael Stewart (the foreign secretary) and Callaghan formulated the government's response to these twin pressures. They agreed that any enquiry into privacy "should be avoided for as long as possible and that if in the end, it proves impossible to resist pressure further thought will need to be given to the method of appointment to be employed and to the selection of the individuals concerned."[37]

This was the political position when the draft *People and Numbers* green papers were issued in June 1969. Wilson, as has been seen, was a great supporter of the work of the Statistical Policy Committee that had given rise to *People and Numbers*, this is why, throughout all this parliamentary agitation, the project was allowed to continue. Moreover, when it was halted in early September, it was not jettisoned rather it was re-routed for a year until the storm had blown over. The group set up to conduct the feasibility study was ready to commence its work under strict "instructions not to go outside the government machine," and Burke Trend noted that it would be a "great pity if we interrupted work which in the interests of economic administration, will undoubtedly have to be done sooner or later."[38]

Over the final months of 1969, Parliament displayed an increasing interest in the subject of privacy. On 29 October 1969, Alex Lyon tabled a motion calling for a right of privacy, on 26 November Brian Walden introduced a bill based on a study by Justice, the British section of the International Commission of Jurists, and on 3 December Lord Windlesham (a seasoned campaigner against press intrusions into privacy[39]) led a debate on computers and privacy. In response to Lyon's motion Gardiner's office wrote to Fred Peart, the new lord president (he had been appointed on 18 October 1968 to replace Crossman) saying "it is clear that there is considerable support for action, but there is no collective view of Ministers at the present time and you will no doubt wish to discourage debate."[40] However, as Windlesham's debate drew near and it was clear that he could not be silenced Gardiner, who was due to reply for the government, became "understandably exasperated."[41] He contended that any private member's bill drafted without government assistance was "bound to be a nonsense" and that what really frustrated him was the absence of any clear ministerial policy on this, the "one branch of our law that I have failed to reform."[42]

However, the reality was that Windlesham's motion was easier for the government to manage than Walden's, because Windlesham's focused on only one aspect of the privacy issue: the role of computers, rather than on creating a general right of privacy. In this debate, Gardiner brought forward three main lines of defence for the government. First, computers would bring huge advantages by standardising, centralising and linking data and, second, that they were safe storage systems because most people could not operate them, and so fewer people had access to them than to paper records. Third, he argued that were a body set up to oversee the use of computerised data, government computers should not be included within its purview because ministers were responsible to Parliament for the information they held, therefore setting up a body to short-circuit this chain of responsibility would be unconstitutional.[43]

The events leading up to this debate in January 1970 had honed the government's thinking and it is possible to distinguish in what ministers said during this period the core elements of the way governments would approach these issues for the rest of the period covered by this book. First, they sought to protect the government's data in general, and that relating to national security in particular and to exclude all of it from examination, justifying this by reference to the constitutional doctrine of ministerial accountability. This, second, dictated their tactics. These came in two broad types: they sought to either, stall requests for such an enquiry by claiming that there was no great demand for one or, if they were forced to set one up, they aimed to manage it by demarcating its responsibilities and handpicking its membership. Third, as will be seen in Chapter 6, governments denied that privacy was an issue of principle and promulgated the view that it should be examined by looking at a series of separate invasions of privacy which could be dealt with by piecemeal changes to various laws thus obviating the need for a general right of privacy.

However, the most immediate and important consequence of these events was that Wilson instructed Moser not to go ahead with the study group on population registration and data linkages, and acting on these instructions, the group's first meeting, scheduled for 2 December 1969, was cancelled. Moser was "most disturbed by this decision" and brought forward three arguments to try to make the prime minister reconsider. First, he tried to make Wilson feel that his government would be something of a laughing stock among progressives: "central government is currently exposed to the risk of appearing to be technically backward in the sense of not even having examined the facts."[44] Second, he pointed out that the pledges, to examine the issue of privacy the government had made in Parliament during Windlesham's debate, could not in all honesty be carried out unless the government had the facts at its command. Moser maintained that since this proposed study was a fact-finding mission, it would provide the government with what it needed to make good on its promises. Third, like Burke Trend, he argued that the tide of modern public administration was running behind his proposals "some work of this kind is ultimately going to be inevitable," therefore, as he put it: the sooner the better.[45] These entreaties fell on deaf ears, but Moser was right on his last point, these proposals would attempt a political comeback, and he, as will be seen in the final section of this chapter, would make sure they did.

On 24 November 1969, Wilson met with key ministers to plan tactics for dealing with Walden's Bill. Their preferred option would have been to stall its progress and so to thwart the whole privacy campaign, however they realised that things had moved beyond that stage and Wilson acknowledged: "the growing pressure for some action would make it impossible to hold out indefinitely."[46] They discussed the possibility of taking over the bill from Walden, but this suggestion was dispatched by Callaghan's objections. Thus, they decided that they would need to set up some kind of committee of enquiry to take the momentum out of the privacy campaign. A week later Burke Trend still hoped that they could postpone doing anything until after the next election before "reluctantly" agreeing that a committee would be necessary.[47] The weeks immediately before and after Christmas 1969 saw the government trying to decide on the membership of the committee, its chair and when to announce it. Their eventual decisions were put to the cabinet on 22 January 1970, the day before the debate on Walden's Bill.

Here Callaghan led the discussion telling his colleagues that during the debate on Walden's Bill he would announce that the government intended to set up an inquiry, with Kenneth Younger as its chair, "to consider whether legislation is needed to give further protection to the individual citizen and to commercial and industrial interests against intrusions into privacy by private persons or organisations, or by companies; and to make recommendations."[48] In cabinet, ministers discussed how they should respond if these terms of reference were criticised for excluding all government bodies. Around the table there was general agreement that here the government could bring forward its arguments about ministerial accountability and the primacy of "the security of the realm." If the growing public concern about the possibility of the government's building databanks was raised, ministers agreed that they would remind the House of Commons that "such information could be obtained by the Government only in accordance with strict statutory requirements and could only be used for the purposes authorised by the statue in question."[49] As a statement of the legal position, this was of course correct. But what this left unsaid, though several ministers including Wilson were well aware of, was the fact that eighteen months before this meeting, the Statistical Policy Committee had discussed introducing a common numbering scheme in such a way as to circumvent this convention. So if, as the cabinet were told, "the government observed these limitations scrupulously" it was not because this was what it wanted to do, but because the privacy campaign had forced Wilson to shelve *People and Numbers*.[50] That the project never emerged fully formed was therefore, not due to either a lack of ministerial conviction, or to a change of heart, rather it was due to the rapidly changing political landscape of the privacy debate throughout the autumn and winter of 1969. In fact, the push to standardise, centralise and link data, which had produced *People and Numbers*, would continue even while the Younger Committee was working under the Conservative government that would come to office in June 1970.

The Younger Committee

The discussion in cabinet and the following day's debate in Parliament saw the government using the arguments about national security and the doctrine of ministerial accountability that it had prepared during the previous year. But, as this section shows, the Younger Committee itself was also part of this strategy. The previous November, when he began to recognise that stalling was no longer a viable option, Trend had run through the various types of committee that could, as a last resort, be set up to examine privacy. He decided that the matter was unsuitable for the Law Commission, which left a choice between a royal commission and a departmental committee. He favoured the latter "because it would be more directly under the control of Ministers": as Gardiner had noted, departmental committees had no real power. Moreover, if as an additional safeguard, such a committee were staffed "by responsible people," Trend thought it would "be the most effective means of reaching the right decisions in the longer term."[51]

Sir Kenneth Younger, who was appointed to chair the committee, had been a Labour MP from 1945 to 1959, he was secretary of state at the Foreign Office during Attlee's second government and became a privy councillor in 1951. At the time of his appointment to the Privacy Committee he was, among his other public roles, chairman of the Howard League for Penal Reform. He was thus an eminently suitable and "responsible" choice as chairman, possessing progressive credentials enough to appear credible, but sufficiently embedded in institutional orthodoxy to reach the "right" decisions. But the government seemed to want to have an additional layer of safety in place because the man who became secretary to the committee, Gerald Pratt, a member of the cabinet secretariat under Trend, had also served as secretary to the *People and Numbers* group. Pratt's appointment was important because, as secretary, he wrote many of the papers the committee discussed. Pratt carried out the normal functions of a committee secretary, but as an observer of the committee's work noted, this role was "especially important in this case because of the wide range of topics to be examined."[52] In particular, he wrote a paper on *Computers and Privacy* that drew attention to the ability of computers to link data, but did not mention, for example, the fact that under *People and Numbers* there had been very considerable discussion of linking data on paper-based records.[53] He was thus part of the growing trend (examined in subsequent chapters) that focused attention onto computerisation and so drew it away from three things: first, data held elsewhere in paper-based files, second, attempts to standardise, centralise and link this data and third, more fundamentally, the purpose of this data.

Despite its pliant complexion, the Younger Committee began its life sparing with the government over its terms of reference and it was not alone in doing so. For example, the Society of Labour Lawyers wrote to Callaghan asking him to consider widening the scope of the committee's remit citing as the basis for this the European Convention on Human Rights.[54] However, Callaghan did not move in response to this and the Home Office set out exactly what the committee could examine. This encompassed four main areas: the use of computers, the use of electronic devices, press and broadcasting activities and commercial and industrial activities. This last was a portmanteau term that included such things as: credit-rating agencies, questionnaires for job applicants, industrial espionage, unsolicited circulars, door-to-door salesmen and private detectives.[55] The committee successfully requested permission to extend this category to include the uncontroversial topics of telephone sales and the use of behavioural sciences to "manipulate employees' social lives."[56] The majority of the committee's members thought that they should also be able to examine public corporations, local government and universities, but there was also broad agreement that they would not ask for more than this because doing so would "encounter immovable political objections."[57]

The reality was, however, that the committee ran into immovable political objections even by asking for this much. Callaghan replied, using the formula that had been rehearsed in the build-up to the creation of the committee, stating that: nationalised industries were governed by statute and so ministers were answerable to Parliament for any breaches of privacy committed by, for example, meter readers working for the gas boards. Similarly, local authorities worked under parliamentary frameworks and were, in addition, democratically controlled by their electors. However, Callaghan pointed out that the fact that the committee's investigations were limited to the private sector did not mean that the areas they would examine were of no importance, and neither did it mean that any legislation that resulted from their findings would need to be limited to the private sector. "I have no doubt," he concluded, "that when the Committee reports in due course, the Government will be very ready to consider any implications which its recommendations may have in relation to the activities of central and local government and of other public authorities."[58]

The issue was more complicated for Callaghan however, because the committee's work covered the high-profile issue of computers and the government was, of course, computerising some of its data operations. The previous February, Alex Lyon (who had since become a member of the Younger Committee) had asked parliamentary questions about computers and privacy and had suggested that the government should "set an example by themselves promulgating regulations" for the use of their own computers. In replying Wilson said that the government was working on a code of conduct for its own computers.[59] As a result, the government set up an enquiry into its own computer systems and since this started work before the Younger Committee, Callaghan was able to inform Younger that work on this aspect of the committee's concerns about government activities and privacy was already in hand. In reality, this government committee's main role would be to refine the government's defence of its data and it would be heavily responsible for the focus of debates about data and privacy remaining fixed on computerisation. This committee will be examined in Chapter 7.

A little more than a month after the Younger Committee held its first meeting there was a general election that returned a Conservative government. Five days after the election, the committee discussed revisiting its acquiescence to Callaghan's stonewalling of their requests for an extended remit. In discussion some members submitted that "the new government would not be inhibited to the same extent as it predecessor from making the sort of concession the Committee wanted."[60] They therefore wanted to ask the new home secretary, Reginald Maudling, for the freedom to examine privacy-related issues in all areas of the public sphere excluding only security matters. They did not anticipate actually commenting on all government operations, but rather wanted the ability to roam across government wherever the evidence led them. However, most of the committee did not agree with this display of post-election assertiveness. They agreed with Callaghan that they were doing valuable work and moreover, stated that they had all agreed to serve on the committee in the full knowledge of its terms of reference. Nonetheless, there was general agreement that they should examine the work of universities, and that as Callaghan had not specifically ruled this out of bounds, Kenneth Younger should take this up with Maudling. Younger did this, and though Maudling followed Callaghan in restricting the committee's work to the private sphere he did agree that they could look at issues relating to universities.[61] The committee accepted Maudling's decision.[62]

This issue, of the privacy of personal information in universities, had made an impact in British politics, shortly after the announcement of the Younger Committee, as a result of events at Warwick University. An occupation of the university administrative buildings, on 11 February

1970, had uncovered evidence of secret files being kept on students and academics. This discovery was publicised and led to a report into the matter by Lord Radcliffe. This report found that the university was entitled to hold the information it had filed and that there was no evidence to support allegations that this was being used to build political dossiers on students and staff.[63] This report was published only a few weeks before the Younger Committee met for the first time and given that the issue was still fresh in the public mind, and that it chimed so resonantly with general fears of data being used to build dossiers, it is hardly surprising that even so biddable a body as the Younger Committee felt it had to insist on including universities within its remit. From the government's perspective, this was something it could offer Younger to placate committee members like Alex Lyon, without unduly threatening its key strategic interests in these matters.

Continuities Under the Conservatives

Some members of the Younger Committee thought that they had more chance of getting an extended remit from the new Conservative government. They thus seemed to think that Wilson's government was more hostile towards the privacy issue and perhaps they therefore commensurately identified Labour as the party of big data. The fact that the new government similarly rebuffed their approaches shows that the issue of privacy was seen as a threat by government as such, rather than by one party. It might be thought that this cross-party similarity was driven by concerns over national security, but although security issues were, as has been seen, very important to governments these had not stopped the Conservative government from abolishing national registration in 1952. More importantly, in the 1960s and 1970s the idea of using population registration and common numbering systems was not connected to security issues as such, but to more prosaic policies related to day-to-day interventions in ordinary lives. Consequently, this refusal by the Conservative government to extend Younger's brief also highlights the fact that the increasing desire by governments to standardise, centralise and link data was not a question of political ideology on a left-right spectrum. Rather it shows how this was connected to a sea change in the way governments of all political stripes thought about the processes of policy formulation and implementation in this period, a process that marginalised diehard old-school tories such as Enoch Powell along with liberals like Shirley Williams. It shows, in other words, that data was becoming central to the increasingly biopolitical processes of governing. This section will highlight how the data-gathering operations begun by Wilson, were very quickly reborn under the Conservatives by presenting the five main consistencies in the data policies of the Labour and Conservative governments. These will show how an established attitude towards data was crystallising across political parties, governments and Whitehall in this period.

People and Numbers had been designed to redraw all of the government's data systems into one standardised and centralised web. The scale of its ambition had so impressed Whitehall departments that they had put their own fledgling schemes for linkage (covering such things as name changes, immigration, divorces, the electoral roll, driving licences and vehicle registration) into abeyance while this metadata project subsumed within its ambit the responsibility for meeting the future needs of all of them. However, when *People and Numbers* was halted by Wilson this left these other needs unmet. So, the first strand of continuity between data plans under the two governments was that these earlier schemes, of more limited scope, were reanimated and just as it had been in early days of the Wilson government, so under the Conservative government, the education system was at the fore of the movement to link data. In August 1970, the Department for Education and Science (DES) received details from the registrar of proposals to rationalise Scottish National Health Service (NHS) numbers. Officials at the DES welcomed this, but they wanted the changes to go further to embrace the introduction of standardised NHS numbers across the whole country and preferably to combine these numbers with the National Insurance (NI) system so that these could be used more widely. Indeed there were discussions about allocating NI numbers at birth, a policy described as "an advance."[64] These proposals, the DES acknowledged, put them back to where they had been in 1964 and they were aware that these suggestions might lead all concerned down the same "long and difficult and dangerous road" that had led to *People and Numbers*. This course might not be politically expedient, but it was clearly where the department's strategic vision was focused. Thus, officials wrote that if the "more limited" policy, of changing NHS and NI numbers, were pursued "we should want to be careful not to take actions which would hamper later developments on the wider issues."[65] As well as witnessing a revival of plans drawn up before *People and Numbers*, the period of the Conservative government also saw new plans being devised. Thus, the Department of Health and Social Security Working Party on medical record linkage envisaged links between medical, criminal and social security records.[66]

Local government also contributed to the impetus behind increasingly linked data during the early years of the Conservative government thus, in March 1970, it was noted within central government that: "computer systems in local government were developing very rapidly."[67] For example West Sussex County Council had recently produced a report that argued strongly for what amounted to a population register and a common numbering system for the county. The council's report claimed that its common number, called a personal reference, would allow the authority to: identify people from minimal information, locate anyone in its area, provide a means of collating information about groups of the population and streamline records by avoiding duplication. The county's version of a population register was called a "personal master index." At its inauguration, the council saw this drawing together information from all the authority's records of anyone the council had dealings with, but its ultimate aim was for the system to encompass everyone in the county.[68] Inside central government these plans received, on the one hand, a positive reception, being described as having a good general approach.[69] However, on the other hand, Moser saw the scheme as a potential strategic setback and the publication of these plans spurred him on. He argued that if these local initiatives were allowed to go ahead unchecked it would be impossible to establish what Nikolas Rose calls "fidelity techniques" (see Chapter 4) because the systems would have been designed to boost the functioning of organisations at the peripheries of power, rather than as a panopticon to subject the periphery to the centre.[70] In January 1971, Moser insisted that central government needed to move ahead with its discussions of record linking before the field was seized by local initiatives like this because, if local systems gathered momentum, they could severely constrain central government's room for manoeuvre.[71] Therefore, the second element of continuity between the Labour and Conservative governments can be seen in central government structures where Moser was still in post and the Statistical Policy Committee was still at work.

In point of fact Moser issued his warning about central government being outflanked by local initiatives in a paper he co-wrote with Michael Reed for the Statistical Policy Committee. This paper was to support a case for setting up a group of statisticians and data processors, under the control of the CSO, to study the needs of departments for data linkage. The reasoning behind this represents the third layer of continuity between this government and its Labour predecessor, because Moser and Reed repeated all the arguments that had been made under Wilson. They outlined the problems that the current structure of government statistics gave planners. Thus, statistics were gathered and kept by individual departments, they were not linked or shared and this meant that data held by government was underused and as things stood, none of it, including the census, could be used to provide a meaningful analysis of society to inform policy making. The solution to this was the linkage of records. This in turn could be made more efficient if a common numbering system were introduced. This would make the various data sets across government "simpler, cheaper to operate, more efficient, more accurate, more compatible with one another and more flexible to use."[72] A common numbering system, they added, might in its turn open the door to a full population register of the type that many other progressive democracies used.

Moser and Reed sent this paper to Francis Graham-Harrison, the deputy under-secretary of state at the Home Office, who amended the document by adding a preface. This stated that the current concern with threats posed by databanks to individual rights "has made it possible to lose sight of the statistical, social, economic and financial advantages of record linkage and of such concepts as common-numbering and a population register."[73] Graham-Harrison was to play a big part in shaping the government's response to the Younger Report and here it is clear that he was firmly behind these plans to boost the government's data operations. This paper also laid out what the authors really wanted: record linkage. They firmly believed in the merits of common numbering (and indeed of population registration), but if this were to be seen as politically unpropitious, then record linkage should be achieved without common numbering. This admission did not, however, mark the end of the idea of common numbering since this, along with population registration, remained a central element of a redrafted version of this paper, authored solely by Moser, that was eventually passed to ministers. When ministers met to consider these proposals, in April 1971, they decided to defer any study of population registration and common numbering, but agreed with his main point and recommended that the study of record linkage should go ahead, going so far as to draft a parliamentary question to the prime minister that could be used to announce this.[74]

The breadth of local and departmental initiatives under the Conservative government, along with Moser's (and others') tireless politicking for a new form of *People and Numbers*, show the continuity between this activity under Labour and its successor. But Moser's paper to the Conservative government also shows that these ideas and policies were produced in response to a more fundamental, fourth, continuity: that of the increasingly widespread biopolitical mode of thought that was discussed in Chapters 3 and 4. Thus, Moser and Reed began the first draft of this paper by pointing out that "governments in all advanced countries" needed increasing amounts of information about citizens and households "in order to maintain effective economic and social policies and to predict the required level and quality of those public services."[75] While Moser's final version, submitted to ministers, phrased this as: "effective decision-making in social and economic policy, with effective monitoring of its results, has increasing need for comprehensive statistical descriptions of society."[76] The biopolitical nature of the thinking that underpinned Moser and Reed's ideas is further exposed by their references to the successful use of record linkage by medical research. Here it is important to note that though these plans were not actually put into operation this was not for want of support from either the Conservative government or officials (see below). It is thus clear that this method of thinking, like the policies with which it was reciprocally intertwined, crossed party political boundaries.

The fifth continuity across both governments, though one clearly not of either of their making, was the privacy campaign. The Labour government's tentative move towards publicity through the green papers had fallen as a result of Wilson's inability to sweep the privacy issue back under the carpet, and so Moser's second attempt too, would have to face an increasing political interest in the subject. This centred on the census taken in April 1971. On 14 April Jeremy Thorpe, the leader of the Liberal Party, made a widely reported speech in which he promised to go to prison rather than answer some of the questions on the census form. This census caused such uproar because it had become known that computers were to be used to process some of the returns. Thorpe objected to this because, he maintained, computers increased the accumulation and spread of information to such dangerous levels that they represented a threat to individual freedom.

Apart from the generalised fear of computers, this particular wave of apprehension may have begun with an article published the previous year in the magazine *Automation*. Here, under the title "Getting a Personal Dossier from a Statistical Data Bank," the authors claimed that it was possible to reverse engineer the purely statistical data from the census to produce results for each individual respondent. This machination had been publicised by the MP and privacy campaigner, Leslie Huckfield in early 1971 when he introduced a Control of Personal Information Bill in Parliament. This unravelling of the census's veil of anonymity could be done, it was alleged, by running the census statistics for a given enumeration district (each of about two hundred households) against information from another databank which would allow the statistics to be de-aggregated. The Census Office pointed out that since their statistical products were of the very simplest kind this process was impossible, but the authorities would require more than this assurance to save the census from falling victim to this story.[77]

In the end Thorpe, along with most other people, completed his form because the pressure generated by this agitation was lanced by the government's shrewd invitation to two outside bodies, the Royal Statistical Society, and the British Computer Society, to appraise the security of the computer systems used for this work. The two societies nominated their own members to these delegations and the reports they produced gave the census security arrangements a clean bill of health and were duly published by the government.[78]

This event had two serious results. First, it occurred while the Younger Committee was sitting and while it was examining the use of computers. The government's acquiescence to popular pressure in allowing its census systems to be subject to outside scrutiny could not have gone unnoticed. Indeed much of what subsequently occurred in the debates over data and privacy focused on this issue: oversight of government computerised data. Second, this campaigning over the census fed into yet more disquiet, this time over a government proposal to follow up the census with a survey of incomes.

This survey of incomes had been mooted by the Labour government, and at the time of the census Moser was strongly in favour of going ahead with it, arguing that such a survey would allow a lot of useful linking of data which would in turn produce a better, factual basis for policy formulation.[79] This survey was to be voluntary and would be sent to a sample 1 per cent of the population with a small fraction of these receiving a follow-up interview. A ministerial committee that reviewed Moser's proposal had some hesitations about this, but in the end gave it the go-ahead.[80] However, on 12 May 1971 *The Guardian* published a report claiming that some government files were open to improper access. Coming hard on the heels of the row over the census, this was enough to halt the incomes survey in its tracks. This was a setback for Moser, but the storm generated by the census spread its fallout more widely and claimed more victims than just the survey of incomes, because it also halted the second attempt to get the government to go ahead with a preparatory study of pan-government record linkage.

Though this feasibility study was cancelled as a result of events spiralling out of the government's control, its response to this unforeseen development shows how Conservative policy in this regard was a continuation of Labour's and thus how data had assumed an increasingly important place in the plans of both parties. Officials wrote to the home secretary advising him to tell the prime minister about the plans that had been stalled because, should he answer questions about the census, he might stray onto the subject of record linkage and say something inopportune and the Home Office wanted to "keep our options open as far as possible."[81] Indeed this was exactly the phrase that Maudling used when he wrote to Heath to advise him on this matter.[82]

The storm over the census had focused attention on computers. Moser had earlier warned against using terms that even reminded the public of computerisation because doing so could have disastrous consequences for his proposals and the census agitation proved him right. However, important as it was at this juncture, in the coming years computerisation would assume an even greater role in the political tussles between the advocates of privacy and those who sought to increase the government's access to data about the British people.

Notes

1. TNA, T 227/4240, Ministerial Committee on Home Publicity, *Green Paper: People and Numbers*, 21 July 1969, 2.
2. Ibid.
3. TNA, CAB 164/392, Isserlis to Reed, 7 July 1969, 1.
4. Bruce Curtis, *The Politics of Population: State Formation, Statistics, and the Census of Canada, 1840–1875* (London: University of Toronto Press, 2001), 40.
5. TNA, CAB 130/427, *Draft Green Paper: People and Numbers*, 12 June 1969, 4.
6. Ibid., 2.

7. TNA, CAB 164/392, *Green Paper: People and Numbers, Fourth Draft*, 3 July 1969, 1.
8. Prof. C. A. Moser, *Evidence to the Sub-committee on Economic Affairs*, 13 June 1966, 1168, 351.
9. *Draft Green Paper: People and Numbers*, 5.
10. Ibid., 10.
11. Ibid., 11.
12. Ibid., 3.
13. *Report of the Committee on Data Protection*, Cmnd. 7341 (December 1978), 264.
14. *Draft Green Paper: People and Numbers*, 4.
15. See, for example, TNA, HO 264/260, *Working Group on Government Computers and Privacy, Meeting 27 September 1971*, 4; "Political Commentary," *The Spectator*, 30 January 1971, 5.
16. TNA, CAB 130/427, *People and Numbers Official Group, Meeting 18 June 1969*, 3.
17. TNA, CAB 139/563, Moser to Reed, 16 September 1968, 2.
18. Ibid., 1.
19. *People and Numbers Official Group, Meeting 18 June 1969*, 2.
20. TNA, CAB 134/3277, Statistical Policy Committee, 7 March 1969, 1.
21. TNA, PREM 13/3257, to Robertson, Cabinet Office, 8 September 1969, 1.
22. Nikolas Rose, *Powers of Freedom: Reframing Political Thought* (Cambridge: Cambridge University Press, 1999), 19.
23. Arthur R. Miller, *The Assault on Privacy: Computers, Data Banks, and Dossiers* (Ann Arbor: University of Michigan Press, 1971); J. Mack Adams and Douglas H. Haden, *Social Effects of Computer Use and Misuse* (London: John Wiley and Sons, 1976).
24. *Working Group on Government Computers and Privacy, Meeting 27 September 1971*, 6.
25. TNA, PREM 13/3102, Jenkins to Crossman, 9 October 1967, 2.
26. TNA, PREM 13/3102, Crossman to Jenkins, 12 October 1967, 1.
27. TNA, PREM 13/3102, Legg to Ward, 11 October 1967, 1.
28. TNA, PREM 13/3102, Home Office to Le Cheminant, 27 October 1967, 2.
29. TNA, PREM 13/3102, to Prime Minister, 1 November 1967, 1 and 2.
30. TNA, PREM 13/3102, *Note for the Record*, 7 November 1967, 2.
31. TNA, PREM 13/3102, *Note for the Record*, 31 January 1968, 1.
32. TNA, PREM 13/3102, to Prime Minister, 2 February 1968, 1.
33. R. H. S. Crossman, *The Diaries of a Cabinet Minister, Vol. 2, Lord President of the Council and Leader of the House of Commons, 1966–68* (London: Hamilton Cape, 1975), 219.

34. TNA, PREM 13/3102, Gardiner to Prime Minister, 22 October 1968, 1.
35. TNA, PREM 13/3102, from Trend, 4 March 1969, 1.
36. See, TNA, PREM 13/3102, M.S. to Prime Minister, 18 February 1969, 1; TNA, PREM 13/3102, L. R. to Prime Minister, *Surveillance and Privacy*, 24 February 1969, 1.
37. TNA, PREM 13/3102, Trend to Ryland, 4 March 1969, 1.
38. TNA, PREM 13/3102, Trend to Prime Minister, *Privacy*, 17 November 1969, 3.
39. Walter F. Pratt, *Privacy in Britain* (Lewisburg: Bucknell University Press, 1979), 137.
40. TNA, PREM 13/3102, Boggis-Rolfe to Peart, 29 October 1969, 3.
41. TNA, PREM 13/3102, to Prime Minister, 14 November 1969.
42. TNA, PREM 13/3102, G. to Prime Minister, *Law of Privacy*, 14 November 1969, 3 and 1.
43. TNA, PREM 13/3102, *Draft Speech*, n.d., ca. November/December 1969, 1–10.
44. TNA, PREM 13/3257, Moser to Trend, 12 December 1969, 1.
45. Ibid.
46. TNA, PREM 13/3102, *Note of a Discussion in 10 Downing St on the Evening of 24 November 1969*, 4.
47. TNA, PREM 13/3102, Trend to Prime Minister, *Privacy*, 1 December 1969, 1.
48. *Cabinet Conclusions* (70), 22 January 1970, 4.
49. Ibid., 5.
50. Ibid.
51. TNA, PREM 13/3102, Trend to Prime Minister, *Privacy*, 17 November 1969, 2.
52. Gerald Rhodes, "The Younger Committee and Research," *Public Administration* 51 (1973): 455.
53. TNA, HO/264/62, Committee on Privacy, *Note by the Secretary, Computers and Privacy*, 2 October 1970, 1.
54. TNA, HO 264/2, Sam to Callaghan, 1 April 1970, 1.
55. TNA, HO 264/57, Committee on Privacy, *Scope of the Committee's Terms of Reference*, 11 May 1970, 1.
56. Ibid., 2.
57. TNA, HO 264/18, Committee on Privacy, *Meeting 14 May 1970*, 1–2.
58. TNA, HO 264/2, Callaghan to Younger, 5 June 1970, 1–2.
59. TNA, HO 411/1, *Code of Conduct for Government Computers, Meeting 4 March 1970*, 1.
60. TNA, HO 264/19, Committee on Privacy, *Meeting 24 June 1970*, 2.
61. TNA, HO 264/2, Maudling to Younger, 23 July 1970, 1.
62. TNA, HO 264/2, Maudling to Younger, 4 August 1970, 1.

63. "Warwick Report Says Files Not Kept," *Times*, 15 April 1970, 2.
64. TNA, HO 411/3, Atkinson to Heaton, 18 March 1971, 1.
65. TNA, CAB 139/563, Redfern to Rennie, 28 August 1970, 1.
66. TNA, HO 264/260, *Government Computers and Privacy, Meeting 10 February 1972*, 2.
67. TNA, HO 411/1, *Code of Conduct for Government Computer Systems, Meeting 4 March 1970*, 3.
68. TNA, CAB 139/563, West Sussex County Council, Computer Steering Group, *Report of the Working Party on Personal and Locational References*, n.d., ca. 1970, 5.
69. TNA, CAB 139/563, Morton to MacLeod, 27 October 1970, 1.
70. Rose, *Powers of Freedom*, 212.
71. TNA, CAB 139/583, Statistical Policy Committee, *The Linkage of Individual Data Held by Central Government Departments*, 21 January 1971, 5.
72. TNA, CAB 139/752, Statistical Policy Committee, *The Linkage of Individual Data Held by Central Government Departments*, 22 December 1970, 5.
73. TNA, CAB 139/752, Graham-Harrison to Moser, 20 January 1971, 1.
74. TNA, HO 411/3, *Proposed Study of Record Linkage, Meeting 5 April 1971*, 3; TNA, HO 411/3, *Draft Written Question and Answer*, n.d., ca. April 1971, 1.
75. TNA, HO 411/3, Statistical Policy Committee, the Central Statistical Office and the Office of Population Censuses and Surveys, *The Linkage of Individual Data Held by Central Government Departments*, 22 December 1970, 1.
76. TNA, HO 411/3, Director, Central Statistical Office, *Record Linkage*, March 1971, 1.
77. TNA, HO 264/81, Redfern to Pratt, 9 July 1971, 1.
78. P. G. Moore, "Security of the Census Population," *Journal of the Royal Statistical Society* 136 (1973): 583–96.
79. TNA, CAB 164/933, Moser to Maudling, n.d., ca. April/May 1970, 1.
80. TNA, CAB 164/933, 1971 *Census, Follow Up Survey of Incomes*, 11 May 1971, 1–4.
81. TNA, HO 411/3, Cairncross to Home Secretary, 26 April 1971, 1.
82. TNA, CAB 139/583, Maudling to Prime Minister, 19 April 1971, 2.

CHAPTER 6

The Younger Committee

The Younger Committee was one of the most significant contingencies to appear around the issues of population registration and privacy in this period. This committee undertook a social survey to discover the nature of public attitudes towards privacy and the findings of this survey are reviewed in the first section of this chapter. These made plain the public's concerns about threats to their privacy and showed how people identified the government as the main culprit in serious breaches of privacy. However, the government (and the Younger Committee) interpreted these findings very differently. From their perspective, these results were seen to bolster the view that privacy was such a broad topic that it was indefinable and that consequently, there was no one agent at fault where breaches of privacy occurred. The rest of this chapter analyses these government views.

The second section concentrates on explaining how, though the government may have claimed to be presenting the facts of British social attitudes, what it was actually doing was stating its vehement political opposition to a general right of privacy. There were three reasons why the government held this view. First, a right of privacy would threaten to pass power over all government data, to the judiciary whose job it would be to interpret such a right. Second, such a right was opposed because it would alienate the media. Third, government could not countenance a general right of privacy because it wanted to protect the bulk of its data, which was held in paper files, from oversight and so insisted that the attention of the Younger Committee should turn to only that

K. Manton, *Population Registers and Privacy in Britain, 1936–1984*,
https://doi.org/10.1007/978-3-030-02753-7_6

data held on computers. Therefore, the government had to argue that the issue of privacy was not the same across all data. Here it is observed that this case was made despite the fact that, within government circles, it was frequently admitted that computerised and paper-based data were actually the same thing.

The third section looks at the issue of computerisation. The fearful attitudes of the British people towards the new technology are examined, but what is drawn out of this is not that the British were technophobes, rather that computers were just one part of a bigger British concern: a fear of government data and dossiers which focused on computers because the existence of the technology was public knowledge. The government did not want this hostility towards its computers but still less did it want this attention to turn on its paper records. The dilemmas this attitude caused the government will be examined throughout the rest of this book, but this section stresses how officials and ministers rubbished both the findings of Younger's social survey and the conclusions of authors who saw the dangers inherent in computerisation.

The People's Attitudes

Throughout the period covered by this book, the British people demonstrated a fundamental ambivalence towards welfare policies delivered through "day-to-day" interventions. They were, on the one hand, attached to these progressive ends, but on the other hand they remained unhabituated towards the means chosen by government to facilitate the increased delivery of these policies: the standardisation, centralisation and linking of data. These popular attitudes form an essential part of the events examined here. This hostility had been excoriated by Sylvanus Vivian, the registrar general during the Second World War, and caused the data planners of the 1960s and 1970s to treat the public in a very circumspect manner. Thus, these views formed the warp and weave of the loose "Anglicized system," noted by Foucault, and so constrained and moulded the forms of data collection that government was able to implement.[1] Parliamentary voices that echoed this wary popular disapproval formed the privacy campaign that derailed *People and Numbers* and, through opposition to the 1971 census, similarly halted attempts by Claus Moser, the chief statistical officer, to get the same scheme adopted under the Conservatives. Moreover, it was plainly from fear of provoking a public backlash that plans such as these were concealed, or couched in terms designed to camouflage registration or common numbering so that they might appear to be an evolutionary extension of trusted institutions such as the National Health Service or National Insurance. The most significant impact of the public's outlook, transmitted to government through those in Parliament who shared it, was the creation of the Younger Committee on Privacy in January 1971. Yet on its inception the committee found itself in the dark as to what these public attitudes actually were because there was a dearth of information in Whitehall on the subject. The Heyworth Report of 1965 had suggested that departments ought to anticipate public concerns by finding out what the people thought on policy matters, but no action had been taken in this regard.[2] This meant that the Younger Committee had to try to sound out public opinion and this section will examine how it did this, what it found out and how this information was reshaped in order to reinforce the committee's fundamental preconceptions rather than to enlighten its enquiries.

The Social Science Research Council secured permission from Younger to attach an observer to the privacy inquiry. This was Gerald Rhodes, senior research officer with the Royal Institute of Public Administration. He noted that from its inception Younger was hampered by the nature of its task. Most committees of inquiry investigated a subject where there was a discernable nucleus to the topic around which opinions could orbit. But privacy, he claimed, was not like that: it was a topic without a definition and where any delineation was often negative, indicating that a breach of privacy had occurred rather than explaining what privacy actually was. Moreover, since these breaches could be anything from gossipy neighbours, to industrial espionage, any examination would almost inevitably blur the outlines of an inquiry by expanding the range of breaches of privacy, rather than bringing the topic into a sharper focus. Whether this confusion really was an essential facet of the topic of privacy, in other words whether privacy really was indefinable, is something that will be examined in the next section of this chapter, but Rhodes recorded that it was this lack of any firm information about the scale and the sources of public anxiety that led the committee to attempt to explore public attitudes.

In August 1970, once the committee had finished wrangling with both the Labour and then the Conservative home secretary over its terms of reference, Younger published an advertisement inviting the public to give evidence. This exercise was judged to have been unsuccessful because it elicited only 214 replies. But the nature of these responses are very interesting and make it possible to see where the public's real concerns were focused since over half reflected concerns about the activities of central and local government or nationalised industries. But this, of course, meant that they fell outside the committee's terms of reference. Looking at the topics mentioned that were suitable for the committee's attention the area most often mentioned was the conduct of the press, followed by unsolicited mail and nosy neighbours. Other categories included credit rating agencies, the opening of mail, telephone advertising, doorstep sales and aerial photography but each of these was brought up by only a few people.[3]

Some members of the committee claimed that the paucity of the data gleaned from this process was proof that the controversy that had established their enquiry had been blown out of all proportion by a few hotheads, whose rabble-rousing did not reflect the reality of popular quiescence on the subject. However, it was agreed that the only way to know for sure was to undertake a survey of public attitudes.[4] The provisional form of this survey was drawn up by Gerald Pratt, the committee's secretary, and had two main aims: first, to see how important privacy was to respondents, and second, to gauge reactions to a variety of examples of intrusions into people's lives. Following Younger's agreement with this in September 1970, Pratt entered into discussions with the Home Office Research Unit, the organisation that would undertake the survey. These talks led to modifications being made to Pratt's format and produced the four-part survey that was carried out in April and May 1971. This looked at: what people understood by privacy, how important they thought it was, whether they felt their own privacy had been breached (and if it had been, what they had done about it) and whether they thought certain hypothetical situations presented to them should be banned. This was all agreed easily, but the survey's provisional findings were not available until July 1971 and the full report not until two months after that. Because significant chapters of the Younger Committee Report were first drafted in November 1971, this meant that the survey results did not have much influence on the bulk of the committee's investigations. As a result, Younger's work was reliant on two sources: the groups who presented evidence to it and the papers prepared by its secretary. This in turn meant that the focus of the committee's work "linked up closely with areas of concern originally identified by the Home Office" which focused on: the press, private detectives, bugging and the question of whether computers posed an actual, or merely a potential, threat to privacy.[5] These were different aspects of the overall problem of privacy and were earmarked for examination as different things thus increasing the likelihood that Younger would not see privacy as a single issue, susceptible to a unified resolution.

However, the survey remains the best indicator of public attitudes on this subject and as such its results are worth examining in some detail. The survey was conducted by interviewing people at selected addresses round the country, a process that produced a total sample of 1596 usable interviews. This was lower than anticipated because the survey got caught up in the bad publicity surrounding the 1971 census that was conducted at the same time.[6] Nonetheless, the survey highlighted three elements of the public's attitude on the question of privacy and the first of these was that privacy meant something to everyone. In fact, 94% of people were able to give a usable answer when asked what privacy meant to them and it would be wrong to assume that the remaining 6% had no opinion because, as the compilers of the results noted, most of these people were badly educated and so might not have been able to verbalise what they meant.[7] The answers given fell into four broad categories: first, not being interfered with, or, being left alone by other people (mentioned by 47% of those surveyed), second, maintaining the confidentiality of one's own affairs (35%), third, the right to do as you wish at home (30%) and fourth, being able to be alone (16%). The totals given here add up to more than 100% because many people gave responses that overlapped these boundaries.

The second main finding of the survey was that privacy mattered to people. The survey asked people to rank privacy on a five-point scale: 16% said it was extremely important, 29% that it was very important, 38% quite important, 15% not very important and only 3% said that it was not important at all.[8] Privacy was seen as less important than economic issues such as controlling prices, reducing unemployment or ending strikes, but of greater importance than building more schools. Moreover, it was the most important of the seven social or civil rights issues presented to interviewees, scoring higher than improving race relations, protecting freedom of speech and protecting the freedom of the press, for example.[9]

Third, the survey found that though most people did not think their own privacy had reduced they felt that privacy in general was in decline. The generalised nature of this concern did not, as the compilers noted, make this fear any less important to people.[10] However, people were given an opportunity to focus their concerns because the survey presented them with thirteen scenarios and asked them to say: whether they thought each one represented a breach of privacy, how annoyed or upset such a breach would make them feel were it to happen to them and whether the situation should be prohibited. These hypothetical situations included receiving unsolicited, sexually explicit material through the post, the actions of credit referencing agencies and nosy neighbours. These three were judged to be invasions of privacy by 67, 46 and 83% of respondents, respectively. These incidents would be labelled "very" annoying (this was the strongest of the three choices offered) by 46, 25 and 53% of interviewees with 72, 37 and 55% stating that these activities should be prohibited. However, the people interviewed were also asked about their reactions to centralised and computerised databanks. Here 87% thought this was an invasion of privacy, 71% said they would be "very" annoyed or upset by this situation, this being the highest total of responses in this category (only 13% said they would not be annoyed: the lowest total for all the situations offered to respondents) and 85% thought they should be prohibited making this scenario the one that most interviewees wanted to ban. To put this level of outrage into perspective, it ought to be noted that the situation that achieved the second highest tally here was that of the receipt of unsolicited sexually explicit material, which was ranked some thirteen points lower. People were also asked which of their personal details they would most object to having published. The four pieces of personal information which people were least concerned about others knowing were: nationality (92% of people would not object to this being published), race (90%), occupation (88%) and maiden name/wife's maiden name (82%). At the opposite extreme, the four pieces of information that most people wanted to keep confidential were: details of their sex life (87% of interviewees would object to this becoming public knowledge), income (78%), medical history (51%) and political views (42%).[11]

When people were asked about incidents where they felt their privacy had been invaded and were prompted to reply with instances that fell within Younger's terms of reference, 14% of people told interviewers that their neighbours had overstepped the mark in the last year, a further 14% said they had been intruded on by doorstep callers (with 5% of all those surveyed singling out Jehovah's Witnesses as the culprits), while 10% of people felt their privacy had been violated by post and 6% by telephone.[12] The compilers of the survey data pointed out that all of this could easily be subsumed within the broad heading of day-to-day hassles, but then added that it would be completely wrong to argue from this that people's concerns with privacy were nothing more than their letting off steam about the petty irritants of modern life. If the answers given focused on the activities of doorstep proselytisers, that was because the Younger Committee's terms of reference excluded the actions of all government departments, local government and nationalised industries. In other words: the survey got answers to the questions it was allowed to ask.[13]

However, despite this awareness the report went on to conclude that "the threats to privacy that are felt to exist are of an extremely varied nature and this fragmentation meant that there was no clearly distinguished enemy of privacy."[14] The report was obliged to reach this conclusion by the nature of its remit, based as it was on Younger's terms of reference. Had its scope been wider then it would surely have reflected the attitudes of the more than half the people who responded to Younger's original advertisement and concluded that people clearly distinguished the government as the enemy of their privacy. But even on its own terms the report could reach this conclusion only by overlooking three things that were self-evident from its own findings. First, that people could say what privacy meant to them and second, that privacy was clearly an issue that mattered to people. But equally the report's conclusion could only be reached by, third, glossing over the clear and specific findings that a very high number of people were concerned about the use of centralised computerised databanks. Moreover, it was admitted within a government committee in 1972 that the public were "more concerned about the threat of misuse of personal information in government computers than in private ones,"[15] which further calls into question the idea that people could not point an accusing finger at a clearly distinguished "enemy of privacy," and therefore highlights the reason why the government wanted Younger to focus only on the private sector. However, all of this was left unsaid by the social survey. Therefore, insofar as the survey had any impact on Younger, it reinforced the committee's belief in the appropriateness of its terms of reference by contributing to the belief that privacy was "a general concern with aspects of almost the whole range of activities within society," in other words, that it was beyond definition and therefore beyond remedy, except through the use of the law to target specific breaches. A general right of privacy would be ruled out by this interpretation of the results of the social survey.[16]

The Committee at Work

In mid-November 1969, while he was anxiously trying to formulate a strategy for dealing with Brian Walden's parliamentary bill, Burke Trend, the cabinet secretary, wrote that part of the problem he faced was that privacy was an "indefinite subject." He contended that though examples ranged from press intrusions into private grief to industrial espionage, the "methods employed in each case are similar; and people are apt to feel, rightly or wrongly, that the principle at stake is basically the same."[17] His concern was thus, that though the topic of privacy encompassed a very wide range of experiences, these could not be parcelled up into separate issues: some to be examined by an enquiry, some to remain outside its remit. Therefore, at this point he was reluctantly forced to concede that: "although it is tempting to try to split off a particular segment of the subject for the purposes of an enquiry, I doubt whether we should in fact get away with it."[18] The danger in this, from Trend's point of view, was that an all-encompassing enquiry into privacy; could produce a recommendation for an all-encompassing right of privacy that would have an impact on state activities even though Walden had accepted that these should remain outside the scope of his bill. Part of the explanation for why this did not happen is to be found in the nature of the Younger Committee and its membership (partly of course, engineered by Trend), but equally important was another element of the strategy that was worked out in the run-up to Walden's bill. This was the way privacy was viewed not as a single issue where "the principle at stake" in various incidents was "basically the same," but as a series of discreet clusters of events each having different causes and therefore open to different remedies, thus obviating the need for a general right of privacy. This view was, from its early days, an essential component of the institutional mindset of the Younger Committee. This section will first examine the nature of this argument and then go on to look at how it was applied to the most important aspect of the committee's work: the use of computers.

The attitude of governments throughout the period studied here towards this aspect of the privacy question was captured by Harold Wilson in a speech to the Liverpool Press Club in March 1976, thus: "what is or should be meant by the right of Privacy is extremely difficult to define, and particularly to define it in legal terms."[19] Discussions in the Younger Committee during the drafting stages of its report phrased this same point even more plainly "the search for an agreed definition of privacy is a waste of time," and so the final report came out against establishing a general right.[20] However, this view was opposed by the results of the committee's own survey of the public. The compilers of this data noted that though the public gave differing and overlapping answers to the question "what do you understand by privacy?" this did not necessarily mean that the topic was a swamp of time-wasting confusion. In fact, they noted "it is possible that the differing types of definition represent differing emphasis or even differing forms of expression of a fairly universal view of privacy rather than fundamentally differing views."[21] Besides which, even if the public did produce competing characterisations this in itself did not constitute particularly good grounds for not choosing one of them, synthesising some of them or proffering a different one.[22] However, the absence of any of these courses of action gives a strong indication of the fundamental predisposition of those examining the issue on the Younger Committee to view privacy as a series of parallel problems: to keep what was once called "the privacy jigsaw" broken up into separate pieces rather than view the big picture.[23]

As might be expected, given that ordinary people could define privacy, the judiciary did not agree with Wilson that this was a difficult if not impossible task. For example, in the run-up to *People and Numbers*, there were at least two attempts to do so. The first came at a symposium in the USA in 1966 where it was proposed that invasions of privacy were not like a trespass onto property, because privacy did not refer to relationships of ownership through purchase or inheritance. Privacy, it was maintained, referred to the social space around an individual that he owned by virtue of his humanity and civility adding that "a society that claims to be both humane and civil" should respect the sanctity of this space.[24] Thus, privacy was here defined as a boundary across which information about an individual ought not to pass without the express consent of the subject of the information: in other words, consent was central to an understanding of privacy. Second, at a meeting in Stockholm in May 1967, the Conference of Nordic Jurists produced a definition of privacy encapsulated as "the right of the individual to lead his own life" protected against interference, though with the important caveat that the state might, in the public interest, need to have a freedom to interfere with people's privacy. Moreover, this judicial activism was not something alien to Britain for, during a 1961 Lords' debate on a privacy bill, Lord

Denning noted that in the USA judges were active in this area of the law, and said that in Britain too, "the judges may well do it."[25] In 1970 Justice, the British section of the International Commission of Jurists issued a report called *Privacy and the Law* that recommended a right of privacy and in 1978 the lord chancellor, Elwyn-Jones received advice from Lord Wilberforce that such a general right of privacy could be drafted, though he was astute enough to realise that the passing of such a right would be wholly dependent on parliamentary politics.[26]

So there cannot be much doubt that a legal definition could be generated. But this is to get to the crux of the problem. Defining privacy was not an objective exercise it was a political process, and equally not defining it was also to make a political judgement. Part of the reason why the government made this judgement, not to define privacy, lay in the fact that it needed to keep a weather eye on two sets of political relationships that influenced and reflected its priorities. The first of these was the relationship between the government and the judiciary. Any right of privacy would need to be underpinned by a definition of privacy, this would need to be interpreted by the courts and this would give, what a 1976 ministerial group on the disclosure of official information would term, "wide discretion to … the judge and jury."[27] Such judicial activism was not without friends. Alex Lyon MP wrote a minority report from the Younger Committee that was based on a vigorous defence of this judicial discretion. He asserted first, that juries were better representatives of public opinion than the Home Office or the police, and so they should have the role of adjudicating in cases that affected such things as whether a private detective should keep his licence. Second, he maintained that judges were accustomed to balancing competing claims and conflicting freedoms and so were perfectly placed, along with juries, to weigh up a right of privacy where it conflicted with, for example, a public interest defence by journalists. Therefore, the courts could and should be trusted to protect privacy, so that "even the weakest of our fellow citizens knows he can call upon the law in his unequal fight with those powerful interests, including the government, who abuse his freedom."[28] But, of course, it was precisely this fact: that a right of privacy could be used to protect people from government intrusion, that caused government to view with extreme caution any attempt at defining privacy. A definition of privacy was consequently seen as a potential Trojan horse that could introduce a right of privacy which might end up including within its remit the actions of the state, because even if such a right were drafted to exclude state actions, there was no guarantee that the courts would not extend this right to encompass these actions at some point in the future. Such an extension could endanger the gathering of intelligence inside Britain and in the process could reveal "the extent to which trespass was involved," in other words it could publicise how often the government broke the law.[29] So, when Gardiner told Wilson, in October 1968 (see Chapter 5) that he had been "converted" from supporting a law on privacy, he replaced his desire for a general law with a safer approach of propounding specific legal remedies to carefully defined particular breaches of privacy such as industrial espionage.

The second element at the heart of the government's unwillingness to concede that it was possible to define privacy focused on the government's relationship with a group that would see itself as losing out if such a definition were to lead to a right of privacy: the press. Walden's bill had met with a hostile reaction from the media and when media moguls and groups that represented sections of the industry gave evidence to the Younger Committee it became clear that "the press would prefer a piecemeal approach to the subject," which is to say that their views coincided with those of the government.[30]

At the Younger Committee, the Press Council argued that a right of privacy would not really protect freedom, in fact it would reduce it, because it would remove the right to free speech and so would be "disastrous for democracy."[31] Privacy laws in the USA, the Guild of British Newspaper Editors claimed, served only as a litigant's charter, whereas the reality of life was, as Lord Shawcross put it, that "the world is a much less private place than it used to be. And those who engage in public life are public property."[32] Public figures knew this, he added, and largely welcomed the oxygen of publicity pumped by the press, as did their readers of course, because "gossip is an integral part of humanity."[33] Summing up a discussion in the committee on all the evidence presented by the media, Kenneth Younger said that: "the majority of members [were] unconvinced on the case for a general right of privacy."[34]

This argument, which was integral to the government's defence of its data and its attempts to expand this up to and including population registration and common numbering, was applied most thoroughly to the most important issue that Younger dealt with: computerisation. Gerald Pratt, the committee's secretary, wrote an extensive paper for the committee on computerisation in which he made this case. In doing so, he reflected and reinforced both the broad trend of the government and

Younger's policy of viewing privacy as a series of separate matters, along with their desire to frame discussion of the issues around computerisation as matters for debate only at a purely technical level. However, the reality was that, just as defining (or not defining) privacy was a political decision not an objective exercise, so too choosing to frame discussions of computerisation as a series of technical issues was also a political decision. As was seen in Chapter 3, William Alonso and Paul Starr note "that political judgements are implicit in the choice of what to measure … and how to present and interpret the results" and the same judgement, that what may be presented as objective or technical is in fact deeply political, can and should be applied to an understanding of how computerisation was adopted, but more importantly for this book, how this process was defended.[35]

In his paper on computerisation, Pratt wrote that the rapid development of computer technology made it possible to envisage an interconnected grid of separate computer systems, which would create a shared pool of all the data nominally stored separately in each constituent system. People may have given permission for personal information to be stored in one system, but the technology would make it available to all the other systems without these data subjects giving their express permission for this linkage to occur. Thus, the issue would be whether individuals should have the final word on how their data was used with it only being exposed to additional systems after full consent had been obtained. Pratt claimed that to insist that information could only be put into a system with the permission of the individual concerned, was to also insist that there be some way of checking that this consent had been given freely and this, he argued, would be extremely difficult to administer.[36]

This may well have been the case and it is beyond doubt that such pleas of administrative difficulties would become commonplace as the debates about controlling computerised databases unfolded. However, what is most notable is that Pratt did not stop at this point, for he went on to make a remarkable admission. Even if such administrative hurdles could be crossed, he continued, doing so would nonetheless fail to deliver a real guarantee of privacy because: "such is the development of technological devices for intrusion and such are the pressures that wealthy organisations can apply, that there is probably no absolute protection that an individual can give to his personal information."[37] But he did not admit this in order to demand yet stronger defences against such intrusion, still less to insist on a right of privacy. In fact having conceded that, in his view, data crime was inevitable, he concluded that because a general right of privacy would not stop this illicit data harvesting there was no point in having one. Thus he concluded: "there seem therefore to be strong practical objections to imposing a ban on the input of personal information" into computers.[38]

Computerisation

Chapter 4 showed how the 1964 report on *Economic and Social Intelligence* presented computer technology as one of the key solutions to the poor provision of data to government policy makers and how computerisation was welcomed as an unambiguously beneficial development by the advocates of standardised, centralised and linked data in their push for population registration and common numbering systems. However, it became apparent that at least some British people were less sanguine about the use of computers when, in 1968, the Society of Conservative Lawyers published a pamphlet: *Computers and Freedom.*[39] This was not the only publication to offer warnings about the new technology and, as the anxiety and upheaval around the 1971 census showed, this unease was not confined to the pages of pamphlets, while the social survey conducted for the Younger Committee made the depth of this unease clear to anyone who wanted it to see it. Moreover, this sentiment was also manifest in Parliament. Leslie Huckfield introduced a private member's bill on the control of personal information in February 1971 and at its introduction said: "action is urgent. Computer men have fobbed me off. Telling me that this is rather a problem for our children's children. But because data banks already operate and more are being set up, we cannot afford to wait for the industry."[40] This section will examine these fears in more detail and then move on to look at how the government opened its campaign in response to them.

In the wake of the furore in the USA initiated by the federal government's proposals to establish a national databank, one author portrayed a dystopian future when computers would have "turned the whole community into the equivalent of an army barracks," suggesting in Foucauldian terms, that "men will live with the constant possibility that they are under surveillance without ever being able to be sure whether this is so."[41] The problems presented by this panopticonism, the author continued, would be exacerbated by the fact that computer technology would be used not only by the government but also by employers, business competitors, insurance companies, jealous spouses and the casually curious. This would create, what other writers referred to as, "an infra-structure of tyranny," or "the imperialism of the social sciences," which was predictably compared to the worlds described by Orwell and Huxley, with the latter's work raising the nightmarish prospect that fully integrated computerised dossiers on all individuals could be put to use by Eugenicists.[42]

The idea that the state could use computers to draw all its data resources for any individual into a dossier detailing each and every aspect of his or her life was central to these fears. Many authors who espoused these concerns stressed how these processes might begin with the best intentions: "more information, more rational judgements. Better data, better decisions" as one phrased it using words that could have come the pen of any progressive such as Wilson.[43] In fact, as was seen in Chapter 4, Wilson saw that an increased flow of statistics to government had "vast potential for … social conscience" further arguing that there were times when what could be portrayed as an invasion of privacy, would be better described as the unveiling of a problem of socio-economic deprivation: finding the "silent community … the legions of the forgotten … So in our capacity at least as passionate statisticians say, let us hear less of this kind of privacy, more of identification."[44] So, it is particularly telling that two of the key British authors who took this critical view of an increase in government data, Malcolm Warner and Michael Stone, went into some detail of how the Swedish system (lauded by Moser) of giving every citizen a unique and permanent identity number worked. But, unlike the British government's data enthusiasts, they concluded that though this system might appear harmless, or indeed beneficial at first sight "once you make any piece of paper obligatory it is a very easy step into tyranny – witness South Africa."[45] The threat was that, given the state's "data mania" (defined as its "predilection toward centralisation and collation of file material"), once the data was compiled, new and malign uses would be found for it: "there is little doubt that technically the state could maintain an integrated dossier on every man, woman and child (and animal, for that matter) in these isles, with the computer equipment now available."[46] Since this was written in 1969, it clearly overestimated the power and practicality of computer technology at that time (see Chapter 4). But though it was prescient rather than observant, it nonetheless voiced a popular fear. This was of a future where "the citizen must be bent round the computer," where "there may be a very real sense in which a person will not exist outside of his computer dossier," encapsulated in the paraphrasing of Jean-Jacques Rousseau by Warner and Stone thus: "man was born free, but everywhere he is on tape!"[47]

These fears were intensified by the increasing marketisation of information: "as a result of the heightened value being placed on information by contemporary society, a substantial portion of information that hitherto has been treated as private is now considered to be appropriate grist for the computer mill and fair game for the data collector."[48] Additionally, there were three anxieties concerning the safety of the technology. The British Computer Society (BCS) gave evidence to the Younger Committee where it stated that: "it is almost certainly impossible to ensure" that computer systems were completely protected from abuse. Computers, the society said, could be accessed from remote terminals, or subjected to "passive threats such as … wire-tapping and the electromagnetic reading of messages," in addition to the illicit copying of data by operatives.[49] The second facet of computer technology underpinning these concerns was that the machines would hold information forever and that it would be ever retrievable: the machines would thus end society's "benign capacity to forget."[50] It was on this basis that *Computers and Freedom* foresaw a dystopian future where minor indiscretions, amorous adventures and youthful misdemeanours would be captured and retained forever by the machines, to remain like a millstone round the neck of the individual who would be trapped in, what another writer called, a "record prison."[51] But arguably even worse than this, it was also maintained, third, that not only would aspects of a person's past be ineradicable once put into a computer, but that the same would apply to erroneous information that was either factually incorrect or taken out of context. *Computers and Freedom* posited the illustration of a person who refused to pay a bill for the good reason that the goods ordered had not been delivered but who, through the act of non-payment, was downgraded by a credit-referencing agency.[52] Another author noted that the defenders of the technology often stated that there was no such thing as "a computer error" since all errors were made by the "human factor," adding that this did not provide much comfort because this type of "old-fashioned typing error made at the input keyboard," could include things which might be serious should they appear in a single-subject, paper-based file but could spell disaster if they were entered in a centralised computer-based "master file."[53]

These were fears of mistaken data being perpetuated, but some saw that events of this nature would arise not as a result of mistakes, but rather because they were inevitable given the nature of computer technology. This was the, perhaps surprising, view of the BCS when it gave evidence to the Younger Committee. The BCS was one of the organisations that had helped the government get out of the political mess it found itself in over the 1971 census. But its Privacy Committee also insisted there was a danger that computerised data could, to all intents and purposes, usurp reality and that, because data gathered on a computer for one purpose would be linked and used for something else, a true picture of reality could get bent or even lost, and a misrepresentation could become accepted as the truth. From this, the society reasoned, that since it was difficult to know which distortions of which pieces of data might cause most harm to an individual, all information should be treated as sensitive and none of it should be used without first obtaining the express consent of the provider.[54]

These authors were not only prophets of doom as they also brought forward solutions to the issues they raised. The authors of *Computers and Freedom* concluded that there needed to be a frank and open discussion of the correct balance between improving the efficiency of public administration and the preservation of traditional British liberal values. It juxtaposed these values, and the British toleration of the irritating slights and pettiness of traditional government administration, with illustrations of the power over the lives of ordinary people that a unified and computerised government databank would give bureaucrats. The authors wrote that the traditional defences of English law were useless against the weight of all this knowledge and power, and they concluded by recommending that: out-of-date information should be regularly purged from computer systems, that officials should only have access to sections of data that were directly relevant to their tasks and most importantly, that there should be independent control and oversight of computerised databanks. These policies would form much of the bedrock of proposals to control computerised data brought forward over the rest of the period studied here. Indeed, Huckfield's bill of February 1971 called for the licencing of all databases that contained data about more than one hundred thousand people and an inspectorate for such licensed operators in order to ensure that they did not breach the civil and personal liberties of their data subjects. These points, and others like them, would be argued back and forth in the considerable debates about computerisation that anticipated and followed the Younger Report and these will be examined in the following chapters, but for now it is necessary to point out that what this argument did was to replace debates about what the BSC called "a social and political matter" with a technical discussion about methods of securing the accuracy and appropriateness of computerised data.[55]

Therefore, the remedies to the issues around computerisation forwarded by Malcolm Warner and Michael Stone were potentially more profound and far-reaching. They began with the premise that privacy needed to be planned into a system. It was not good enough to refuse to recognise that a problem existed until it caused incalculable harm and then attempt to tinker with the system that caused it. Computer systems were very expensive and this, along with technical difficulties would mean that it would be all but impossible to retrofit meaningful modifications once a system was running.[56] The BCS agreed and told Younger that legislation was needed to protect computerised data and to make operators of databanks register their systems because only this would oblige all users to invest in the expensive systems that were needed to protect privacy.[57] However, before real safeguards for privacy could be designed into systems, it would be necessary to know what privacy really was, so this approach was expressly built upon the need to define privacy. In fact, the BCS was adamant about this: "failure to do so could result in existing bad practices becoming more firmly established and some existing safeguards being relinquished without public discussion of the issues involved. This we would deeply deplore."[58] However, any such discussion was ruled out by the parameters drawn round the topic by the institutional dogma across government that held as an article of faith that privacy was indefinable.

Like the BCS, Warner and Stone argued in favour of a general approach to data held on computers, treating all of it with the same high degree of respect and caution. But even so they still focused on data that was computerised, rather than data in general and so ignored that held on paper files. In fact, they associated society's "benign capacity to forget" with the traditional paper filing of data and warned that computers would link data together to produce a panopticon of all-encompassing and all-seeing power that would render all people open to what was elsewhere termed "the scrutiny of all-seeing government."[59] This focus on computers was entirely understandable for two reasons. First, the furore that had erupted in the USA had drawn public attention to the technology and more importantly, second, none of these authors, and indeed no one in Britain outside of a tight government circle was aware of plans such as *People and Numbers* that would have led to the creation of an interlinked database through population registration or the common numbering of paper-based files. On this latter point, it is obvious from Younger's survey that what people were worried about was the effect of computers: their perceived ability to link data and create dossiers, rather than the computerised methods by which these links and dossiers might be created. Indeed, Max Weber (see Chapter 3) had warned of the tendency of bureaucrats to "parcel out the human soul" long before computers were ever invented.

Moreover, the government knew all of this, thus in 1972 it was admitted in government circles that: "it was easier to build dossiers on manual files than on computers."[60] Furthermore, the year before this it was noted first, that "there is a potential threat to privacy when data provided for one purpose is used for another" and then, in a different forum it was concluded that: "the problem is essentially one of the propriety and confidentiality of personal record keeping by 'authority' and not one of the use of computers per se to handle data."[61] This point, that the public feared data as such, rather than its computerisation was reiterated two months later in a speech to the BCS when Frederick Corfield, the minister for aerospace, said: "experience has shown how strong are the fears that information given in confidence to one Government body will find its way to other parts of Government."[62] Additionally, it can be seen that this recognition was not something new to government, indeed the *People and Numbers* draft green papers had admitted that people were "rightly uneasy" about the prospect of greater record linkage.[63]

Since the government saw computers as being the technology of the future, it did not want to tie its own hands and so sought to defend their use, all the while being aware that any scandal concerning data on government computers would "provoke a storm of protest [which] … would expose the government to severe criticism" and, more importantly, would also inhibit "the increased use of computers in government with consequent adverse effects on efficiency."[64] But there was a much more important issue at stake because the government saw computerised and paper-based records as essentially the same and was desperate to prevent the attention attracted by computers from falling onto its paper files. This is hardly surprising when it is remembered that in 1971 it was noted from the heart of government that: "much, if not most personal information held in Government Departments is not yet on the computer."[65] In order to protect its paper-based data, the government might allow some discussion of the use of safeguarding mechanisms for computerised data, though even where this narrowly defined set of technical issues was concerned it would mount a staunch resistance to protect its use of computers. But what it could never sanction was a general right of privacy that might lead to an all-encompassing approach to the gathering and use of data regardless of how it was stored.

The nature of the government's defence of its data will be examined in the next chapter, but this process focused at least some of its attention on addressing the dissenting views outlined here. Warner and Stone's work was dismissed as "adding nothing new" while Pratt forwarded the BCS's submission to members of the Younger Committee with a covering summary that spent longer telling committee members that the BCS proposed that it should be used as the registration body for organisations holding computer databases than it did summarising their views.[66] By comparison, none of the submissions from the newspaper industry were forwarded with such a clear indication of the self-interest that may have motivated them.

However, the Younger Committee's social survey came in for particular scrutiny and was the subject of a meeting, held under Home Office auspices soon after its publication in September 1971. This centred on four themes. The first of these concerned the nature of not only the public's answers to the survey questions, but also the questions themselves. Thus, early in this discussion it was stated that the survey "did no more than confirm the emotional responses to a weighted question which might have been expected from uninformed people," and that it "indicated the superficiality of the public reaction."[67] The language here was more restrained than Sylvanus Vivian's 1946 tirade against the "primitive taboos" of the opponents of the wartime National Register, but it clearly came from the same mindset.[68] The second theme of this meeting therefore, looked at what could be done about this situation. Here the fact that the people were "uninformed" seemed to offer a way forward: they could be informed. "Education of the public was essential," but the meeting seemed to think that this should not be too difficult to achieve since "the public was obviously malleable and a report emphasising the benefits of computers might help to sway public opinion in favour of more computerisation for greater efficiency."[69] Third, the meeting stressed how the public's fears as expressed to the survey were just that:

fears and apprehensions. These, it was said, were based on stories coming to Britain from the USA: "no actual incidents of invasions of privacy have been cited."[70] Here it is important to point out that this is hardly surprising since the extent of computer use by the government was, according to this same committee, kept concealed from the British people. Moreover, this also ignores the more fundamental issue, that given the raw state of the technology in the early 1970s, most government plans to standardise, centralise and link data focused on achieving these aims through paper records, and these were never included in any discussion. Fourth, when these civil servants read the Younger Committee's social survey they saw what they wanted to see: a variety of fears clustered around computer technology, such as the indefinite storage of information, the use of information for purposes other than which it had been obtained and the dangers of unauthorised access.[71] They thus used the survey to move the whole debate onto terrain where, to use Burke Trend's phrase, the government could "get away with it": by focusing on the technical aspects of computerised data rather than the political realities and purposes of data as such, and in so doing avoiding any discussion of the paper records which still held most government data.

Notes

1. Michel Foucault, *The Birth of the Clinic* (London: Routledge, 1989), 48.
2. Gerald Rhodes, "The Younger Committee and Research," *Public Administration* 51 (1973): 459.
3. TNA, HO 264/3, *List*, October 1970, 1; Rhodes, "The Younger Committee and Research," 451.
4. Rhodes, "The Younger Committee and Research," 451.
5. Ibid., 455.
6. TNA, RG 25/501, Research Bureau Limited, *Report on Survey of Public Attitudes to Privacy*, September 1971, 1.
7. Ibid., 3.
8. Ibid., 8.
9. Ibid., 1 and 6.
10. Ibid., 10.
11. Ibid., 23 and 24.
12. Ibid., 11.
13. Ibid., 29.
14. Ibid., 37.
15. TNA, HO 411/17, *Control of Government Computers, Note by the Home Office*, n.d., ca. 1972, 4.

16. Research Bureau Limited, *Report on Survey of Public Attitudes to Privacy*, 37.
17. TNA, PREM 13/3102, Trend to Prime Minister, 17 November 1969, 1.
18. Ibid.
19. TNA, CAB 164/1327, Wilson, *Speech at the Liverpool Press Club, Friday 5 March 1976*, 7.
20. TNA, HO 264/7, Pratt to Younger, 2 November 1971, 4.
21. Research Bureau Limited, *Report on Survey of Public Attitudes to Privacy*, 5.
22. D. N. MacCormick, "Privacy: A Problem of Definition?" *British Journal of Law and Society* 1 (1974): 77.
23. Gerald Dworkin, "Reports of the Committees: The Younger Report on Privacy," *Modern Law Review* 36 (1973): 406.
24. Edward Shils, "Privacy in Modern Industrial Society," in *Censuses, Surveys and Privacy*, ed. Martin Bulmer (Basingstoke: Macmillan, 1979), 36.
25. Quoted in, C. H. Rolph, "Privacy," *The New Statesman*, Vol. 61, 12 May 1961, 746.
26. TNA, PREM 16/1857, Rees to Prime Minister, *annex*, 7 April 1978, 5.
27. TNA, PREM 16/1855, Ministerial Group on the Disclosure of Official Information, *Privacy, Contempt of Court and Defamation*, 30 July 1976, 4.
28. A. W. Lyon, "Minority Report," in *Report of the Committee on Privacy*, Cmnd. 5012 (July 1972), 211 and 212.
29. TNA, PREM 13/3102, Foreign Secretary to Prime Minister, 18 February 1969, 4.
30. TNA, HO 264/22, *The Press and Privacy, Notes of a Talk to the Committee, 29 July 1970*, 6.
31. TNA, HO 264/18, The Press Council, *Memorandum to the Committee*, n.d., ca. 1970, 1.
32. TNA, HO 264/66, The Guild of British Newspaper Editors, *Written Evidence to the Committee, 20 November 1970*, 5; Lord Shawcross, *Speech, 6 October 1970*, 1.
33. The Press Council, *Memorandum to the Committee*, 3.
34. TNA, HO 264/257, *Extract of the Minutes of a Meeting Held on 18 May 1971*, 8.
35. William Alonso and Paul Starr, "Introduction," in *The Politics of Numbers*, eds. William Alonso and Paul Starr (New York: Russell Sage Foundation, 1987), 3.
36. TNA, HO 264/62, Committee on Privacy, Note by the Secretary, *Computers and Privacy*, 2 October 1970, 5.
37. Ibid.
38. Ibid.
39. Society of Conservative Lawyers, *Computers and Freedom* (London: Conservative Research Department, 1968).

40. Leslie Huckfield, "Know Your Neighbour's Bank Balance for a £7.00 Fee," *New Scientist*, 18 February 1971, 364.
41. Harry Kalven, "The Problems of Privacy in the Year 2000," *Daedalus* 96 (1967): 877.
42. Michael Stone and Malcolm Warner, "Politics, Privacy and Computers," *Political Quarterly* 40 (1969): 260; Kalven, "The Problems of Privacy in the Year 2000," 879; Arthur R. Miller, *The Assault on Privacy: Computers, Data Banks, and Dossiers* (Ann Arbor: University of Michigan Press, 1971), 39.
43. Malcolm Warner and Michael Stone, *The Data Bank Society: Organizations, Computers and Social Freedom* (London: George Allen & Unwin, 1970), 258.
44. Harold Wilson, "Statistics and Decision-Making in Government—Bradshaw Revisited," *Journal of the Royal Statistical Society. Series A* 136 (1973): 9 and 11–12.
45. Warner and Stone, *The Data Bank Society*, 77.
46. Miller, *The Assault on Privacy*, 22 and 211; Stone and Warner, "Politics, Privacy and Computers," 228.
47. Antony A. Thompson, *Big Brother in Britain Today* (London: Michael Joseph, 1970), 53; Miller, *The Assault on Privacy*, 49; Warner and Stone, *The Data Bank Society*, 80.
48. Miller, *The Assault on Privacy*, 23.
49. TNA, HO 264/121, The British Computer Society, *Submission to the Younger Committee*, March 1971, 10.
50. Warner and Stone, *The Data Bank Society*, 73.
51. Society of Conservative Lawyers, *Computers and Freedom*, 4; Miller, *The Assault on Privacy*, 40.
52. Society of Conservative Lawyers, *Computers and Freedom*, 3.
53. Thompson, *Big Brother in Britain Today*, 56.
54. TNA, HO 264/121, The British Computer Society, *Submission to the Younger Committee*, March 1971, 17–18.
55. Ibid., 2; Nikolas Rose, *Powers of Freedom: Reframing Political Thought* (Cambridge: Cambridge University Press, 1999), 205.
56. Warner and Stone, *The Data Bank Society*, 73–74.
57. The British Computer Society, *Submission to the Younger Committee*, 11.
58. Ibid., 6.
59. Warner and Stone, *The Data Bank Society*, 73; Stone and Warner, "Politics, Privacy and Computers," 259; TNA, HO 411/18, *Government Computers and Privacy, Draft Report to Ministers (2), v Education of the Public*, n.d., ca. January 1972, 1.
60. TNA, HO 264/260, *Government Computers and Privacy, Meeting 10 February 1972*, 3.

61. TNA, HO 411/2, *Discussion Paper, Code of Conduct for Safeguarding Personal Information on Central Government Computers*, n.d., ca. June 1971, 5; TNA, HO 411/16, *Computers and Privacy, Background Note*, n.d., ca. August 1971, 2.
62. TNA, HO 411/16, *Speech Notes for the Minister of Aerospace for Dinner of British Computer Society*, 27 October 1971, 8.
63. TNA, CAB 164/392, *People and Numbers, Fourth Draft*, 13 July 1969, 6.
64. TNA, HO 264/260, *Government Computers and Privacy, Extent of Public Interest, a Note by the Home Office*, 27 September 1971, 8.
65. TNA, HO 411/2, Spain to Graham-Harrison, 11 June 1971, 1.
66. TNA, CAB 164/392, Isserlis to Reed, 7 July 1969, 1; TNA, HO 264/121, Summary, March 1971, 1.
67. TNA, HO 411/17, *Government Computers and Privacy, Meeting 27 September 1971*, 1.
68. S. P. Vivian, "Identity Cards and Liberty," *National Review*, August 1946, 143–48.
69. *Government Computers and Privacy, Meeting 27 September 1971*, 5 and 4.
70. *Government Computers and Privacy, Extent of Public Interest, a Note by the Home Office*, 5.
71. Ibid., 7.

CHAPTER 7

Defending Data

Although the government had set the Younger Committee up in as pliant a form as possible, there was still concern along the corridors of power about what the committee might recommend. Thus, the government put a lot of effort into preparing its defence in advance of the Younger Report, and this work is examined and analysed in this chapter. The first section looks at the work of a committee chaired by a senior Home Office civil servant, Francis Graham-Harrison, and shows how this committee's real function was not, as ministers often stated, to prepare a report on government computer use, but rather to buttress the defences around government data. This section provides a broad overview of the committee's thinking and the plans it laid for the government's response to popular opposition to computerisation.

The second section considers the committee's thinking on government computers and lays bare the wholly political nature of the reasoning that led it to state that computer-based records were qualitatively different to paper files. It is shown how this assertion realised the committee's interconnected aims, first of removing paper-based data from the realm of any oversight regime that might be introduced by Younger and, second, of focusing the attention computers were receiving onto purely technical matters. Further, this section shows how the assurances offered in the committee's report: that computers were safe storage systems and that computer operators were thoroughly vetted were both known to be false. Additionally, it demonstrates that though the report presented computers as stand-alone machines, Graham-Harrison himself

K. Manton, *Population Registers and Privacy in Britain, 1936–1984*,
https://doi.org/10.1007/978-3-030-02753-7_7

was very well aware that they were increasingly being linked together to form data grids.

The last section looks at the Younger Report's chapter on computers and how the government's response to this was built on the findings of the Graham-Harrison Committee. But it also highlights the fragility, indeed the artificiality, of the barrier built by Graham-Harrison between computers and paper-based records. This was manifest when the prime minister, Edward Heath, called it into question. However, the resolve of officials to defend their data by keeping paper-based records out of Younger's spotlight was made clear by the way they speedily and effectively marginalised Heath's objections.

Preparing for the Younger Report

The Younger Committee was announced during the parliamentary debate on Brian Walden's bill, on 23 January 1970. The government had not wanted this committee and had only established it when, having prevaricated for as long as it could, it was backed into a corner by the privacy campaign, so the government did all that it could to draw the sting out of the committee's work. It set Younger up in the form of a departmental committee because this was the most powerless of the possible forms for an enquiry and, more importantly, most of the committee's membership, concurred with the government's framing of the privacy debate as a series of more-or-less unconnected breaches of the law that, insofar as they needed remedying, would be best dealt with by ad hoc changes to existing laws and did not need a general right of privacy. The committee was therefore, in many respects, a paper tiger: "responsible people … reaching the right decisions in the longer term" as the cabinet secretary, Burke Trend, had phrased it.[1] So it might seem that the government had no reason to worry about the Younger Report, but any enquiry into issues of privacy would always touch a raw nerve with any government in this period. There was too much at stake for any complacency because the government was not only trying to protect its existing data holdings from scrutiny, it was also trying to build an environment that would allow it to introduce schemes such as *People and Numbers*. The Younger Committee's brief excluded all state activities and bodies, but it covered the use of computers and the government was aware that the committee's findings on this topic could ripple out to effect its own machines; moreover, it was always aware of the possibility that its worst-case scenario could become reality were any control regime suggested by Younger to also oversee the government's use of paper-based records.

However, this general sense of unease was brought sharply into focus by a parliamentary exchange on 5 February 1970 when, during supplementary questions on the subject of the government's computerised records, Alex Lyon suggested to Wilson that the government should "set an example by themselves promulgating regulations for the way in which this information is acquired and by the way which it is dispersed." Wilson replied that he would consider whether it would "be possible to work out some code of conduct in which the government could give a lead."[2] These comments by the prime minister exacerbated the already cagey attitude to Younger within government circles because they seemed to proffer some hope of legitimising demands for oversight of government records. As a result, the government made thorough preparations for the Younger Report, and studying these can divulge its fundamental priorities and concerns. This section presents the main issues that perturbed the government and how ministers and officials sought to manage these by examining the work of a committee charged with this defensive task. It looks at the political views of this committee, how it anticipated the Younger Report and how it viewed the likely response of the public.

A few weeks after Wilson's parliamentary comments, the Home Office reconvened the group of officials that had first met to consider Lord Windlesham's parliamentary motion on computers and privacy in November 1969 (see Chapter 4). This group was again chaired by Francis Graham-Harrison, but its brief was now to consider "the more philosophical problems of the proper limits of confidentiality and the evolving of a code of conduct" for computer use.[3] The group at this provisional meeting would remain together as a committee enquiring into whether such a code of conduct was necessary and if it were, how it should be framed. The government would refer to this body whenever it was quizzed about its use of data processing. For example, in November 1970 Lord Hailsham said: "the government have set in train a comprehensive survey to find out by the end of this year what categories of information are held, or are likely to be held, in the computer systems of each Department and the rules governing its storage and use; we shall then proceed to decide what shall be done." Additionally, the following summer Mark Carlisle, speaking for the Home Office in

Parliament, said: "this is not merely a paper exercise. We propose to put into practice the results of that inquiry."[4] It was entirely in keeping with this general view of the committee that, as will be seen in the next chapter, its report would be portrayed as representing an objective statement of fact. However, both the real purpose of this committee and its real findings were very different to the picture presented by ministers of both this Conservative government and its Labour successor.

This committee's chair, Francis Graham-Harrison, had been involved in delineating the scope of Younger's enquiry; he had also been one of those who had defended government data by arguing that as there was not an acceptable definition of privacy, Younger needed to focus on a series of discreet phenomena and their separate solutions rather than make the case for a general right of privacy.[5] Under his lead, this new committee would insist that "nothing should be done to inhibit" the increasing flow of statistical data across Whitehall.[6] Moreover, he regarded increased data linkage as an inevitable feature of administration and at the committee's first meeting spoke of "data constellations": natural, informal clusters of data sets held by different ministries.[7] But Graham-Harrison not only accepted data linkage, he also actively promoted it. He had been a stalwart supporter of attempts by the chief statistical officer, Claus Moser, to reanimate *People and Numbers* after the Conservatives took power and so it was not surprising that, once invited to attend this meeting to discuss computers, Moser seized the opportunity to make his case yet again. He reminded his ally Graham-Harrison of the suspension of the feasibility study and pointed out that since the coming meeting could not consider the use of computers by government if it did not know the facts, that this was an ideal opportunity to resurrect that study. He added that he felt strongly "that it would be inadvisable and very nearly impossible to formulate a code for government computers in the absence of a firm policy about future development of such matters as record linkage."[8]

Though Moser did not get his feasibility study, it was abundantly clear that he was among kindred spirits at this committee. At the meeting, representatives of his Central Statistical Office received strong support from the Department for Education and Science's officials who stated that any code of conduct for government computers would, of necessity, be based on current practices and technology and so could seriously inhibit future developments. Moreover, far from examining how to control the increasing stockpiles of data in government computers, the view was expressed that "in the interests of progressive administration there should be more exchange of information than at present took place."[9] Thus, though the government presented this enquiry as one that was examining how to monitor or even check the spread of computerisation, what Graham-Harrison was actually doing was orchestrating the defence of government data gathering, this will be seen here by examining two broad aspects of the committee's work.

The first of these concerned Graham-Harrison's general approach to the likely conclusions of the Younger Committee. Graham-Harrison's committee was aware that any possible findings that Younger might reach about computerised systems would apply only to the private sector, but knew also that Wilson had committed government to taking account of Younger's recommendations and so was very interested in what those recommendations might be. It was thought that Younger might recommend the adoption of a code of conduct to govern the use of computers for storing data. Such a framework could be the best outcome for ministers, since they could accept it, and thus show that they were subjecting their machines to the same rules as those in the private sector, while avoiding the need for any external oversight of what they were actually doing. However, what caused alarm on the Graham-Harrison Committee was the notion that Younger might recommend the creation of a non-governmental body, a standing commission, to draw up a code of conduct, or even to operate one. Yet worse still, from the government's point of view, would be the scenario where Younger recommended that the role and duties of such a body be framed in legislation.

The depth of this concern was made plain in November 1971 by when it seemed likely that Younger was going to recommend the establishment of a standing commission to investigate whether certain basic principles were being observed by computerised processes in those private sector areas that fell within its remit. When this became clear, Graham-Harrison was concerned about the impact that even this, without the force of legislation, would have on government's computers and wrote to the Exchequer and Audit Department that this would be "unacceptable."[10] Subsequent discussions of this proposal in the committee threw up two different approaches, which although following different vectors, both clearly began from the same point: a need to defend government data from real oversight. On the one hand, the committee thought that it might not be necessary to accept that anybody established by Younger should be able to oversee government too.

Ministers, it was argued, had already publically stated that operations in the private sector were qualitatively different to those of the government, and so they could justifiably claim that a one-size-fits-all policy would be inappropriate.[11] In fact, the committee concluded that across government computers performed tasks that were so different from each other, that even government machines could not realistically be subjected to the same oversight regime.[12] But, on the other hand, it was suggested that any such a body might not be such a bad idea. It would only be able to investigate complaints made by the public, and since the public did not know very much at all about government computers there would be little for them to complain about. Any oversight body would therefore be able to oversee only what the government was prepared to let it oversee and would "in practice, be useless"; nevertheless, it would have one great advantage: it would be "presentationally desirable."[13] However, in the end, the committee came to see that this would have left the government too exposed and their draft report ruled it out by stating categorically that it was "highly undesirable for the government to subject any part of its administration to … regular oversight."[14] Their final report made the same point even more forcefully stating: "it would be virtually unprecedented for the Government to subject a part of its administration to the oversight of a body such as the standing commission proposed by the Younger Committee."[15] Were such a body to be proposed, Graham-Harrison recommended that the government reply by, first, using the argument of ministerial accountability and, second, by pointing out that the public could already complain about government computers by using the parliamentary commissioner for administration who they could access through their MP.

The second general aspect of Graham-Harrison's work concerned this presentational aspect of policy, in other words how those gathered here viewed the public. This was seen as "crucial": "ministers … should get clear advice about the quality of the alleged problem, the way it could be handled by the government, and the information that could be made public so that people would understand the issues involved."[16] There was some discussion of whether it was advisable, to inform the public of, for example, data transfers between departments with the argument being made that this publicity, although issued in the name of protecting privacy, would actually endanger privacy because telling the public that data had been transferred between departments would reveal the data's existence and so reduce its security.[17]

But more usually the committee recognised that the people were in need of reassurance and were prepared to provide it, subject to the proviso that nothing they suggested unduly interfered with the processes of government.[18] These processes, it was generally accepted, were moving all government departments "towards a greater interchange of statistical information" and rather than watch people obdurately stand, Luddite-like, in the way of progress the committee's members thought that they had a duty to "condition" the public to accept the inevitable.[19] One solution brought forward was to fall back on the doctrine of ministerial accountability, which it was maintained, would offer two advantages. First, it "should reassure the public" because they could be told that all data transfers would be cleared by ministers, but, second, it could actually significantly expedite such transfers, since ministers could simply sign a blank cheque allowing officials to transfer anything unless there were "exceptional circumstances."[20] However, this did not solve the problem that had dogged all their predecessors: how to sweeten the deal so that the British public would accept data linkage and an increased efficiency of government administration and not demand that anything Younger suggested for the private sector be rigorously applied to government as well.

During wartime and in the post-war period, the registrars, Sylvanus Vivian and George North, had tried to condition the public to accept registration by emphasising how the National Register allowed the necessary sacrifices of the war to be shared equally across society. But, while they stressed the necessity of an efficient system to guarantee that people could not avoid giving what they should to the country, Graham-Harrison thought that "it would be presentationally helpful" to pick up another aspect of North's post-war advocacy of common numbering (see Chapter 3) to emphasise how an increase in data linkage across departments would help prevent some people taking too much, in his words, to prevent them "abusing the social services."[21] This in its turn could be presented as the corollary of the government's determination to provide help to those who merited it. Abuse of the social security system would be the subject of a separate government report in 1973 (the Fisher Report) but this thinking found its way into the final report of the Graham-Harrison Committee. Here, it was suggested that the government might want to publish white papers on the subject of computerised data (these will be examined in the next chapter) and that these could mention how computerisation could "ensure the distribution of obligations and benefits."[22] This is worth mentioning here for two reasons. First, because it was the first time that such discussions in the 1970s attempted to justify increasingly linked government data holdings on the basis that they could solve the problem of abuse of the social security system. Second, because it was further suggested that when announced by the prime minister, this could be introduced as a measure designed to promote administrative efficiency and that such an announcement could include under this rubric a population register and common numbering of government files.[23]

This committee's thinking thus ranged quite widely across the whole issue of government data to encompass its gathering, storage and use. But the central focus of its work was the government's use of computers and Graham-Harrison had as clear a view of his role in this regard as he did when considering privacy legislation. The committee's job was to prevent discussion of the Younger Report "turning on" computers in the public sector and imposing "restrictive" systems.[24]

Government Computers

Discussions at the committee's first meeting raised the "philosophical" question of what computers actually were: whether they represented "a change of kind rather than degree."[25] On one side of the debate, there were those writers with dystopian opinions, examined in the previous chapter, who paradoxically found themselves in the same corner on this point as the technophile Tony Benn. He had written in 1969 that: "the computer is more than a tool to enable existing policies and systems of working to be carried out more easily and more cheaply: it opens up possibilities of pursuing policies which could not otherwise be followed."[26] However, this view was rejected by the Department for Trade and Industry which having analysed the functions performed by automatic data processing found that the important differences between the new systems and the traditional paper-based methods were all ones only of degree.[27] Interesting though such a debate was, it did not occupy much of Graham-Harrison's time because this discussion could not alter the fact that the political reality was broadly the same whichever philosophical position was adopted. This was so because if computers represented something qualitatively new; then, it could be argued that they needed controlling, with the additional threat that there was no way of knowing whether any code of conduct, or oversight regime could be confined to computerised processes. However, if computers were not a new departure, then they might be seen as identical to traditional filing methods and these might attract the same unwanted attention albeit for a different reason. The committee's real tasks were, therefore, to keep attention away from the government's paper files while simultaneously ensuring that only minimal attention and oversight fell onto its computerised systems and so to defend the government's standardisation, centralisation and linking of data. This section demonstrates how the committee achieved this strategic aim and how in doing so it not only treated the facts exposed by its own investigations into computer security in the most cavalier manner imaginable, but also ignored what it knew about the networking of computers.

Reaching a conclusion that ring-fenced the government's paper-based files against any oversight of its computer systems would be a long process because, in order to do this, it was necessary to demonstrate that the two systems, the one using computers and the other based on paper, were so different that they should be subject to totally different regimes. To do this, the committee would need to define the technical differences between paper systems and computers. But right from their first meeting the members found it hard to decide whether or not computers presented their own set of unique problems.[28] This discussion exposed the crux of the dilemma faced by the committee and the government, because as far as they all understood the issue, the reality was that they were in pursuit of a Will-o'-the-wisp because such a fundamental difference between the two systems did not exist. Therefore, though they would have liked to do so, it would prove extremely difficult to frame the debate about computerisation in purely technical terms. Indeed, they spent a lot of their time concerned that they would not be able to keep the debate focused on computers and that it would, almost of necessity, expand to consider manual filing systems too.

Members of the committee, as has been seen, were strongly opposed to any legislative backing for a code of conduct for private sector computers, part of their reasoning being that if this were imposed, then it might also affect government computers, which of course they were determined to avoid. However, the much more serious issue was that they could not "see how such legislation could be confined to the use of computers instead of covering the whole field of government administration," something which it almost went without saying "would clearly be unacceptable," with one committee member describing it as "opening wide floodgates to the disadvantage of all personal information held by government."[29] Thus, at their first meeting it was noted that "it was largely agreed that the main problems … and the relevant principles of conduct were the same for manual and computerised systems" while eighteen months later, as they approached the drafting of their report, they discussed "once again … the unreality of separating computer systems from manual systems."[30] Indeed, the two forms of filing were so similar that it was once noted that this might even work to the government's advantage. Thus, the "obvious fact" was, that if computers fell under the sway of an oversight commission which insisted that data be deleted once the task for which it had been gathered was complete, "there was nothing to stop the transfer of information from a computer to a manual system" where it could be stored indefinitely.[31] Although this process was elsewhere described by officials as "subterfuge," it was added that this could even become recognised as best practice since, given the state of the technology at the time, data on computers deteriorated if it were not used regularly.[32]

However, more usually the committee found that the correspondence of paper to computerised records was extremely problematic and raised three major difficulties. First, the committee's draft report made much of the safety of computerised systems. But when the committee considered this draft it was pointed out that though it was vital "to indicate that computer safeguards were more intensive than those now applying to manual records," it was nonetheless necessary to find a way of doing so that did not imply that the safeguards that applied to manual systems were substandard.[33] In other words, they could not simply say that computers were safer than manual systems. Second, on the one hand, the committee acknowledged that there was concern about the transfer, or linkage, of data and that the public thought this was more likely to happen in computerised systems. But, on the other hand, the committee also wanted to point out that people could reap a tangible benefit from the government's computerisation, because this would allow linkage of data across departments which would lead to them being pestered less often to provide the same data to government. In order to solve this obvious predicament, Graham-Harrison suggested that the public should be told that such transfers between computers would only be made if they abided by the current rules governing the transfer or linking of data between paper filing systems. However, this brought the committee up against the third, and largest, problem that came from any comparison of computerised and paper-based data because, as will be seen, Graham-Harrison was well aware that these rules governing paper records were often vague within departments, inconsistent across departments and often subject to, at best, only lax enforcement.[34]

In order to defend manual files from any criticism directed at computers, the Graham-Harrison Committee needed to know about the standards that applied to such files across Whitehall. Thus, it was decided at a meeting in July 1971 to ask the Management Services Section of the Civil Service Department to investigate the type of personal information held in manual systems by various departments, along with the systems in place to protect the confidentiality of this data and the rules governing its transfer or disclosure. The report of this investigation was given to the Graham-Harrison Committee two months later.

This investigation examined the manual records of various departments and covered twelve tasks selected to span the breadth of the confidentiality spectrum. These ranged from the registration of births, marriages and deaths and the registration of driving instructors at one extreme to prisoners' records and details of cancer treatment at the other. The investigators were tasked to assess the rules and regulations that governed the disclosure of this information and to assess how this compared to information stored on computer. Disclosures were divided into three types: first, those that were routinely performed to aid the completion of a separate administrative task, for example information gathered in assessing family allowances was, as a matter of course, passed to those allotting welfare foods; second, ad hoc authorised disclosures to bodies or individuals outside the civil service; and third, unauthorised disclosures. These latter were outside the terms of reference of the investigation, but the report was able to indicate the likelihood of their occurring by reviewing the level of staff access and the general security arrangements surrounding the data.[35]

This investigation found that there were only three sets of records where the rules governing disclosure of information were bound by law. These were personal tax returns, the registration of births, marriages and deaths and medical records. Apart from these, all other departments "relied on what they considered to be well understood guidelines and precedents."[36] But when these were examined the investigators could not find one instance where the data subjects were even notified of, never mind consulted about, the transfer of their data. The investigators were part of the Whitehall machine and so accepted that these transfers were made in the interests of administrative efficiency and therefore, also for the greater good of the individuals concerned. But even so, they maintained that people should at least be told that this was happening especially when the information contained subjective judgements.[37] During the course of their enquiries, they were told several times that such transfers were legitimate because they had had been publicised in court decisions or written into statutes. The investigators, however, regarded this as nothing but falling back on legalistic formulations to cover up a glaring dereliction, concluding dryly that: "the reading of parliamentary Acts is not yet a common pastime."[38]

Moreover, the investigators did not find a single instance (bar one slight change to do with the storage of one aspect of the records of the unemployment benefit system) where these policies and practices had been changed by the introduction of computerisation, which meant that computerised data was treated in the same way as data in traditional paper systems. It was for sure the case that, because computer technology was still in its infancy in 1971, only the most easily codified data had been put onto the machines and that since this was simple factual material its disclosure would not pose a serious threat to the privacy of the data subject. However, the corollary of this was that the more subjective and sensitive material was still largely held on manual files "which indicates that manual records are potentially more dangerous than computer held records."[39] This matter was made worse by the investigation's findings concerning the security arrangements provided to protect against unauthorised disclosure. Here, they found that the records of births, marriages and deaths, which were perhaps the least sensitive material they looked at, were stored in underground rooms, while the records of the Prisons Department in the Home Office were, to all intents and purposes, open to anyone with access to the building. This forced them to conclude that: "at the risk of stating the obvious … lax internal security can make a nonsense of any disclosure policy."[40]

The report of this investigation must have been unwelcome news to Graham-Harrison. Certainly, it contradicted the publically stated view of the government that, in the words of Lord Hailsham, "government Departments have over the years … worked out effective procedures which ensure that information they hold about individuals is safeguarded against unauthorised or improper disclosure."[41] The Graham-Harrison Committee had shared this sanguine view, thus at its first meeting it had noted: "the Government's good record on confidentiality," how "strict" rules of confidentiality were applied to data across Whitehall and how these admirable safeguards "would not be altered by the adoption of computers."[42] Speaking in the House of Lords, Hailsham had said that the job in hand was to "make sure that equal or more effective safeguards are applied to information held on computers."[43] The investigation threatened to expose the fact that in reality these safeguards were ineffective and so increased the importance for Graham-Harrison of deflecting all attention away from paper-based records. To do this, the Graham-Harrison Report airbrushed the results of the investigation and invited its readers to continue to believe Hailsham's words writing that: "the rules bearing on the confidentiality of information in computer files were at least as stringent as those applying to comparable information in the department's manual files."[44] This form of words clearly led the reader to construe that this was a comparison of equals at the top of a scale of security even though the committee knew that in reality the opposite was the case.

The committee used a similar modus operandi when it came to consider computer operators. Graham-Harrison had begun work by suggesting that the remedy to security problems that might arise with computers "lay in the most careful selection of officials and severe penalties for those who betrayed their trust."[45] However, the committee came to realise that computer staff were not specially trained in security and neither were they subject to any special vetting procedures.[46] Nonetheless, the draft report stressed that computer personnel were all civil servants, subject to the same recruitment, training and security measures as all staff and that therefore they were as trustworthy as any other civil servant, particularly when it was remembered that they would also have signed the official secrets act.[47] Thus, through the sleight of hand of concealing the reality of what happened when ordinary civil service operations used paper records, Graham Harrison's report initially sought to draw, what at first sight would seem to be, a favourable comparison between the computerised and conventional records of the civil service, thus giving the government's computer usage a clean bill of health.

Nevertheless, this positive outcome could only be reached by making a direct comparison with paper records. Doing this might have got Graham-Harrison out of a bad tactical position but it did not resolve the fundamental strategic issue of the need to draw down a veil over the entirety of government manual files. To do this, Graham-Harrison made a political decision to sweep the revelations of the investigation back under the carpet by mobilising one of the tactics used by the government in the build-up to the creation of the Younger Committee. Thus, the draft report was altered to remove all comparisons between the paper files and the computerised data used by civil servants. More importantly, the final report was amended to deny that there was any popular clamour for manual record systems to be examined at all. In this, it not only ignored the results of the investigation, it also flew in the face of Younger's social survey and the government's own admissions, since this section of the committee's report began: "if public concern were with the privacy of personal records as such, it would be logical to consider the confidentiality of government records as a whole." It then continued that this was not the case, in fact "the whole emphasis, in relation to privacy has been on computer records and there has been no indication of lack of public confidence in the handling of manual records." Given this, the report stated that there was nothing to be gained from examining manual records and accordingly the rest of the report dealt only with computer records.[48]

The Younger Committee has not attracted much attention from historians but when it has, the common approach has been to show how the committee scrutinised computerisation and then to examine the results of its work. Thus, for example, Edward Higgs has shown how Younger responded to popular "apprehension" that was "especially strong because the potential of the new technology caught the imagination of the public." While Jon Agar has written how the Younger Report did not satisfy critics "who insisted on targeting the computerised data base as the principal threat."[49] Given that it clearly wanted to protect its computers from oversight, these outcomes might be seen as a defeat for the government. But what such a view cannot draw out is the manner in which public disapproval of the government's increased amassing of data was consciously channelled into the already mounting opposition to computerisation in order to protect the vast majority of the government's data that remained on paper. The fact that Younger had been allowed to look at computers, and that this position was exacerbated further by Wilson's remarks, meant that some commentary on government computerisation was inevitable regardless of the government's strong preference for keeping its technology behind closed doors. Forced into this position, the government developed a two-pronged strategy. It wanted to keep attention away from its paper-based records by limiting the debate to computers, and it wanted to ensure that any discussion of this computerisation was confined to technical matters and did not stray onto the political purpose of the data stored on computers. In other words, it wanted to keep the debate focused on the alternatives that threatened it least. The government had laid the outer ramparts of its defensive positions by its structuring of the Younger Committee and its successful political campaign to resist a definition of privacy. It added further buttresses by developing a strategy for how to present its data gathering to the public. What it needed to secure its position was a political method to make sure that the focus of the debate about data and privacy stayed firmly on computers. This was difficult because, as everyone at the committee's first meeting had conceded, it was "unreal" to discuss computer and manual systems as though they were totally different; nevertheless, Graham-Harrison was eventually able to provide this inner bulwark around the government's paper-based data stockpile.

Thus, though the Graham-Harrison Committee was trumpeted as an enquiry into computerisation, the reality was that it was responsible for organising the government's defence in the face of the Younger Committee and, having taken the government's paper records off the agenda, this committee aimed to de-politicise government data in general, and its computers in particular, by fixing debate on the technical aspects of computerisation. The report held that computerised data was protected by the facts that the technology was beyond most people's understanding and that the data was stored on tapes that were kept under lock and key away from the machine.[50] The public could also be reassured that rather than perpetuating data that was inaccurate or out-of-date, computer systems would actually protect them from these dangers. Computers regularly purged themselves of material that was no longer needed and would notice any inaccuracies in data, but in any case government departments had special systems in place to ensure that inputs were accurate.[51] Additionally, Graham-Harrison's report highlighted the four normal outcomes of large-scale computerisation all of which, it said, protected data stored by machine. First, computerisation reduced the number of people involved in handling data. Second, it also reduced the amount of attention these people gave to each piece of data. Third, these people could only access limited sections of the total data stock, and indeed, fourth, in many computerised operations no one had contact with the total record.[52]

During one of its meetings, the Graham-Harrison Committee had noted that critics of government computers overestimated both the extent to which the technology was used and its capabilities.[53] But here the committee veered to the opposite extreme because its portrayal of the safety of computers also presented them as stand-alone, unlinked machines and seemed to want readers to assume that they would stay this way. In fact, as was shown in the previous chapter, in 1970 Gerald Pratt, the Younger Committee's secretary, had written a paper for that committee in which he pointed out that "it is technically feasible to link" all computer systems.[54] Indeed, this possibility had been suggested to Tony Benn in May 1968,[55] and in January of that year, Claus Moser had sat on a committee that reported on the topic of allowing computers to be linked to share data (see Chapter 4). Moreover, three months before Pratt made his assertion, officials had met to discuss Ministry of Defence proposals to establish, by 1977, a defence computer network called Grid77.[56] Interestingly, while the Graham-Harrison Committee was meeting, a US report proposed the creation of "wired cities" and a "wired nation" but these ideas were rejected by the administration with the government's spokesman suggesting that the plans had "big brother implications."[57] There were also, as was shown in Chapter 6, many dystopian projections of the power of linked computer databases, but more importantly Graham-Harrison himself was well aware of these possibilities. He was in the chair of the committee considering Lord Windlesham's motion in November 1969 where discussion of computerisation had noted that: "more important than the sheer mass of information which could be kept available was the possibility of inter-linkage between different systems. … the time could be foreseen when all the information recorded about an individual in all his dealings could be made available through one computer network."[58] But, in order to portray computers as safe systems, all these insights were pushed to one side when the Graham-Harrison Report was written. In addition, this process also omitted the evidence of the British Computer Society to Younger (see Chapter 6) where it had warned of threats to computer data holdings "such as … wire-tapping and the electromagnetic reading of messages," things that were elsewhere described as "the electronic burglar."[59]

As a result of the work of the Graham-Harrison Committee, the government completed the arguments it would use in defence of its data. The political decisions reached by Graham-Harrison's arduous trails of reasoning meant that the government had finally worked out a method to keep the attention of privacy campaigners away from its paper-based records and onto the unwelcome, but less dangerous, topic of computerisation. This had allowed it to marshal its arguments and to encourage apprehensions to centre on the new technology where the public could be comforted by a list of technical reasons why computers were safe. Additionally, it had produced a new tangible benefit to offer the public in the form of a reduction in social security fraud. The Graham-Harrison Report was ready in the spring of 1972, and the Younger Report came out a few months later, in July.

The Younger Report

This section surveys both the most important conclusions of the Younger Report and the government's response to it showing how, for all Graham-Harrison's twisting and toiling, the issue of the similarity between the government's paper-based and computerised records could not be hidden under the carpet.

Because the Younger Committee was rooted in a fundamental denial of a need for a general right of privacy its work covered a patchwork of often banal issues and its report focused on providing specific remedies to selected problems that were presented as the most urgent needs.[60] In order to justify this, the Younger Report was very selective in its interpretation of the conclusions of its own social survey. As was seen in the previous chapter, this survey noted how many of the people interviewed complained about rather petty breaches of their privacy, and from this, it drew conclusions at two different levels. First, it noted that these were given in reply to the type of questions they had been asked and that people's attitudes to privacy deserved to be given more respect than these replies might seem to merit, because "if we had probed for concern at the actions of official bodies, there is no doubt that more concern would have been found."[61] However second, it then went on to conclude, in line with Younger's brief, that there was no clear enemy of privacy in the public mind and that, therefore, there was no need for a general right of privacy. It was this latter view that the Younger Committee chose to foreground in its report. In doing so, the report presented the statistics drawn from the survey (see the previous chapter) but made no mention of the survey's first set of conclusions. Moreover, in order to ensure that it was this view that of the Younger Report that caught the attention of the media, the Home Office press release that accompanied publication of the report used a quotation from the survey so selectively that it gave the impression that the broader conclusions of the survey (that people were "most often concerned [about] the collection of information by official government departments") did not exist at all and stated that: "the researchers concluded that many of the incidents which were mentioned could often have been interpreted as the petty annoyances of day-to-day life."[62]

The use of computers stood out from the wide range of activities reviewed by Younger both because the technology had aroused public concern, and because this was the aspect of the committee's work that threatened to encroach on government. However, on this important subject the committee drew, what Burke Trend would have described as, the "right conclusions." Crucially, in its chapter on computers, the report made only one passing reference to paper-based filing systems and this was a recognition that people who were really determined to do so could exploit any system and as such even this mention was designed to reassure people that all that could be done to protect computerised data would be done.[63] In pinning the debate down to computers, the report concurred with Graham-Harrison's view (see Chapter 6) and concluded that "the computer problem as it affects privacy in Great Britain is one of apprehensions and fears and not so far one of facts and figures."[64] Moreover, it insisted that it was of paramount importance to weigh "the scanty evidence of their serious abuse" against "the immense gains to human welfare which computers can bring," and that "once the problem is dispassionately analysed, adequate safeguards can almost certainly be devised and applied."[65] Thus, the report resolved the issue by turning it into a discussion of the "technical means … to provide a very high degree of security over the handling of information by computers."[66]

Younger set out the basic principles that should underpin the operation of any computerised database. These were: that data should be used only for the purpose for which it had been obtained and any linking of datasets should be authorised. Only authorised people should be able to access the data, and the data subject should be aware that this data was stored. Only the required minimum of data should be stored, this should be kept for only as long as it was needed for the original task, it should be accurate and, if it was kept only for statistical purposes, it should be anonymous. The security arrangements for the computer should be specified in advance, there should be a monitoring system to prevent unauthorised activity on the system and care should be taken in putting subjective judgements into a computerised system.[67]

Younger rejected all the calls to enshrine these principles in law and instead recommended they should form the basis of a voluntary code of conduct. However, it recognised that computer technology was advancing rapidly and so also recommended that the government should set up a body, which it labelled a "standing commission," capable of responding to these changes. This should collect information about the use of computers and review the relevance of the principles governing computer use in the light of technological developments. It should receive complaints about invasions of privacy driven by computer use and, based on all this, it should make recommendations to government about any required changes in the law. In accordance with the committee's general terms of reference and government statements on the matter, the Younger Report concluded by recommending that: "the Government should consider including both the public and private sectors within the purview of the proposed commission."[68]

The Graham-Harrison Committee had prepared the ground for the government's response to the Younger Report, and by October 1972, the Home Office had started to convene meetings with other departments to finalise the government's proposals for publication in a white paper. These meetings picked up the thread of Graham-Harrison's work and were initially even more hostile to Younger's conclusions. Their early meetings were adamant that not only was there no need for the government to introduce legislation, but also that there was no need for Younger's proposed standing commission. These meetings decided that, were it created, this body would be a permanent thorn in the side of government, constantly seeking to justify its own existence by keeping the issue of privacy in the public eye and promoting the idea of legislation. However, it was recognised that something needed to be done to allay public fears, so meetings proposed that the government's National Computing Centre could draw up a voluntary code of conduct. If this policy were followed, it was accepted that the government would have to play its cards very carefully. This was because, though on the one hand, it would be useful for the government to have an input into this code of conduct at the drafting stage in case it later became necessary to adopt this for its own machines, on the other hand, it was possible that government involvement in this drafting could be seen as an invitation by privacy campaigners to demand that this code of conduct also be applied to government machines.[69]

The Younger Committee had not been set up to conduct a wide-ranging inquiry into privacy as such; in fact, it had been set up to deflect attention away from demands for a right of privacy, and the departments at these meetings after the Younger Report's publication all recognised "that there are good reasons why the Government is unlikely" to accede to demands for such a right. But the participants in these discussions went beyond this position and recognised that their conclusions "represent a considerable watering down of the Younger proposals." Indeed, it was expressly noted that because government was not going to need to introduce legislation, it might as well "have the practical advantage of not lumbering itself with another mini-Younger (the standing commission), whose raison d'être it is to keep privacy issues in the public eye."[70] Instead, these meetings proposed that government announce piecemeal changes to the most high-profile examples of organisations where abuse was thought to occur, such as credit referencing agencies and universities.

However, these were not the views of those who would be subject to any computer oversight regime. Having adopted the most aggressive posture against Younger, the Department of Trade and Industry (DTI) surveyed fifty-five computer users in industry and found that forty-two of them were actually in favour (with seven saying "no," and four "don't know") of a voluntary standing commission to carry out the tasks delineated by Younger. This caused "reflection" at the DTI and subsequently led to a reversal of the hostile policy that had emerged from the earlier meetings, with the grudging acceptance that "some body with some at least of the functions of the standing commission if only for presentational reasons" should be incorporated into the white paper.[71] This, it was planned, would now contain a brief account of the type of personal information held on government computers, the safeguards in place to protect this data, a general description of how this information aided government and "an outline of the considerable advantages derived from this both materially and in enhancing the quality of life," along with indications of how government proposed to act on Younger's proposals "as they concern the public."[72]

In all of this, it is clear that these meetings followed the path mapped out by Graham-Harrison and that this work was designed to protect government computers from oversight, only accepting Younger's minimum position when obliged to. Graham-Harrison had experienced a lot of difficulty in devising a method to focus attention away from paper records and onto computers, and the inherent artificiality of this distinction is further highlighted by discussions in these meetings to formulate the white paper. These meetings began by adopting a very hard line towards Younger, but paradoxically they also threatened to expose the fundamental fault line that ran beneath all Graham-Harrison's conclusions, with the Home Office pursuing what the Treasury would describe as "a somewhat independent line."[73] This was discernable at the outset with the Home Office noting, that though computers were probably the most sensitive and high-profile component of the privacy issue, and also the only practical thing for the government to turn its attention towards, it was still the case that they were only part of the problem. Thus, "the real question" was "whether information stores or data banks of any kind are a threat to privacy."[74] However, any discussion of this point of principle was abandoned as these meetings turned to consider the practicalities and a series of technical issues. Ministers and officials met and, with a view to publishing a white paper in the autumn, approved the proposals from these meetings at the Home and Social Affairs Committee late in May 1973. The prime minister, Edward Heath, was not able to comment on this discussion until after this meeting but, when he did, his words threatened to drag the discussion about whether computers really were different to paper records back out from under the carpet where Graham-Harrison had swept it and where many others wanted it to stay. Heath stated that "if the government were to publish a White Paper confined to the computer aspect of privacy they would be accused of bad faith."[75] In addition to this, he also seemed to reject the notion of introducing only piecemeal reforms. He did not go so far as to advocate a right of privacy, but he did state that the government needed "a central and co-ordinated policy" and thus that it "would be wrong for Departments with an interest in the specific recommendations of the report of the Younger Committee to consider them individually."[76]

Many officials were hostile to the Younger Report from its publication and regarded even the minimum oversight regime it recommended as something that the government should avoid being "lumbered" with. Therefore, they must have regarded Heath's remarks as a major setback since these seemed to reject the basis of all their discussions since Graham-Harrison had shown the way. They responded to the prime minister by pointing out that the Home Office was coordinating the work of all departments in response to Younger and was also responsible for drafting the white paper.[77] This did not actually address Heath's criticism of a piecemeal approach to the issue of breaches of privacy, but it did sidestep his point effectively. When it came to addressing the prime minister's point about limiting discussion to computerised records, they attempted to focus him on the job in hand, which was responding to the Younger Report. Paper records had not been discussed by Younger, and the committee's report had not made any recommendations that concerned paper-based systems. Therefore, they could assure Heath that the planned white paper would do all that it was required to do. However, this relationship between computerised and paper files was the fundamental weakness in the government's defences against Younger. Thus, it is hardly surprising that the issue resurfaced. Indeed, it did so again in September 1973 when Kenneth Baker, parliamentary secretary in the Civil Service Department, wrote that "we are at present concentrating, naturally on the computer. It would be prudent to recognise, however, that the distinction between personal information held on computer files and that in manual files is a somewhat artificial one."[78]

These arguments from Baker and Heath (along with the "somewhat independent" views of the Home Office) were important, but they need to be put into context. Neither Baker nor Heath was opposed to the collection, storage and use of data by the government. They were not, like Enoch Powell and Shirley Williams, opposed to either increasing the government's stockpile of data, or to its standardisation, centralisation or linkage, and unlike Jeremy Thorpe, they were not hostile to computerisation. In fact, the Conservative government had welcomed Moser's plans for the revival of *People and Numbers* and it was under this government that all the preparations for the Younger Report had been made. These Conservative politicians were not defenders of the people's privacy. Rather, it is perhaps the case that they were picking up on an obviously contentious point in the debate because they had not been at either the meetings of the Graham-Harrison Committee, or the meetings where the draft white paper was discussed. In fact, rather than highlighting a point of rupture with the Labour government, what happened to the issue raised by Heath and Baker (and the nascent independence at the Home Office) can be seen as clear evidence of the continuity of a drive to gather data, particularly where the civil servants involved in the policy were concerned. The stark comparison is thus not between officials and ministers under these two governments, but between those in the post-war period who had abandoned national registration, and these ministers and officials in the 1960s and 1970s who wanted to re-instate it.

This can be seen in two developments. First, as will be examined in the next chapter, in the way the Home Office would close ranks with the rest of officialdom against any meaningful independence of thought even when it came from one of its own junior ministers in the Labour government elected in 1974. Second, this is noticeable in the way the white paper was re-drafted to respond to Heath's points. By January 1974, the wording of this new version was becoming clear. The new draft stated that the final version of the paper would now include Heath and Baker's point, but did so only by paying lip service to it in the most shrewdly non-committal phrasing. Thus, it was stated that the paper was still going to focus on computers in the first instance; however, when it was eventually finalised it would recognise that "any 'rules' which are elaborated may be of more general application" and that the intention now was "to consider at a later stage whether they should be extended to other kinds of information stores."[79] The comparatively rapid introduction of this prevarication and circumspection marked so thorough a diminution of Heath's views that this was virtually a return to the status quo ante of Graham-Harrison's position. This clearly demonstrates the strength of the attachment to data across government and the determination to defend it. However, it would not be Heath's Conservatives that would carry any of this through, for on 4 March 1974 the Labour Party took office. Under this government, the Home Office would acquire a junior minister who would try to perpetuate its "somewhat independent line," but ultimately it would be the government's data, not the people's privacy that would be defended.

Notes

1. TNA, PREM 13/3102, Trend to Prime Minister, *Privacy*, 17 November 1969, 2.
2. TNA, HO 411/1, from Graham-Harrison, 20 February 1970, 1.
3. TNA, HO 411/1, *Code of Conduct for Government Computer Systems, Meeting 4 March 1970*, 2.
4. TNA, HO 411/18, *Government Computers and Privacy, Draft Report to Ministers (2), New Paragraph 6 for Inclusion in Annex 1*, n.d., ca. January 1972, 1.
5. TNA, HO 264/57, Graham-Harrison to Younger, 8 May 1970, 1.
6. TNA, HO 411/17, *Government Computers and Privacy, Meeting 9 November 1971*, 1.

7. *Code of Conduct for Government Computer Systems, Meeting 4 March 1970*, 2.
8. TNA, HO 411/1, Moser to Graham-Harrison, 24 February 1970, 1.
9. *Code of Conduct for Government Computer Systems, Meeting 4 March 1970*, 3.
10. TNA, HO 411/17, Graham-Harrison to Pitblado, 11 November 1971, 2.
11. TNA, HO 411/17, *Government Computers and Privacy, Meeting 3 November 1971*, 5.
12. TNA, HO 411/18, *Government Computers and Privacy, Draft Report to Ministers (2), iv Safeguarding Computerised Information*, n.d., ca. January 1972, 1.
13. *Government Computers and Privacy, Meeting 3 November 1971*, 3.
14. TNA, HO 411/18, *Government Computers and Privacy, Draft Report to Ministers (2), vi Recommendations of the Younger Committee on Privacy*, n.d., ca. January 1972, 2.
15. TNA, HO 337/264, *Government Computers and Privacy*, n.d., ca. March/April 1972, 19.
16. *Government Computers and Privacy, Meeting 3 November 1971*, 5.
17. Ibid., 3.
18. TNA, HO 411/17, Home Office, *Control of Government Computers*, n.d., ca. early 1972, 5.
19. *Government Computers and Privacy, Meeting 3 November 1971*, 2.
20. *Government Computers and Privacy, Meeting 9 November 1971*, 2.
21. Ibid.
22. TNA, HO 337/264, E4 Division Home Office, *Revised Draft Report to Ministers, Government Computers and Privacy*, n.d., ca. March/April 1972, 15.
23. *Government Computers and Privacy, Meeting 9 November 1971*, 3.
24. Ibid.
25. TNA, HO 411/2, Home Office, *Discussion Paper, Code of Conduct for Safeguarding Personal Information on Central Government Computers*, n.d., ca. June 1971, 16.
26. When he was first elected and held government office, Benn was known as Anthony Wedgewood Benn. For the sake of simplicity, he is referred to as Tony Benn throughout the text of this book, but where necessary in endnotes, his name is given in the form of the publication. TNA, HN 1/60, Minister of Technology, *Data Processing and Government*, 4 March 1969, 1.
27. TNA, HO 411/71, Department of Trade and Industry, *Effects of Computers on Privacy*, n.d., ca. April 1973, 1.
28. *Code of Conduct for Government Computer Systems, Meeting 4 March 1970*, 2.
29. TNA, HO 411/17, *Government Computers and Privacy, Meeting 3 November 1971*, 2; TNA, HO 411/2, Spain to Graham-Harrison, 11 June 1971, 1.

30. *Code of Conduct for Government Computer Systems, Meeting 4 March 1970*, 2; TNA, CAB 164/829, Meeting, 19 October 1971, 1.
31. TNA, CAB 164/829, *Government Computers and Privacy, Meeting 19 October 1971*, 2.
32. TNA, CAB 139/779, Kevin to Carr, 22 August 1973, 2.
33. TNA, HO 264/260, *Government Computers and Privacy, Meeting 10 February 1972*, 3.
34. TNA, HO 411/17, *Government Computers and Privacy, Meeting 27 September 1971*, 5.
35. TNA, HO 411/17, *Government Computers and Privacy, A Report by C.S.D. on Some Manual Systems of Personal Information*, September 1971, 1.1–1.7.
36. Ibid., 14.3.
37. Ibid., 14.7.
38. Ibid., 14.8.
39. Ibid., 14.2.
40. Ibid., 14.9.
41. *Government Computers and Privacy, Draft Report to Ministers (2), New Paragraph 6 for Inclusion in Annex 1*, 1.
42. *Government Computers and Privacy, Meeting 4 March 1970*, 3.
43. Quoted in, *Government Computers and Privacy, Draft Report to Ministers (2), New Paragraph 6 for Inclusion in Annex 1*, 1.
44. E4 Division Home Office, *Revised Draft Report to Ministers*, 5.
45. *Government Computers and Privacy, Meeting 4 March 1970*, 3.
46. TNA, HO 411/17, *Government Computers and Privacy, Meeting 12 October 1971*, 4.
47. TNA, HO 411/18, E4 Division Home Office, *Revised Draft Report to Ministers, Government Computers and Privacy, iv Safeguarding Computerised Information*, n.d., ca. March/April 1972, 1.
48. E4 Division Home Office, *Revised Draft Report to Ministers*, 13.
49. Edward Higgs, *The Information State in England: The Central Collection of Information on Citizens Since 1500* (Basingstoke: Palgrave Macmillan, 2004), 170; Jon Agar, *The Government Machine: A Revolutionary History of the Computer* (London: Massachusetts Institute of Technology Press, 2003), 361.
50. E4 Division Home Office, *Revised Draft Report to Ministers*, 10.
51. Ibid., 12.
52. Ibid., 7–8.
53. *Government Computers and Privacy, Meeting 27 September 1971*, 5.
54. TNA, HO 264/62, *Note by the Secretary, Computers and Privacy*, 2 October 1970, 2.

55. TNA, FV 49/2, S. Gill, *Computer Technology, Government Actions Required*, 20 May 1968, 1.
56. TNA, CAB 134/2636, *Meeting of Officials on Computers in Central Government, 2 July 1970*, 9.
57. J. Mack Adams and Douglas H. Haden, *Social Effects of Computer Use and Misuse* (London: Wiley, 1976), 129.
58. TNA, HO 411/1, *Lord Windlesham's Motion, Meeting 21 November 1969*, 2.
59. TNA, HO 264/121, The British Computer Society, *Submission to the Younger Committee*, March 1971, 10; A. A. Thompson, *Big Brother in Britain Today* (London: Michael Joseph, 1970), 57.
60. TNA, HO 264/14, Home Office Press Release, *Technology's Threat to Privacy, Report of the Younger Committee*, 12 July 1972, 2.
61. TNA, RG 25/501, Research Bureau Limited, *Report on Survey of Public Attitudes to Privacy*, September 1971, 29.
62. *Report of the Committee on Privacy*, Cmnd. 5012 (July 1972), 31–32; TNA, RG 25/501, Research Bureau Limited, *Report on Survey of Public Attitudes to Privacy*, September 1971, 29; Home Office Press Release, *Technology's Threat to Privacy*, 2.
63. *Report of the Committee on Privacy*, 182.
64. Ibid., 179.
65. Ibid., 180.
66. Ibid., 181.
67. Ibid., 183–184.
68. Home Office Press Release, *Technology's Threat to Privacy*, 3.
69. TNA, HO 411/70, Littler to Witney, *White Paper on Computers and Privacy*, 6 November 1971, 4–6.
70. Ibid., 7.
71. Ibid., 8.
72. Ibid., 1.
73. TNA, T 353/141, Copeman to Howard, 23 May 1973, 3.
74. Littler to Witney, *White Paper on Computers and Privacy*, 2.
75. TNA, T 353/141, Copeman to S. G. Norris, 30 May 1973, 1.
76. Ibid.
77. TNA, T 353/141, Butcher to C. W. Roberts, 12 June 1973, 1.
78. TNA, CAB 139/779, Baker to Carr, 7 September 1973, 2–3.
79. TNA, CAB 139/779, Taylor to Benner, 3 January 1974, 7.

CHAPTER 8

The White Papers

The Younger Committee was set up under Labour in 1970 and reported under the Conservatives in 1972, but it fell to the Labour government elected in 1974 to do something about the committee's findings, and to this end, it drafted two white papers on computers. The proponents of these papers sought stronger safeguards for people's privacy, and the first section of this chapter analyses their thinking to show how this came up against arguments that had been formed by the Graham-Harrison Committee. These were now propounded by a united officialdom that was four square behind the government's defence of its data and were determined that though they might be obliged to allow some oversight of government computers, the government's paper-based files should be protected against any such monitoring regime.

The second section interrogates the contents of the two white papers, published in December 1975 after these confrontations, and details how they were a very considerably watered down version of the initial proposals. This analysis of these papers details the degree of dissimulation, obfuscation and indeed the fundamental dishonesty of much of their contents and how this positioning had its roots in the work of the Graham-Harrison Committee.

In May 1976, the government set up a new committee, under Norman Lindop, to pave the way for a Data Protection Authority. The third section of this chapter shows how by the time Lindop's report was published; in December 1978, it was irrelevant due to the accession of Jim Callaghan as prime minister and Merlyn Rees as home

K. Manton, *Population Registers and Privacy in Britain, 1936–1984*,
https://doi.org/10.1007/978-3-030-02753-7_8

secretary. Their ideas are examined here but, more importantly, this section explains how Lindop accepted at face value the assurances his committee received that Whitehall did not have any plans in the pipeline to create a common numbering system. As a result, its report contained recommendations that would be problematic for the subsequent government of Margaret Thatcher's Conservatives.

The Government's Proposals

There were two general elections in 1974. The Labour Party manifesto for the second of these, in October, was called *Britain Will Win with Labour* and contained a pledge to "protect the citizen from unwarranted and mischievous intrusion into the citizen's private affairs."[1] Though this was only a headline pledge that did not give any detail of how its aim might be achieved, it indicated that a Labour government intended to make a response of some kind to Younger. The process that led to this commitment began after Labour took office following the March 1974 election, when Wilson appointed Alex Lyon (a dissenting voice on the Younger Committee and a long-time privacy campaigner) to a junior position in the Home Office. From here, Lyon invited the human rights lawyer and law reform campaigner Paul Sieghart to assist with drafting the government's two white papers: *Computers and Privacy*, and *Computers: Safeguards for Privacy*.[2] This section will outline the proposals made by Sieghart and Lyon and then go on to look at the aggressive defence of the government's data that was mounted in response.

The white papers were published in December 1975, and the following year Sieghart wrote a book, *Privacy and Computers* outlining his ideas. Sieghart broadly agreed with the pamphlet *Computers and Freedom*, written in 1968 by the Society of Conservative Lawyers, which had been adamant that it was necessary to construct a regime to protect people's privacy from the threat posed by electronic data. Unlike others, such as Tony Benn, he argued that computers were a continuation, not a break with the past.[3] Bankers had always had their ledgers, hotels their guest books and doctors their case notes, so computers had not invented the storage of personal data, rather what they offered was a vast increase in the speed with which this data could be manipulated. Moreover, Sieghart was well aware of the potential for computers to be linked together. To illustrate the possible shape of such developments, he presented the case of the shopper who wrote a list on a piece of paper and paid by cash, arguing that, after a few days, neither the shopper nor the shopkeeper would be able to remember what had been bought or how much it had cost. He contrasted this with systems that were being introduced in the USA where the shopper paid by "plastic money." With a few refinements, he added, the company's computer could retain and collate information on who bought what at each of its stores, "indeed, it may pay our supermarket company to collect and record all this additional information because, with it, it can keep lower stocks, choose lines which sell well and make more accurate plans for the future."[4] With further prescience, he imagined connected webs of computers allowing people to, for example, book hotels and flights and permitting the post office to analyse the phone calls of every user.[5]

Though Sieghart was at pains to point out that none of these developments were "necessarily an infringement of anyone's privacy," this did not mean that computerised data was safe.[6] In fact, most of Sieghart's work on the subject was designed to draw attention to the threats to privacy that could arise were computerisation allowed to proceed uncontrolled. As well as highlighting the threats from unauthorised access to computerised files, Sieghart repeated the more fundamental problems, previously listed by *Computers and Freedom*, which flowed simply from the fact that files were computerised. Thus, he pointed out how data stored on tape needed to be relevant, accurate and complete. Irrelevant data was exemplified in Sieghart's book by out-of-date criminal convictions that remained in computer databases, while one of the dangers of inaccurate data was that it could lead to the results of confidential medical tests being sent to the wrong address. Writing about the problem of incomplete data, he argued that it could lead to erroneous inferences being drawn to the detriment of the data subject giving the same example as *Computers and Freedom*: that of someone who was given a bad credit score because a bill had not be paid, even though the reason for this non-payment was that the bill had been wrong. Sieghart's point was that because computers could store data indefinitely, such problems as these would inevitably arise were plans not drawn up, while the technology was still in its infancy, to prevent them. Moreover, since computers were expensive, there was a financial incentive for owners to use them to the maximum, which would mean that more data would be stored. This, of course, would have the knock-on effect of making the computer a more attractive target for data thieves.[7]

Important though these points were, they were not the main thrust of his thinking. This centred on data linkage and this focus ensured that his proposals would be criticised within government circles. Sieghart cited the constitutional norm that people gave data to the state to be used only for the purpose for which it had been sought. This was the basis on which data was provided, so people were entitled to think that they would be told were two sets of information, provided separately to the state, to be subsequently merged. Sieghart argued that just because data subjects might, for example, willingly tell a political canvasser their voting intentions and also tell a consumer survey their preferences in washing powder, it did not follow at all that they would be happy for the detergent manufacturer to know their political opinions.[8] Still less did it follow that people would want their medical, criminal or tax records linked to other databases such as the electoral register.

From all of his reasoning, Sieghart concluded that, any progress made towards protecting the privacy of people's computerised data needed to begin by first defining "a comprehensive set of 'principles' which reflect the entitlement of the data subject to assurances about the privacy of his data … and which can be implemented by appropriate safeguards."[9] In saying this he concurred, to an important extent at least, with the views of the British Computer Society and the writers Malcolm Warner and Michael Stone (see Chapter 6) who had all insisted that the main task in protecting the privacy of computerised information was to lay down first principles, since without these, there would be little but a series of unconnected ad hoc measures drawn up in response to specific breaches. Sieghart's thinking informed the draft white papers where these principles were called "ends" and were designated as separate to the means of achieving them. These ends would be immutable, whereas the means would necessarily change in response to technological developments, and could also be expected to vary between contemporaneous systems performing different functions.

The government's longer-term proposal was to set up an agency, to be called the Data Protection Authority (DPA), to oversee the use of computers and to act to protect the interests of all parties particularly the public.[10] In the interim, while the legislation to establish the DPA was making its way through Parliament, the government proposed to set up a non-statutory body to prepare the way for the DPA, which it called the Data Protection Committee (DPC). The DPC would be guided in all its work by the ends drawn up by Sieghart, so his ideas would be put into practice straight away. As originally drafted there were six of these ends. First, the public should know of the existence, purpose and scope of computer systems and who had access to them. Second, people should be told what would happen to information they gave to be held on computer, how long it would be kept, who would have access to it and if, and for what purposes, it might be transferred, and that these transfers, or linkages, should only occur if authorised by law, or with the consent of the data subject. Third, data should be held only if it were relevant, accurate and up to date. Fourth, there should be adequate safeguards against unauthorised access. Fifth, the public should be able to discover what information was held about them, why it was held and if and to whom it had been transferred. They should also be able to correct, amplify or delete data that was incomplete or misleading, and finally, the last of these ends stipulated that all data transferred for statistical purposes should be anonymous.[11] An early draft of one of the white papers stated that: "there is no disagreement about the ends to be pursued."[12] However, this judgement would prove to be extremely optimistic as these proposals galvanised resistance against the serious limitations they would impose on the state's ability to standardise, centralise and link data.

Following on from the work of the Graham-Harrison Committee, it was resolved in government that any oversight should be applied only to computerised data, not to paper-based, manual systems. But the first thing to note about the response of officials to the Sieghart-Lyon proposals was that this did not mean that they wanted, or indeed even accepted that government computers should be subject to this supervision. In preparing for the Younger Report, the Graham-Harrison Committee had attempted to deflect attention from paper records, but it definitely did not want to forgo the increased administrative efficiency that could flow from computerisation. That those facing the Sieghart-Lyon proposals in 1974/1975 concurred with Graham-Harrison's conclusions became clear when, soon after the October 1974 election, meetings were held to agree a position to be adopted in the face of the white papers. The basic position agreed at the first of these meetings, in January 1975, was that any oversight body established should not inhibit the development of computers. One official wrote that he was "fearful" of such an outcome, while another wrote: "I do not need to reiterate our view that if 'ends' are to be included in the White Paper it is most important that they should not create hostages to fortune for Government computers."[13] Computer applications were "of an evolutionary nature" since they could be adapted to fit new purposes as the need arose.[14] This meant that any oversight of a system might tend to limit its application by permitting it to be used only for the function for which it had been originally registered, thus putting an artificial brake on technological progress and impeding the centralisation of government data through computerisation.

Even the Younger Committee, it was stated, had accepted that the technology could deliver great benefits to society, and since the threats posed to privacy were potential rather than real, preventing these threats (which might not arise) needed to be weighed against the real benefits to be derived from computerisation. The example offered here of such tangible benefits was of computerisation in the service of medical research. Here, it was argued that the opportunities for the increased linking of data offered by computers would be to the advantage of both the individual data subject and society as a whole.[15] This point got to the crux of official opposition to the Sieghart-Lyon proposals, because though much of these debates focused on technical matters, such as the accuracy, completeness and relevance of computerised data, it is important to remember that the real issues under discussion were the standardisation, centralisation and linking of government data. In order to fully utilise this data it had been argued, since at least Wilson had come to power in 1964, that this data needed to be spun into a connected web. Linking data was Whitehall's cause célèbre, plans such as *People and Numbers* had focused on this, and increasingly computers were advocated as the future means to deliver this end.

But if this computerised future were to be checked by the DPC/DPA, then maintaining the ability to link paper records would become even more important. This raised a second aspect of the Whitehall response to the Sieghart-Lyon proposals. It was noted that Sieghart's ends suggested that the data subject's permission would be required before personal information could be stored on a computer. But the point was raised that at least some, if not most of this information would already be stored in manual systems. It was maintained that the sale of credit referencing data, which had been the subject of a recent furore in the press, would not have been prevented by any of the proposals in the white papers since the data was not computerised. But, it was suggested that if the Sieghart-Lyon proposals had been law, they might have encouraged demands to extend such controls to cover paper-based credit records.[16] Additionally, the draft white papers made mention of "mechanical, electrical ... and other devices" and one official saw that this could have an impact on the use of, for example, the mechanical card indexes found in many offices.[17] One broadside against the idea of any monitoring of computer use argued that such measures could only be necessitated were the existing safeguards shown to be inadequate. But, it continued, these were the same safeguards that applied to paper records. Therefore, there was no logical reason to limit the reach of oversight to those areas that were computerised. This was of course a point that had been raised before, it had been one of the main preoccupations of the Graham-Harrison Committee and by pursuing this line of reasoning the writer concluded that the only thing "which will satisfy an informed public" would be oversight of all government data.[18] Not for the first time officials went in fear of the spectre haunting Whitehall: a control regime designed for computers alone that somehow crept beyond its remit to govern all government data.

But even if this cataclysmic situation did not come to pass, those in government were still fearful of the effect of these proposals. The third aspect of this opposition was, as one official wrote from the Treasury, a concern that "we might tie our hands unduly in gathering statistical data which might be wanted for social and economic policies."[19] He might have been reassured by the reply he received informing him that officials from other departments shared these fears and that there was a cross-departmental determination to thwart Sieghart.[20] This considerable degree of hostility led officials onto two paths of resistance. First, there were attempts to modify the draft white papers which will be examined presently. Second, this belligerent attitude towards data protection also underpinned two lines of criticism that went beyond seeking to modify the proposals by calling the whole process into question. The first of these concerned the cost of the exercise.

Unsurprisingly, it was the Treasury that directed fire onto the costs of these proposals. The Treasury was angered not only by the proposals themselves, but by the way Lyon had initiated them. The Home Office had not shown these proposals to their own finance division and had not informed the Treasury that they were planning to publish white papers containing spending commitments. "It may be no coincidence that this issue is in Mr. Lyon's bailiwick" was one Treasury official's acerbic indictment of this breach of Whitehall rules.[21] But, more importantly, when Treasury officials looked at Sieghart's ends they saw vaguely defined commitments to spend money. For example, Sieghart's fifth end would give people a right to know what information was held about them. The Treasury argued that, as it was drafted, this would give the DPC/DPA a "substantial" workload that could only be dealt with by a large staff. However, the draft "contains no detailed assessment of the public expenditure implications of the proposals."[22] In fact, it was worse than this from the Treasury point of view, because in addition to paying the start-up and running costs of the DPC/DPA, the government would also have to comply with any rules made by these bodies, but it had no idea of how much this compliance would cost. This, it was argued, was because Sieghart's proposals were so vague that no one had a clear idea of what criteria the DPC/DPA would actually mandate computer users to follow, so it was impossible to estimate what the costs of adapting government machines might be. It was felt the home secretary might argue that the DPC was an interim body that would not be expensive. But these officials argued that this was not the point at issue because once the DPC had been set up, the government would be unable to back out of its commitment to establish the full DPA. Any move towards realising Sieghart's vision would therefore inevitably incur costs, anyone who argued differently was, it was stated on another occasion, talking "nonsense."[23] The Treasury's position was therefore that the home secretary ought to fund the DPC/DPA by making savings out of his existing budget. In addition to these extra costs on the government purse, there were also the costs to industry. In arguments that foreshadowed those that would be brought out by some ministers after 1979, Treasury officials argued that the whole data protection project would impose unacceptable costs on industry and commerce to the detriment of the economy.[24]

These were increasingly strained times for the government's budget and the Treasury was explicitly looking for "an opportunity to argue that this project ought to be abandoned in the face of a worsening economic situation."[25] In Chapter 3, it was shown how austerity was one component of the argument that ended national registration after the war. Here, in the 1970s, the same economic argument, austerity, was again brought forward, but this time it was mobilised in order to achieve the opposite end: to further the standardising, centralising and linking of data by opposing innovations in data protection. This highlights the point, first made in Chapter 3, that between the early 1950s and the mid-1960s governments increasingly adopted a biopolitical mode of thought as they, regardless of their party, came to view data about people as a vital necessity for the formation of policies that were designed to have impacts on the day-to-day lives of ordinary British people. Thus, while in the early 1950s officials had been able to wind up the National Register by saying that data about the British people could be obtained "if need be" from the census and electoral register, in the 1960s the perceived need was to revive at least some form of population registration.[26] Similarly in the 1970s, rather than "setting the people free," they sought to set up new data systems and to stymie attempts to protect the public against these data harvesting exercises.

The second line of attack on demands for the establishment of the DPC/DPA was a further application of a tactic that had been used in the late 1960s (see Chapter 5) to stall an enquiry into privacy: denying that there was any popular demand for it. Home Office officials wrote to the Treasury on behalf of Lyon, saying that "we have to bear in mind that it is now nearly three years since the Younger Report was published" in which time computerisation had continued apace. As a result "the pressure for government action has grown" so that "the government must be seen to be taking really effective measures." This meant "a commitment to legislation."[27] The recipients of this letter, however, flatly rejected all its premises. They did not accept that the simple fact that time had passed meant that more time could not be allowed to drift by in the same way, because as far as they were concerned, there was not a "widespread public demand for remedial action" to curb computers in order to protect privacy for the simple reason that computers were not really threatening anyone's privacy.[28] This attitude was shared even by officials in Sieghart and Lyon's own department, and thus, in April 1975 Sieghart wrote telling an official in the Home Office that action was "already grossly overdue" but the recipient of this letter underlined this phrase and wrote in the margin "where is the demand? Who is pushing that idea: Mr. Lyon."[29] Other officials wrote of "a spurious sense of urgency" generated by "frenzied activity" that did not even have "a shred of evidence" to legitimate it.[30]

This stalling tactic by the opponents of the proposed DPC/DPA was not simply a combination of bureaucratic inertia and wishful thinking because one official at the Treasury had heard from Gerald Pratt, who had been the secretary to the Younger Committee and had backed the chief statistical officer, Claus Moser's, schemes for population registration and common numbering. Pratt was, by this time, working in the

Home Office, and the writer stated that Pratt had informed him "that the Home Secretary [Roy Jenkins] is said not to feel as committed to this project as he is to the Equal Opportunities Commission, [EOC] and pressure to slow down the pace at which this [data protection] project is being pursued might have some success."[31] Regardless of Jenkins's commitment to the EOC, two of his biographers have commented that he and Lyon had a fraught relationship and that Jenkins was a greater advocate of free speech than of privacy.[32] So there may well have been some truth in the gossip Pratt was spreading. This idea, that the proposals could be successfully stalled, led at least one opponent to contemplate a method of achieving this. It was suggested that proponents of the data protection scheme might have the wind taken out of their sails by the publication of the white papers. This might convince most people that the government was doing something, and so allow the issue to be shunted into the Whitehall sidings and be quietly forgotten.[33] In the end though, opponents of the Sieghart-Lyon proposals concentrated on the other path of resistance: attempts to modify the proposals.

These attempts came to a head at a lengthy meeting held at the Home Office early in May 1975. At this meeting, Sieghart presented the "ends" to officials from 11 departments in an experience that plainly put him in the midst of a hostile environment. A Home Office official chaired this meeting; however, this did not make the environment any more hospitable because he was the person who had scrawled "where is the demand?" on Sieghart's letter the previous month. There were seven other Home Office staff there, but one of these was Gerald Pratt whose letter to the Treasury informing them of Roy Jenkins's attitudes towards the DPC/DPA had been sent only 3 days before this big meeting with Sieghart. The minutes of the meeting show the remainder of the Home Office delegation being largely quiet throughout. In other words, Sieghart was left on his own.

What he was facing was a united phalanx of Whitehall officials none of whom wanted his ends to be passed into law because they all wanted to protect, or indeed to increase, the standardisation, centralisation and linking of government data holdings. Whereas during the Second World War, some officials had been indifferent towards registration and some (e.g. those within the Ministry of Food) had been actively hostile to it; by the mid-1970s, official minds saw data as a necessity. The conduct of this meeting epitomises the attitudes and behaviour of officials towards Sieghart's proposals and runs counter to Edward Higgs's view that there was some "hesitation, or at least ... divided counsels" within the British state concerning computerisation in this period.[34] Thus, whereas the point made by Jon Agar (see Chapter 2) that the state was a fractured entity capable of holding competing views about data was to some extent valid during and immediately after the war, by the 1960s and 1970s minds across Whitehall had melded to form a solid coalition of data enthusiasts. And it was to these people that Sieghart had to present his "ends."

The first end suggested that people should be aware of the existence of computer systems that held their details. The data enthusiasts in the Departments of Health and Education objected to this on the grounds that it might not be possible to state clearly in advance all the uses to which data might be put. There was also concern about how much detail should be provided when identifying the existence of data in a system. But the thorniest problem was what constituted "an individual" data subject. The question was raised whether this signified a person only, or whether the term included organisations. The meeting would suggest that Sieghart go back to the drawing board on this.[35] The second end concerned the public's right to know details about the data itself, such as how long it would be kept and under what conditions it could be linked or transferred. Concern was expressed at the meeting that "people might be more reluctant to provide necessary information if they had to be given what could appear to be a frightening list of purposes for which it might be used," thus putting officials in the "invidious" position of having to refuse to help people who would not provide this data.[36] To get round this apparent problem, it was suggested that, rather than telling everyone about the planned uses of their data, this information should only be provided on request, which would "considerably reduce the administrative burden."[37] The third of Sieghart's ends, focusing on issues such as the accuracy of the data, remained comparatively unscathed, though questions were raised concerning what constituted a "minimum" amount of data and how the phrase "up to date" could be defined.[38] The fourth end stipulated that no one should have unauthorised access to data and since the majority of those at the meeting were there to prevent anyone, including the public, accessing this data, this end was unchallenged. The fifth end concerned the public's right to know if their data had been transferred. As with many other points, the discussion here raised the issue of how to confirm that the person asking for information about the data actually was the data subject. But the most important point secured by interventions at the meeting was that this end would not prevent or limit the transfer of data in anonymous statistical form. This use of statistical data was covered by the sixth end, which was broadly accepted by the meeting. How these arguments changed the contents of what was eventually published in the white papers is reviewed in the next section.[39]

The White Papers

The key passage in the two white papers published on 16 December 1975 was paragraph thirty-four of *Computers and Privacy* because it was here that the government addressed Sieghart's ends. The first of these, that the existence of data should be acknowledged, and the fourth end's stipulation against unauthorised access were both in this passage. However, all his other points were substantially watered down. This white paper stated that the public would have the right to check on what was stored about them, not a right to be told of this information's existence. But even this right was qualified because the white paper limited its application to "many cases" where Sieghart had wanted it to be universal. Additionally, what people could expect to be told, should they ask, was very considerably reduced in scope. Thus, the white paper made no mention at all of the public being told how long data would be kept. Neither did it mention that data stored should be up to date. The white paper stated that data transfers should not occur unless they were "authorised," whereas Sieghart had recommended that they should only occur if sanctioned by law.[40]

The white papers thus represented a victory for those across government who had resisted calls for action since privacy first appeared as a political issue in 1960s Britain. This is all the more obvious when it is realised that the second of these white papers: *Computers: Safeguards for Privacy* was based to a very large extent on the work of the Graham-Harrison Committee. Indeed, this work was so central to the whole project that the main white paper, *Computers and Privacy*, began with a reference to how Graham-Harrison had not found any "evidence to suggest that fears about the improper use of computers in the public sector are justified by present practice. These systems are operated in accordance with administrative rules and procedures which provide substantial safeguards against the realisation of any such fears."[41] After this opening, the white paper listed all the reasons why computers were beneficial to administration and therefore to society, before returning to the familiar refrain that a computer-driven threat to privacy had yet to materialise. Despite this, it added, the government was alive to people's fears and so had decided to set up the DPC to advise it on how to establish a permanent authority to oversee the use of the new technology.

This reference to the findings of the Graham-Harrison Committee blithely ignored the reality of what this group had actually found out about the ramshackle security arrangements for government data stocks and this policy, of accepting Graham-Harrison's report as a statement of fact, was continued later in the paper thus: "in the long run some of the best protection lies in … keeping different information systems segregated from each other."[42] The second white paper, *Computers: Safeguards for Privacy*, repeated this point: "the Government fully recognise that the uncontrolled transfer of personal information, even within Government, is undesirable."[43] This may have repeated Graham-Harrison's findings, but it must be remembered that these had only been produced by Graham-Harrison's turning a blind eye to the truth of the many detailed plans and projections for linking computer systems across Whitehall that were discussed in the previous chapter. However, even this does not get to the heart of the matter. For even if these papers had acknowledged the paucity of data security in government departments and the clear desire to construct pan-departmental databases, this would still have only concerned computers. Thus, if these admissions had been made, the white papers would still not have made any mention of plans, such as *People and Numbers*, to introduce population registration or the common numbering of files, either of which would have spun all government paper-based data into a unified web. Indeed, it is essential to recall that though the government had never wanted its computers to receive this level of public attention, Graham-Harrison was not alone in thinking that once this spotlight had been turned on, it was his job to keep it pointed away from paper files. The importance of paper filing systems across government in this period cannot be overstated. In fact, even two of the greatest data enthusiasts in government circles, Claus Moser and Michael Reed (Reed was the registrar general), were well aware of the shortcomings of computer technology in this period (see Chapter 4) and saw their data plans as reliant, at least for the short and medium terms, on the standardisation, centralisation and linking of paper records and worked hard to keep their plans for such a paper-based data grid out of the limelight. This contextualisation is necessary in order to appreciate the full audacity of the white paper's statement that "some of the best protection" should be rooted not only in avoiding any linking of computers, but also "in dealing honestly and openly with the subjects of the information."[44]

All of this was a result of political decisions the origins and development of which have been traced throughout recent chapters: decisions to isolate computers from the broader context of government data operations and to present the issue of the privacy of computerised data as a technical, rather than a political problem. Given this, the contents of the second white paper were entirely predictable. This focused mainly on reassuring people that computer technology was safe. This safety, it was stated, flowed from the technical characteristics of computers: fewer people were involved in computerised systems than in traditional filing, access to the machines was restricted, not many people could operate them and their data tapes were kept under lock and key away from the machines. Further, repeating Graham-Harrison's findings, and again doing so as though this committee's report represented the truth of what it had uncovered, it was stated that computerised data was also safe because it was governed to the same standards and by the same rules as paper files. Moreover, both types of data were held subject to parliamentary approval and ministerial accountability with a similar layer of democracy being present when data was held in computers operated by local government. This second white paper concluded by noting that despite all this, the government recognised that people were still apprehensive about the technology and so had "decided" that its own computers should be subjected to the same oversight as those in the private sector.[45] Of course, the reality was that the government had not made any such decision, rather the concessions it had made had been wrung out of it when it had been backed into a corner by contingencies beyond its control and this fact is made very clear by what happened to the white papers. For had they been produced as the result of decisive action in favour of protecting people's privacy, then it would not be unreasonable to expect to see some action taken to implement their recommendations. However, the government did not simply neglect to take any action; rather, it made a series of deliberate decisions to do nothing at all to protect people's privacy. These decisions and the manoeuvrings within government that produced them will be examined in the next section.

After the White Papers

In February 1976, Kenneth Younger was appointed to the chair of a new committee, one that was designed to pave the way for the establishment of the DPC. However, he died three months later. The committee was subsequently reformed under a new chair, Sir Norman Lindop, and began work in July. It would report in December 1978 but by then its findings had been so overtaken by events that they were irrelevant. This section will chart the complexities and twists of these events focusing on the impact of the change of prime minister from Wilson to Callaghan.

On 5 March 1976, Wilson made a speech to the Liverpool Press Club where he reiterated his government's "commitment to open government" and offered the press what became known as a "package deal."[46] This was an amalgamation of Younger's findings with the reports of two committees that had been set up, in June 1970, to look into the behaviour of the press. These were the Phillimore Committee on Contempt of Court (its report was published in December 1974) and the Faulks Committee on Defamation (March 1975). This "package deal" offered, with one hand, the carrot of "changes in the law on Contempt and Defamation which would, in the interests of the press and the public, increase the right of the press and broadcasting authorities to comment on issues of public concern," while holding, in the other hand, the stick of "voluntary measures, agreed with the Press, to guarantee the individual citizen and his family an effective right of Privacy."[47] The press had been a political factor throughout the government's considerations of privacy (see Chapter 6) and so the fact that Wilson's speech received "a less than cordial reception" would have always been important.[48] However, on this occasion it was even more so because the real purpose of Wilson's speech was to test for the water for a green paper on "protection for the individual." The first draft of this paper was ready a few weeks after the Liverpool speech.

This draft summarised the Younger, Phillimore and Faulks reports and congratulated the government on the various piecemeal changes it had brought in as a response to Younger. Thus, the white papers on computers, action on credit referencing agencies, legislation to control private detectives and a code of conduct for employment interviews were all lauded. It then went on to note that, though Younger had concluded that relying on the self-regulation of the press to control its more extreme tendencies might be overly optimistic, the government was awaiting another report, from the Press Council, before deciding what to do.[49]

However, any progress towards the type of policies indicated by the draft green paper would have to cross three political hurdles. The first was that both Wilson's speech and the paper it trailed, sought to link three reports that, according to one official, were, in reality, only "tenuously" connected. Second, the press would never accept such a package without a clear commitment from the government to reform the Official Secrets Act.[50] These two points were acknowledged in private Whitehall correspondence, but the third and most important point was soon public knowledge, because less than two weeks after his Liverpool speech, on 16 March 1976, Wilson announced his resignation.

Jim Callaghan became prime minister on 5 April 1976 and after less than two weeks in this new role, as a result of a row over race relations policy, he sacked Alex Lyon who returned to the backbenches (he would remain in Parliament until losing his seat in 1983). Since Lyon was acknowledged as the driving force behind the move to data protection and had also "apparently advised Wilson behind the scenes," this dismissal must have come as a relief to many across government.[51] But the issue of privacy was not dead yet. In July, Callaghan wrote to the lord chancellor, Elwyn Jones, asking for his view of Wilson's green paper. The chancellor replied saying that he would rather proceed separately with the reforms outlined in the plethora of reports, both published and outstanding. The officials who reported these discussions to Callaghan noted that they thought the home secretary would concur with this approach.[52] The home secretary at this point was Roy Jenkins, but he resigned and was replaced by Merlin Rees in September 1976. Jenkins, who had worked at Bletchley Park in the Second World War, was as keen an advocate of computers as anyone in the Labour government.[53] However, Rees's position on the issue of privacy would be pivotal. Until this point, the white papers had been borne by (albeit junior) ministerial backing, and opposition to the proposals had mostly been organised by officials. But with Rees in the Home Office and Callaghan in number 10 this position would change completely.

Merlin Rees had risen to this position riding on Callaghan's coat-tails. He had been Callaghan's junior at the Home Office having taken up his role shortly before Callaghan arrived there late in 1967 (they both remained in these posts until Labour lost the 1970 election), and their political relationship was sealed when Rees organised Callaghan's leadership campaign after Wilson resigned. During his time as home secretary, Callaghan had already shown that he prioritised data collection and the work of the security services over any advances towards protecting people's privacy (see Chapters 4 and 5). Now ten years later, Rees would demonstrate one reason why he and the new prime minister were such close political associates by following suit on this issue.

In April 1978, Rees wrote to his mentor Callaghan, saying that he and the lord chancellor had discussed whether the government needed to publish a white paper based on the Younger Report. He told Callaghan they had concluded that: "it was neither necessary nor desirable to take" any action on the issues it raised and set out his reasoning.[54] He began by pointing out the Conservative government, which had received the Younger Report, had not acted on its recommendations and gave three reasons why the Labour government of which he was now a vital part should likewise not take any action. First, Labour had followed through on a list of separate issues raised by Younger. Second, the parliamentary timetable was congested. Third, and most importantly, action along the lines indicated by Younger would open a can of worms since such a white paper "could hardly avoid dealing with the troublesome and controversial question of whether there should be a general right of privacy."[55] Though the Younger Committee had not advocated a right of privacy, this issue was still in play and any action the government took in granting or opposing such a right would have an impact on a host of other interlocking issues still under consideration, most notably: defamation, contempt of court, breach of confidence, official secrets and the freedom of the press. Taking just this last example, officials wrote that, on the one hand, the press were aware that Younger had come out against a general right of privacy so, were the government to propose one, it would attract the "antagonism" of the media. However, on the other hand, it was "not an opportune moment to come out positively against it" because doing so would impact the other issues. In other words, the government's best policy was to do nothing.[56]

One of the government's arguments against granting a right of privacy, honed during its criticisms of the public's attitudes as expressed to the Younger Committee's social survey, was that because there were a variety of opinions on offer, it was impossible to choose between them and therefore, privacy could not be defined. It was noted in Chapter 6 that this was not indecisiveness but rather represented a choice: a choice to deploy an excuse rather than to act. On this occasion, in 1978, Rees and Callaghan (and others) did the same thing. They refused to prioritise the public's privacy over the other issues and claimed that the degree of interconnectedness between these issues made choosing impossible. In fact, the reality was that government had allowed the issue of privacy to become enmeshed in what Rees called "a complex," and after having done so, it presented this situation as a fait accompli seemingly beyond anyone's control and used this complexity as an excuse to finally shelve the issue of privacy.[57]

A few days after hearing from Rees, Callaghan's office circulated a note stating that: "the Prime Minister is content with the course proposed by the Home Secretary," which meant that nothing would happen.[58] This was the political situation in which the Lindop Committee published its report in December 1978. The following May, Labour lost an election to be replaced by the Conservatives under Margaret Thatcher. One thing these two governments had in common was their attachment to data gathering and a commensurate hostility towards data protection. How this all played out under the Thatcher government will be examined in the next chapter, but for now it can be seen that the Callaghan government had set its mind against developing any further data protection measures a year before this election and eight months before Lindop's report was presented.

Lindop's remit was far more limited than Younger's had been but its focus on data protection offers an insight into the workings of the official mind on this issue. However, paradoxically Lindop's acceptance of this orthodoxy also led it to make several highly contentious recommendations that would be part of the reason why the report would later be rejected by Thatcher's government. This is not to say that had Callaghan's government had time to consider it, they would have reached a different conclusion. Far from it, in fact given what has been shown about the attitude of Labour under Callaghan, it is clear that the Lindop Report was destined to fall on stony ground.

The most interesting section of the Lindop Report was Chapter 29 which discussed what was here called "a universal personal identifier" (UPI), in other words, the use of a common number to catalogue files for each data subject across all government departments.[59] This began by listing all the ways a person's data was identified: by name, by both name and date of birth, or in the case of large systems such as the NHS, by giving everyone a number. Broadening out from this, the report suggested that there could be huge savings in administrative costs along with an added convenience to the public, if all datasets referred to each person by using the same number: a UPI. However, the greatest advantage to using a common numbering system like this would be that "it would make it easier and cheaper, especially with the use of computers, to relate or merge the information about individuals held in different sets of records." However, the report continued, though this might yield substantial gains for administrators, it would "also present a considerable threat to the privacy, and perhaps the freedom of, the private citizen."[60] The report showed how moves towards such a common numbering system had led to protests in many other states. In France, for example, the government had been forced not only to abandon its system for linking records (the system was called "Safari"), but also to inaugurate a data protection law as a result of such protests. Similarly, when the Lindop Report was being written, the passage through the federal Parliament of a data bill containing clauses to introduce a UPI across West Germany was becoming increasingly difficult. There had also been protests against the US government's data plans and even in Sweden, the government was said to be reconsidering how it used its UPI system.[61]

However, Lindop was able to conclude that what Foucault described as Britain's "much looser, Anglicized system" was still intact.[62] Thus, Lindop's report stated that its research did "not suggest that the UK Government has any plans at present to introduce either a population register or a UPI."[63] These had been "contemplated from time to time," Home Office witnesses had told the committee, but as witnesses from the Central Statistical Office (CSO) phrased it, the advantages of such systems "had always been outweighed by objections of principle."[64] What was actually going on in the world of Whitehall data plans at this time will be examined in the next chapter, but for now it is necessary only to point out two things. First, the clear dissimulation involved in using the phrase "contemplated from time to time" to describe projects such as *People and Numbers*, which had been pursued doggedly for over two years with the support of two different governments, and second, the plain deceitfulness of the CSO's claim that such projects were abandoned on a point of principle. However, the main outcome of this campaign of camouflage was that it concealed the truth from Lindop, and the committee went ahead and made its recommendations in the apparently certain knowledge that no one would object, since these recommendations were proposing nothing but a codification of what the committee assumed actually was the current best practice across a Whitehall that, it really believed, did not want to use a common numbering system.

Thus, the report concluded that were a UPI to be introduced, it "would greatly reduce the British citizen's traditional anonymity."[65] Building on this, it counselled very strongly against allowing a UPI to be developed by stealth through, for example, a creeping use of NHS numbers for other purposes (an interesting choice as an example, and given what was seen in Chapter 4 about how staff at the General Register Office had been doing just that with NHS numbers, an example that also showed how successfully the truth had been concealed from Lindop). Indeed, Lindop went so far as to suggest that the DPA should have the power to restrict by codes of practice, the use to which any given identifier could be put. A common numbering system, the report concluded, should only be introduced openly through legislation. This proposal alone would have been enough to cause Whitehall to seek to disarm the Lindop Report. However, doing so would become more complicated because consideration of the report would fall to the Conservative government of Margaret Thatcher, and though that government would share the attitudes of Callaghan and Rees, it would, unlike these Labour ministers, be faced by a new contingency that would force it to do something about data protection.

Notes

1. The Labour Party, *Britain Will Win with Labour* (London: The Labour Party, 1974), 11.
2. *Computers and Privacy*, Cmnd. 6353 (December 1975); *Computers: Safeguards for Privacy*, Cmnd. 6354 (December 1975).
3. When he was first elected and held government office, Benn was known as Anthony Wedgewood Benn. For the sake of simplicity, he is referred to as Tony Benn throughout the text of this book, but where necessary in endnotes, his name is given in the form of the publication.
4. Paul Sieghart, *Privacy and Computers* (London: Latimer, 1976), 60–61.
5. Ibid., 62–63.
6. Ibid., 60.
7. Ibid., 67–68.
8. Ibid., 69 and 73.
9. Ibid., 137.
10. TNA, T 353/141, *Draft Chapter 9, The Government's Proposals*, n.d., ca. April 1975, 4–5.

11. TNA, T 353/141, *Draft, Table 11*, 29 April 1975, 1 and 2.
12. *Draft Chapter 9*, 4.
13. TNA, HN 1/14, Geall to Aylward, 13 May 1975, 1; TNA, HN 1/14, Aylward to Kent, 14 May 1975, 1.
14. TNA, CAB 139/779, *Computers and Privacy, Meeting 30 January 1975*, 3.
15. Ibid., 4.
16. Ibid., 5.
17. TNA, HN 1/14, Aylward to Kent, 14 May 1975, 3.
18. TNA, CAB 139/779, V. Dunleavy, *Computers and Privacy*, 25 April 1975, 1.
19. TNA, NH 1/14, Baldwin to Cairncross, 6 May 1975, 1.
20. TNA, CAB 139/779, Cairncross to Baldwin, 22 May 1975, 3.
21. TNA, T 353/141, Kent to Copeman, 15 April 1975, 1.
22. Ibid., 2.
23. Ibid., 1.
24. Baldwin to Cairncross, 2.
25. TNA, T 353/141, Kent to Copeman, 12 May 1975, 2.
26. TNA, WO 32/21649, *Report of the Committee on National Registration*, February 1950, 4.
27. Cairncross to Baldwin, 1.
28. TNA, T 353/141, Kent to Copeman, 15 April 1975, 2.
29. TNA, T 353/141, Sieghart to Cairncross, 30 April 1975, 2.
30. TNA, T353/141, Kent to Copeman, 5 May 1975, 1.
31. Ibid., 2.
32. Anthony Lester, "The Home Office Again," in *Roy Jenkins: A Retrospective*, eds. Andrew Adonis and Keith Thomas (Oxford: Oxford University Press, 2004), 154; John Campbell, *Roy Jenkins: A Well-Rounded Life* (London: Jonathan Cape, 2014), 435.
33. Baldwin to Cairncross, 1.
34. Edward Higgs, *The Information State in England: The Central Collection of Information on Citizens Since 1500* (Basingstoke: Palgrave Macmillan, 2004), 170.
35. TNA, T 353/141, *Computers and Privacy, Meeting 8 May 1973*, 2–3.
36. Ibid., 3.
37. Ibid., 4.
38. Ibid., 4–5.
39. Ibid., 4–6.
40. *Computers and Privacy*, Cmnd. 6353, 9–10.
41. Ibid., 3.
42. Ibid., 8.
43. *Computers: Safeguards for Privacy*, Cmnd. 6354 (December 1975), 6.
44. *Computers and Privacy*, Cmnd. 6353, 8.
45. *Computers: Safeguards for Privacy*, Cmnd. 6354, 9.

46. TNA, CAB 164/1327, *Speech by the Prime Minister at the Liverpool Press Club, Friday 5 March 1976*, 12; TNA, PREM 16/1855, Cairncross to Neil, 23 March 1976, 1.
47. *Speech by the Prime Minister at the Liverpool Press Club*, 5.
48. TNA, PREM 16/1855, Cairncross to Neil, 23 March 1976, 1.
49. TNA, CAB 164/1328, *Green Paper, Public Discussion and Protection for the Individual*, 23 March 1976.
50. TNA, CAB 164/1328, McIndoe to Hunt, 26 March 1976, 1.
51. Lester, "The Home Office Again," 154.
52. TNA, PREM 16/1855, Hunt to Prime Minister, 29 July 1976, 1.
53. Asa Briggs, "Bletchley," in *Roy Jenkins: A Retrospective*, eds. Andrew Adonis and Keith Thomas (Oxford: Oxford University Press, 2004), 20.
54. TNA, PREM 16/1857, Rees to Prime Minister, *Privacy*, 7 April 1978, 1.
55. Ibid.
56. TNA, PREM 16/1857, Vile to Meadway, 17 April 1978, 2.
57. Rees to Prime Minister, 6.
58. TNA, PREM 16/1857, Private Secretary to Morris, 17 April 1978, 1.
59. *Report of the Committee on Data Protection*, Cmnd. 7341 (December 1978), 260–64.
60. Ibid., 261.
61. Ibid., 261–63.
62. Michel Foucault, *The Birth of the Clinic* (London: Routledge, 2003), 48.
63. *Report of the Committee on Data Protection*, 263.
64. Ibid.
65. Ibid., 264.

CHAPTER 9

The 1984 Data Protection Act

It fell to Margaret Thatcher's Conservative government elected in 1979 to deal with the Lindop Report and this chapter will demonstrate how it approached this task with both a mindset and policies, for the standardisation, centralisation and linking of data, that were, to all intents and purposes, the same as those of its Labour predecessor. Understanding this however, raises a central conundrum: why did this government pass the 1984 Data Protection Act? This chapter charts the ideas and politics that led to this legislation. It begins by examining the opinions of ministers, showing how these were no different to those of their predecessors and, on this basis, it demonstrates how Conservatives did not warmly embrace data protection out of conviction, but only grudgingly accepted it under the force of international pressure.

Following this, the second section establishes how once the government was in this position two ministers, Sir Keith Joseph and John Nott, produced a form of data protection that conformed to their free market metanarrative and which triumphed over an approach to the issue that seemed to have been agreed on within the government. This discussion of these debates indicates how the outcome was a greatly reduced role for the data registrar, and how this reshaping of the initial proposals for data protection legislation jettisoned more traditional conservative approaches to this question.

The last section presents the two main effects the 1984 act. First, it gave government carte blanche to exclude from oversight anything which it defined as relating to national security. Second, the act also

K. Manton, *Population Registers and Privacy in Britain, 1936–1984*,
https://doi.org/10.1007/978-3-030-02753-7_9

achieved its unwritten aim of safeguarding the vast bulk of government data that was still held in paper-based files since these were excluded from the oversight of the Data Protection Authority. By thus focusing attention exclusively on computerised data, the 1984 act realised the strategic aim of governments since at least the time of the Younger Committee: it turned political debates about the nature and purpose of data, into discussions about the technical safety of computerised systems.

The Attitude of the Conservative Government

After Margaret Thatcher's Conservative Party took office, following the election on 4 May 1979, the new ministers began to formulate their views on Lindop. By November of the next year, Home Office officials could conclude that Lindop's "basic approach contained serious flaws" and that "ministers were likely to have different priorities from those of the Labour Administration under which earlier schemes had been formulated."[1] Thus, on the issues of data gathering and data protection, it would seem that the Thatcher government conformed to what is often seen as its general metier: breaking the mould of the social democratic consensus and ushering in a new wave of policies designed around the axis of a free market and a strong state.[2] Though, as will be seen, these views were important within the government, such a perception of a difference between it and its Labour predecessor cannot explain how the politics of data protection unfolded under Thatcher's government because, in reality, her government and Callaghan's were, as this section will first show, in agreement on all the important areas of data policy. Second, this discussion of the government's thinking also observes how ministers shifted from objecting to Lindop because of its perceived implications for national security to what they came to see as the report's constitutional repercussions. Third, this section provides an overview of how this Conservative government came to enact a data protection law only because it was obliged to do so as a result of European legislation.

Two months after officials had noted the apparent difference between the new government and its predecessor, it was observed in Whitehall that the range of ministerial opinions towards data protection could be comfortably accommodated on a scale that ran from "the lukewarm," at one extreme, to "the downright sceptical" at the other.[3] This chapter will not dispute this classification of Conservative government opinion, but it is important to note that this was not something new. As was shown in the previous chapter, it was Callaghan and Rees who stalled progress on data protection, while earlier Labour governments had initiated drives to standardise, centralise and link an increasing pool of government data. Thus, with the exception of a very few ministers, such as Alex Lyon (a junior minister whose brief period at the helm is probably best seen as an aberration in the long-term vector of data policy), the record of Labour governments on this topic was as firmly located on the lukewarm/sceptical continuum as anything witnessed under Thatcher. This similarity was demonstrated across a range of ideas and issues thrown up by data protection under the Conservative government.

Shortly before the 1979 election, officials in the Home Office prepared a briefing paper for whoever would be home secretary after the election and it fell to the Conservative William Whitelaw to read it. This paper stated that "we have a number of reservations about some of the recommendations" of the Lindop Committee.[4] At this early stage in the Conservative administration, the reservation that dominated discussions was national security. Officials foresaw "major difficulties over the application of the [Data Protection] Committee's recommendations to computers used by the police and security services."[5] The police agreed with this, ruling that Lindop's proposals were "unacceptable," indeed the only facet of the report that met with the Association of Chief Police Officer's (ACPO) approval was the section that downgraded the Sieghart-Lyon proposal that data holders should have to tell data subjects what data was held about them.[6] The security services in general maintained that there were two major difficulties with the proposals. First, that the data commissioner and his staff would need very high security clearance were they to oversee the computers used for national security and law enforcement. Second, given that this level of clearance was unworkable, there would need to be both a very wide definition of "national security" and a commensurately wide range of exemptions from the oversight of the Data Protection Committee/Data Protection Authority (DPC/DPA). This would involve, for example, a blanket exemption from the rules of the DPC/DPA to allow any other government body to share data with the security services or police special branches beyond the purview of the oversight body.[7]

There cannot be any doubt that the Conservative government took this security issue seriously. But here again it is clear that this concern was not something new, rather it was a continuation of the policy of all the governments studied here since the 1960s. However, national security did not remain at the forefront of the government's opposition to the DPC/DPA, and though it come back into discussions as the 1984 act took shape, it rather faded from view for the intervening years. In this period, security was superseded by a variety of issues the first of which had been highlighted by ACPO. This was the constitutional position of the proposed DPC/DPA. This body was pointedly and melodramatically described as a "self-financing, non-accountable quango having more than the usual number of teeth and claws."[8] The constitutional position of the DPC/DPA "evoked the strongest comments" from government departments, with the Lord Chancellor's office, the civil service and the parliamentary commissioner for administration being "utterly opposed to a DPA independent of ministers."[9] This furore was produced because such an arrangement would challenge the constitutional supremacy of Parliament. Lindop proposed giving the DPC/DPA power to prepare codes of practice that would have the force of law and carry criminal sanctions. However, according to constitutional norms, "the creation of legal obligations had to be a function of Parliament and could not be entrusted to an independent administrative authority."[10]

This raises the question of why Lindop suggested such a scheme in the first place. The DPC/DPA was designed like this so that it would have the flexibility to respond to rapid changes in technology.[11] It has already been seen (Chapter 6) how the British Computer Society was in favour of the regulation of computer databases and in 1980 it was because this system would be flexible that, according to officials, "many in the computer world" concurred with Lindop's plan.[12] Unfortunately for the cause of data protection, this allowed the government to describe the DPA as a form of Star Chamber, a "judge and jury in its own cause."[13] Arguments against data protection, as has been seen in previous chapters, often brought up such constitutional issues. However, it is important to realise that this government could be as cynical about its use of constitutional rhetoric as any other. Indeed even while this Conservative government was raising the defence of the constitution it, like all its predecessors studied here, continued to produce plans to network its records, contrary to the constitutional convention outlined by Lord Gardiner in 1966 (see Chapter 4).

The previous chapter showed how the dissimulation practised by officials concealed the truth of data linkage plans from Lindop and successfully convinced the committee that there were no plans to advance record linkage. This is in turn led the committee to recommend that what it had been told was the principled Whitehall practice of not linking databases should continue. The report thus argued that if a common numbering system (using what Lindop termed a universal personal identifier, [a UPI]) were contemplated, it should be introduced openly by act of Parliament. However, members of the Conservative government continued to make covert plans to increase the breadth and depth of record linkage. For example, in July 1980 the minister of health, Patrick Jenkin, wrote to his colleague William Whitelaw specifically to point out how Lindop's proposals would inhibit his department's plans. He noted how Lindop had praised his department for using different numbering systems for its records of Supplementary Benefits, Pensions and Child Benefit and further, how the committee's report had applauded the absence of plans to connect these systems. But, he wrote, the Department for Health and Social Security was now planning to use the National Insurance number as a common number for everyone having any contact with any aspect of the social security system, and also mentioned that the Inland Revenue had plans to use this number as a common number for tax records. Therefore, he was moving ahead with a plan, to develop a common numbering system by stealth, in the full knowledge that this was completely contrary to Lindop's recommendations.[14] To protect these plans, Jenkin did not want any data protection system introduced to be answerable to Parliament. He wanted data protection to be firmly under the control of ministers. In other words, the solution to his problem was for the government to undermine the very constitutional principle (the supremacy of Parliament) that it claimed to be upholding by opposing Lindop.

Plans for record linkage systems like these were, as has been seen throughout many of the previous chapters, common within government. Government wanted data about the British people but obtaining this data was easier said than done because government could not keep asking people to provide more information, while popular opposition meant that it could not realistically hope to obtain everything it needed from a population register. The opposition generated by government computerisation and the tangible public fears of a consequent increase of data centralisation, clearly demarcated the limits of what government could achieve openly. Governments had been aware of this since at least the time when Wilson put *People and Numbers* into abeyance but the demand for data for day-to-day interventions had not subsided. In fact, though it might seem paradoxical, under Thatcher's

Conservatives the demand to reduce the size of the state went hand in hand with a desire to strengthen the state's ability to discharge its functions.[15] The state could only be reduced in size by the action of the state: by, in other words, following highly interventionist policies. For example, redrawing the welfare system to force people to behave differently was to be achieved partly by targeting social security fraud, but this could not be done without knowing more about individual claimants.[16] In Chapter 4, it was shown how, under Wilson, progressives embraced the use of statistical data as the underpinning for policy producing what Nikolas Rose called, a "new form of government of the economic, social and personal lives of citizens."[17] Under Thatcher this same form of government, similarly reliant on the standardisation, centralisation and linking of data, would be applied at least as vigorously, albeit to very different ends.

As well as shielding their plans to link the data at their disposal, Conservative ministers, along with their officials, displayed a second continuity with their predecessors because they were similarly preoccupied with the thorny problem that had long obsessed Whitehall: how to keep paper records away from the oversight of a data protection regime. The problem now, under this Conservative government, was the same as it had always been that, in the words of one Home Office official: "the argument against controlling manual systems" did not rest on "logic."[18] This was so because of the obvious fact that the data was the same however it was stored. On this basis, Whitelaw, whose preferred line of action on data protection was to do nothing, was worried that if legislation were presented to Parliament, the National Council for Civil Liberties (NCCL) "would stimulate amendments of a very restrictive kind as well as promote hard their view that data protection must apply to manual as well as computerised information."[19]

This issue, and others thrown up by the close correspondence between computerised and paper-based systems, is exemplified by the commotion it produced in the prime minister's office over the winter of 1982/1983. Number 10 was concerned that plans to computerise its honours and appointments records would have to be put on hold because it seemed that this data could not be exempted from the oversight of the proposed DPA. This material was highly sensitive so Robin Butler, Thatcher's principal private secretary, wrote "we could not … contemplate" allowing the subjects of this information to have access to it.[20] Thus, it seemed that the only way to circumvent this problem was to keep the records on paper. Butler was a keen advocate of computerisation. He had led the team that had installed the government's computerised financial information system in 1975–1977 and now, in February 1983, he vented his spleen on this issue to Thatcher.

> I am afraid that the trouble is the principle that a person can only be protected in respect of computer information held about him. … In my view that is a silly principle: why should people be given access to computer records about themselves but be denied access to manual records? The effect of it is that records which could have been stored efficiently … will have to go on being kept manually, not just in this office but in hundreds of comparable offices. It is maddening to think how that will inhibit the use of more efficient methods of storage and retrieval which computers give – and how much business will be lost to the computer industry as a result.[21]

Thatcher was a sympathetic ear for this tirade. Her government had designated 1982 as "Information Technology Year" and, in her own words, she "took a particularly close interest in IT [information technology]."[22] But where Butler counselled "with great reluctance" that they should acquiesce to the demands of the data protection lobby, her government would, as will be seen, find a way to circumnavigate these demands.[23]

The third element of the thinking of this Conservative government where it is clear that, rather than blazing a new political trail, they were progressing along an administrative and political track that had been well-trodden by their predecessors, concerns their attitude to more general rights for the public. One reason why William Whitelaw was opposed to data protection was that he was afraid that if legislation were presented to Parliament, the NCCL would take the opportunity to encourage sympathetic MPs to pressurise the government to yield more ground. Officials agreed that: "such a step could also lead to unwelcome demands for similar rights to be extended in other fields."[24] Indeed a month later it was noted that it was "unrealistic" to expect that the introduction of data protection would do anything other than open the floodgates to a deluge of demands for rights.[25] Fifteen months later, this panic had snowballed with Whitelaw writing that: "the introduction of legislation on data protection will inevitably raise again the general issues of privacy and freedom of information."[26]

In all of these ideas and patterns of resistance to data protection, Thatcher's Conservative government was operating with the same mindset as all governments over the previous fifteen years. Indeed, the only way in which this government's views diverged from those of previous office holders was in its focus on the costs of data protection, but even here it is important to note two things. First, that any difference between this government and its immediate predecessor was only a difference of degree. Thus, under the Callaghan government the Treasury had brought the costs of the Sieghart-Lyon proposals to the centre of the argument. Second, the reason why there is a contrast on this point between the Thatcher government and the administrations of Wilson and Heath, in other words why the Thatcher government constantly cavilled about the costs of data protection, is because these earlier governments had not had to contemplate these costs. If there had been serious proposals to limit computerisation, it seems reasonable to assume, given what has been seen of their behaviour, that these earlier administrations would also have baulked at having to pay to subvert their own data-gathering operations.

Nonetheless, it is still a fact that the Thatcher government was determined to reduce public spending and that the issue of costs was always at the centre of discussions about data protection. Thus, the government wrote that "it is essential that the additional costs of data protection in the public and private sectors should be kept to a minimum" and Timothy Raison, a junior Home Office minister, was briefed to answer a parliamentary question by stating "we want to avoid unnecessary cost."[27] These costs were estimated at, for example, one million one hundred thousand pounds to establish the initial systems in the DHSS with a subsequent annual operating cost of nine and a half million pounds.[28] To alleviate the burden of this expense, Patrick Jenkin insisted that any system of data protection ought to be phased in, arguing to Whitelaw that: "anything else could involve substantial expenditure in my Department which we just could not afford."[29]

Consequently, as far as this government was concerned, there was a plethora of reasons for following Whitelaw's instincts and the behaviour of Callaghan and Rees, and doing nothing about the Lindop Report. Therefore, this raises an obvious question: why was it was this government that passed the 1984 Data Protection Act? The answer is that the Thatcher government was obliged to do this because of changes in European rules. The previous chapter showed how, across Europe in the late 1970s, protests about government data-gathering proposals had built up a head of steam. Following these, in October 1980, the Council of Europe approved a *Convention for the Protection of Individual with Regard to the Automatic Processing of Data*. This had two purposes. First, to encourage states that did not have data protection legislation to adopt some and second, to ensure that these measures were compatible across signatories thus facilitating trade by reducing unilateral or restrictive measures. It was open for member states to sign from the start of 1981 and Britain signed in May of that year but could not ratify the convention until it had passed domestic data protection legislation.

There are three reasons why this convention was so important for the way data protection legislation took shape in Britain. First, most obviously, because it was this convention that obliged the government to think about some form of data protection. Without this spur, it seems reasonable to assume that Whitelaw's policy of doing nothing would have won the day and data protection would have gathered dust on the shelf where it had been placed by Callaghan and Rees. Second, there was the nature of the issue at stake. This international dimension was important, as Andrew Gamble has shown, because for many British Conservatives the free market was not only a national institution, but also an international bulwark against Soviet hegemony.[30] Moreover, some key Conservative ministers were determined not only to protect this international economic order but also to extend its openness, and this European convention, with its hostility towards restrictive national measures, seemed capable of aiding this forward international march. The third reason why this convention mattered was because it was new. It presented a blank slate onto which ministers could write a new policy, relatively unencumbered by institutional vested interests apart from rival Conservative visions for data protection. Moreover, not only would this policy directly affect a modern and dynamic sector of British business (the sphere of influence of Sir Keith Joseph and John Nott, two of Thatcher's closest fellow travellers in the cabinet) but it could also be presented as defending the interests of the public.

Once this European instrument was operational, Whitelaw's preferred option of doing nothing was no longer viable because without government action, it was stated: "British firms may be excluded from valuable markets."[31] Sir Keith Joseph, the minister for industry, listed the three ways in which the British economy could suffer. First, not passing data protection measures would hit the British IT industry, which needed to penetrate overseas markets if it were to keep up with its international competitors. Second, all British businesses that used IT and traded abroad would suffer were the UK to maintain different standards to its trading partners. Third, it was necessary to harmonise standards to attract international companies to invest in Britain since they would fight shy of having to adjust to a separate legislative framework.[32] None of this was idle scaremongering, in fact four months earlier it had been noted that British firms had already experienced difficulties trading in Sweden where different data protection systems were in use.[33]

For this Conservative government (but not only this government), data protection might best be described as a necessary evil. Indeed, Mark Carlisle, the minister for education, wrote to Whitelaw noting that though proposals for data protection had been accepted within government, this was only because "many people had assumed that legislation of some sort is inevitable, there was no great display of enthusiasm."[34] Based as it was on this very grudging acceptance, the government's discussions on how to proceed sought to achieve a balance between what it understood to be two equally bad policies. The first of these was not doing anything, which would have detrimental economic outcomes. The second was doing too much, imposing too tough a protection regime, which would also have harmful consequences.[35] Striking this balance involved the unfolding of an empirical (albeit ideologically driven) process of political twists that will be examined in the next section of this chapter.

The Government's Proposals

The previous section outlined the ideas that circulated within the Conservative government that would lead to a watering down of the proposals of the Lindop Report. This section will outline how this dilution was achieved by examining the political arguments within government circles during the drafting of the 1984 Data Protection Act, illuminating how the eventual shape of this act was brought about by the intervention of some of the most vehement free marketers in the government, and how they sought to sell this scheme to the British people.

The government's initial data protection proposals, drafted in September 1980, centred on a power that would be given to the minister to decide that certain types of computer system should be subject to statutory provisions that were referred to as "designation orders."[36] Systems covered by designation orders were to be entered into a public register, maintained by the data registrar, that would also specify the type of data held. However, the most vital feature of this proposed system was that designation orders would need ministerial backing and parliamentary approval. In this way, the system was designed to uphold the constitutional convention that only Parliament could approve legislative penalties and so it was based on what was, at this point, the government's most important consideration. Other features of the designation order scheme were that: data on registered systems could only be used for the purpose for which it was registered unless a change of use had been agreed with the registrar, stored data should be accurate and up to date, it should be only as extensive as necessary and the data subjects should be able to check that data held in registered systems met these criteria.[37] Some data, however, would be exempt from designation orders.

Indeed these proposals gave the secretary of state carte blanche to include or exclude anything from the scope of designation orders, this meant that any system connected to national security or criminal intelligence could be removed from oversight at the discretion of the government. This of course is exactly what happened, and in 1987 Home Office officials wrote to senior police officers stating that: "the Home Secretary has a similar interest to that of chief officers in ensuring that the confidentiality of national security data is not prejudiced by proceedings under the [Data Protection] Act."[38] Lindop had suggested that the DPA employ a special security consultant to advise the registrar, but these proposals maintained that such a person would be unnecessary thus leaving all the power ultimately in ministerial hands. Statistical data was the second type to be excluded from designation under these proposals. But since much statistical data, though in an anonymous form, was related to identifiable individuals whose details were held in other databases, these other databases were also to be exempt. The third type of data to be exempted was medical records. These were to receive this classification because it was thought that meeting the anticipated level of demand to verify the accuracy of records would be too expensive and time consuming.[39] Subsequent discussion also suggested that it would be preferable to exclude social work records, because otherwise social workers would not officially record sensitive information and subjective opinions, but rather would keep these in unofficial notes. Therefore, it was argued that in order to preserve their integrity, social work files needed to be excluded from oversight.[40]

It was suggested that some aspects of these proposals, such as striking a balance between the use of civil and criminal penalties still needed "further work," and there was still the issue of phasing in the new system to be discussed, but these were not issues of principle and so the proposals received a generally warm welcome.[41] In fact Thatcher's policy review staff described them as treading "a nice line between Lindop and voluntarism," and the only issue outstanding seemed to be the timing of an announcement of the government's plans.[42] There was some concern (perhaps recalling the fuss ten years earlier, see Chapter 5) that this might cause problems for the census planned for 5 April 1981, but a month after the census was taken the plans were announced by Timothy Raison, minister of state at the Home Office.[43] Towards the end of the following month, reflecting the ideas that had been discussed across government, a white paper was drafted noting that "designation orders will be the central feature" of the scheme and so the issue of the form of the government's policy seemed to have been settled.[44]

This policy had been drawn up and approved at meetings that were held under the auspices of the Home Office. But even while these meetings and the drafting process were underway there was a feeling among some officials that the Departments of "Trade and Industry had not been properly represented" in these discussions and that therefore, the views of the businesses that would be effected by any data protection regime had not been given a full hearing.[45] As a result, over the winter of 1980–1981 the secretaries of state for trade and industry, John Nott and Sir Keith Joseph respectively, worked on their own version of a data protection system. Nott left this ministerial position early in January 1981, and Joseph left the Department of Industry in September of the same year. However, this new scheme would continue to carry the strong imprint of the free market thinking of these two ministers and highlighted their perception of several shortcomings in the draft proposals. The essence of which was that "many designation orders and codes of practice would prove burdensome and expensive to prepare for Government and users alike."[46] The letter bringing this critique arrived at the Home Office from the Department of Trade, but its author wrote that its new proposals also enjoyed the backing of the Department of Industry, the Foreign Office and the Cabinet Office. Since these proposals came with such heavyweight backing, they could not be shrugged off by the Home Office, which duly acquiesced to the Department of Trade's request for a meeting to discuss them.

This meeting was held just before Christmas 1981. Here the Home Office reiterated its belief in designation orders. These would all be approved by Parliament and so would both conform to constitutional norms and place the power of regulating computer use under the control of the government. To this, the Department of Trade replied that these designation orders would be "an onerous and continuing procedure involving lengthy consultations with a number of sectors and possibly even individual companies ... there were, therefore, considerable resource implications for both Government and users alike."[47] Moreover, as the Department of Trade was keen to show, the resources that would be used up by approving designation orders were not only financial, indeed precisely because this process stressed parliamentary oversight it would also consume a lot of parliamentary time.

The Department of Trade proposed a scheme that became known within government circles as "the registrar scheme." Under these proposals, it was argued, no user of data would be any worse off, foreign states would find the British system easier to understand and, above all, data protection would be more flexible: it would allow the introduction of different standards, perhaps set to a higher level if the public were to demand that. Moreover, while it would require a long time to draw up a designation order, which might then soon need to be modified to cope with rapid technological change, the registrar scheme would allow systems to be altered more quickly and with less red tape.[48] This was so because under this scheme it would not be the computer system that was registered but rather the data. From the point of view of those who initiated this plan, its advantage lay in the fact that it would create a business environment more akin to a free market. But, as Andrew Gamble has shown, there is an important point to note here: that in doing so, these free marketers came "into conflict with the conservative disposition to defend existing institutions," which in this case meant an attachment to the constitutional doctrine of parliamentary responsibility.[49]

After reflecting on the Department of Trade's view, the Home Office conceded that there was a need for "a balance to be struck between greater Parliamentary accountability which favours designation orders, and greater flexibility, which favours control by the Registrar." It then concluded that: "the advantage lies with the Registrar scheme."[50] In other words, it did not seek to strike a balance at all rather it gave in to the Department of Trade on what had always been described as the key constitutional point at the heart of the discussion: parliamentary responsibility. But the Department of Trade wanted more.

In January 1982, this department wrote that "we are still disturbed by the scale and cost of the bureaucracy we believe may be necessary to implement your scheme."[51] It now argued that the draft plans gave far too active a role to the registrar. The registrar would be the first point of call for any member of the public seeking information or redress. Indeed, a statement from the registrar that a data holder had been in the wrong would be a prerequisite for any legal proceedings. The point made here was that though it was difficult to foresee how often the registrar would be called upon, "to be convincing the Registrar will have to have a suitably large staff."[52] The Department of Trade was thus seeking a diminution of the data registrar's role. Other departments fell into line behind this plan, perhaps partly spurred on by the knowledge that they all needed to agree to a scheme of data protection that would be as cheap as possible, since ministers had already decided that there would be no extra money available to fund departmental compliance with whatever system was adopted.[53]

In this system, which without any apparent hint of irony was still referred to as "the registrar scheme," the registrar would register data sets on computers, but would not be expected to police them. Therefore, it would not be his/her job to assure the public that these systems conformed to any overarching principles. Instead, the data subject would have a statutory right of access and a similar right to have errors corrected. The registrar's job would thus be to liaise with foreign data authorities and, within Britain, to hold information and provide it to the public: to guide data users rather than to shape their behaviour. The registrar would only be expected to intervene in the workings of data systems in major cases of public interest.[54] Under this new scheme, anyone shown to be misusing data would incur a no-fault liability. The Department of Trade did not argue that criminal sanctions be dropped altogether, "but rather that they should be confined to 'black and white' areas, with reliance being placed on civil remedies in other cases."[55] This was the preferred method of remedy because it would go a long way towards removing the courts from interpreting any guidelines or principles underpinning the regime. Such a system would therefore, conform to the general position of British governments (see Chapter 6) of wanting to keep their data protected from judicial oversight, while commensurately conforming to the neoliberal agenda by obliging citizens to be free and responsible: to look after their own data protection rather than relying on the state to do this for them.

Indeed, it was argued that the sum total of these actions by individuals would bring a powerful instrument, "the sanction of publicity," into play against data users who behaved irresponsibly.[56] Thus, ministers envisaged data users being tried, not in courts of justice, but in the court of public opinion. But public opinion would not be blind on this topic as it would be informed by the registrar's annual report. Ministers wrote that they anticipated that this would be an instrument of indirect power that could shape public perceptions of data use and data protection through its annual presentation to Parliament.[57] In fact, even before the registrar scheme appeared, ministers had publically aired the view that legislative sanctions alone would not achieve the desired aim of raising standards. The best way to do this, it was suggested, was to foster the "development of a climate in which data handlers will come to view observance of data privacy principles as desirable in itself … The gradual development of good ethical practice will do much to ensure that the principles of the legislation are followed in spirit as well as in the letter and … may offer even higher standards and safeguards for privacy than the legislation itself."[58] All in all, it would seem from this that faith in the superior ability of the hidden hand, or the panopticon of public opinion, to construct a data regime that functioned within socially agreed norms, was shared beyond the ministries of trade and industry under Thatcher.

But removing the courts from the process still left a need for some body to adjudicate appeals against the data registrar's decisions. The registrar scheme proposed an appeals tribunal to fill this gap. This would have the added advantage that, unlike the courts, its constitution could be written so as to include technical experts alongside its three lay members and a legally qualified chairman.[59] Its services were to be free to appellants and it would be expected to respect the confidentiality of data users' systems.[60]

In common with all their predecessors, this government thought that the British people really neither wanted nor needed data protection. But it was nonetheless the case that the cause of data protection, recognised in the early 1980s as an urgent commercial necessity, had begun as a campaign to protect personal privacy.[61] Thus, while "on the one hand" government (singing from the same songbook as its predecessors) claimed: "there is little if any evidence of computerised intrusion into privacy amounting to a misuse of personal information," on the other hand it also recognised that there was a "case for reassuring the public on this score."[62] This realisation underpinned a comment that the government's proposals should be redrawn "so as to dispel any suggestion that the sole concern was the preservation and promotion of commercial activities."[63] In other, more modern terms, they suggested that the policy needed to be spun. It was noted in Chapter 7 that the Graham-Harrison Committee gave a lot of attention to what, in this period, was called the presentational aspects of policy, and this awareness continued thus ensuring that a great deal of effort went into the "the presentational advantages" of data protection policy.[64] Consequently, when the government was working out which parts of its data to exempt from oversight it was urged to remember the necessity of maintaining a "balance between acceptance and credibility."[65] It was a fact acknowledged across government that the existence of the office of data protection registrar was, in itself, something that had a "presentational role."[66] Indeed, it was with these presentational benefits in mind that the Treasury agreed "exceptionally" to pay the registrar from the consolidated fund, rather than insisting that it be funded from the Home Office budget.[67]

However, this reassurance was not delivered to benefit the public, but rather to aid the government. The reasoning here was that government's uptake of the new technology was being held back by public anxieties. Therefore, if the people could be placated by some scheme of data protection they would be more sanguine about an increase in government computerisation.[68] These presentational points were all woven into government thinking and when the white paper was finally drafted it began by giving two reasons why data protection was necessary. These were: to protect the privacy of the individual and to aid British business in international markets and, tellingly, these reasons were listed in that order.[69]

Data Protected

The passage of the Data Protection bill into law was delayed by the election of June 1983, but it eventually received royal assent in July 1984. This legislation was a pale shadow of the government's initial plans, but even these had been described by the Central Statistical Office as: "quite different from (and weaker than) Lindop."[70] This is, of course, hardly surprising since Lindop sought to apply a permanent legislative brake to the engine of the government's data machine. Indeed, one of the few things that survived the attentions of Nott and Joseph's departments was the inclusion of exemptions in the eventual legislation. These exemptions to data protection fell into two types, the first of which consisted of those made on the grounds of national security.

ACPO's initial reaction to Lindop's proposals was to describe them as dangerous "draconian powers" which were not balanced by "sufficient accountability."[71] However, by September 1982 they were "pleased to note that the current proposals take a more straightforward approach to the problem and as a result some of our earlier objections no longer apply."[72] The police chiefs were particularly pleased that the revised proposals permitted two things. First, "derogation from the general principles in the interest … of the suppression of criminal offences," and second, exemptions from registration for "data held for the purpose of protecting State security."[73] The police maintained that their computers were already subject to an advanced code of practice and moreover, that their adherence to this was monitored by the police inspectorate. ACPO further insisted that the new proposals would impose operational costs on police forces and was keen that the legislation should include penalties to deter mischievous or malicious applications for access to data, but overall the association was relieved by the work that had gone on behind the scenes in Whitehall to limit the impact of data protection.

Two months later, the government altered the proposal that had placated ACPO. This was part of the presentational effort to convince the public that the legislation had teeth by reducing the extent of exemptions from its provisions. Thus, it was stated that: "under the new approach to exemptions, the clear watch-word is 'trust the registrar.'"[74] This trust had become possible because it was now accepted that the registrar would be content with the broadest generic descriptions of police data such as "reports and details of suspected criminals," and that it was "inconceivable that he would require the police to be so specific as to register a purpose as 'the bringing to justice of the Kray brothers.'"[75] Moreover, if the registrar were to insist that the police reveal operational details like this, officers could appeal to the tribunal. The government was thus happy that while the alterations were beneficial to its presentational campaign, "protection for the police under this approach is considerable."[76]

After the bill became law, the security services sought clarification on how they should respond to requests for data. The Home Office told them that they should simply tell an applicant that: "no data are held to which he is entitled."[77] A certificate of exemption from the home secretary would only be needed if the data subject appealed to the tribunal. However, the issue was more complex where data from other departments were concerned. The security services used data from, for example, the National Health Service and this would be open to oversight but the security service was assured that any indication of its interest in this data would be exempt.[78]

In March 1983, as part of the preparations for questions in the House of Lords, Lord Elton (under secretary of state for home affairs), was briefed to reply to questions over national security exemptions from the 1984 act by saying that "those who keep national security data will not be totally free from challenge or control, even though the Registrar may not play any role in that monitoring process."[79] This accountability came from the fact that the intelligence service was answerable to ministers at the highest level of government: the home secretary, or the prime minister. But this meant that their words were writ on security issues. Indeed, this was literally the case as an exemption certificate signed by the home secretary was, under the terms of the 1984 act, evidence that such a certificate was necessary. This system was designed to be an "effective defence against ... probing" and certificates would be worded in such a way as "to dispose of" matters arising without confirming or denying the possession of any data.[80]

What this meant in reality was made plain by the example of the Immigration Service Suspect Index. This was a confidential list of about nine thousand people who the Home Office considered to be of "significant interest." It was a bound volume and was consulted by immigration officers before giving people, who were subject to immigration controls, permission to enter the country. About half the names were on this list at the request of the security services and the rest were included because they were considered to be "political dissidents whose admission to the UK may be dangerous or at very least result in embarrassment to the government."[81] In April 1987, this ledger was computerised. The Conservative home secretary, David Waddington, saw trials of this new version of the index at Dover East car ferry terminal where it was greeted with enthusiasm by immigration staff. While it was being trialled there was no need for the immigration service to register this system with the DPA, but with its imminent adoption across the country, the implication of the 1984 act for this system had to be drawn to Waddington's attention.

Officials made the case to the home secretary that the index needed to be exempt from oversight by the DPA. This was despite the fact that some of the material in the index was not sufficiently connected to national security to be covered by earlier exemptions under section twenty-seven of the act. The case for exempting this newly computerised data rested on the fact that, if it were listed by the DPA it would reveal the extent to which this index relied on information from other government databases. In other words, this index needed to be exempt to avoid exposing the linkage of government data. At a meeting with his officials in June 1987, Waddington concurred with this judgement and stated that he was prepared to certify this fact should any proceedings arise concerning this system.[82]

Andrew Belsey has described actions of the Thatcher government, where the government alone defined national security, as part of an erosion of civil liberties that was underpinned by the Prevention of Terrorism Act and the Official Secrets Act.[83] Although these actions, similar to this use of exemption certificates, had clear antecedents in the determination of previous governments to conceal the work of the security services, it is nonetheless the case that this analysis is correct. Yet at the same time, given these antecedents it can be seen that the use of these exemptions is hardly anything more than would be expected from a British government in the Cold War period, particularly one facing down large scale industrial unrest and a mounting campaign of Irish terrorism. Thus, what really needs emphasising is the second type of "exemption": the 1984 act only applied to computerised data and so totally exempted paper-based files.

It has been seen throughout this book that, since the beginning of the privacy campaign, governments put a great deal of time and effort into thinking up ways to keep public attention focused on computers, despite the fact that it was widely admitted within government circles that doing so had no basis in logic because the data was the same regardless of how it was stored. Nevertheless, as a result of governments successfully concealing plans to standardise, centralise and link paper-based data this exemption for paper-based records became wound into the warp and weave of the legislation. Thus, because plans such as *People and Numbers* remained concealed, anyone interested in the issues of data collection and privacy, whether they were political campaigners or dystopian writers, saw computers as the main driver behind the creation of a government data web.[84] Indeed the most recent overview of surveillance in

Britain presents the 1984 Data Protection Act as defying the trajectory of Orwell's *1984* precisely because it applied to computers.[85] To restore balance to this misinterpretation, it is necessary to re-state two things here.

First, in Chapter 4 it was shown how, in 1968, even the strongest advocates of computerisation did not see widespread computerisation as possible even in the medium term, and they were right. Number 10 Downing Street was dependent on paper records in 1982/1983 and the same was true for the governing party. In November 1982, Michael Spicer, a member of Parliament and vice-chairman of the Conservative Party, wrote to Timothy Raison at the Home Office, to ask what implications data protection proposals might have for the party's plans to get a computer for Conservative Central Office. He was concerned that party records, including comments written about prospective parliamentary candidates would have to be revealed to the data subjects and that this could lead to appeals procedures unearthing embarrassing statements from the party's files. He was reassured by replies that told him that though this material would need to be revealed to data subjects, it could not be challenged by an appeal because it represented the opinion of the party and did not purport to be a factual record.[86] This doubtless came as a relief to Spicer, but the important point here is that this enquiry was made, late in 1982, as a preliminary to the party getting its first computers. So, for the Conservative Party, as for much of the government machine, the period up until this point, and indeed also for some years beyond the early 1980s was characterised mainly by the use of paper records.

Thus, the second point here is that though, with the benefit of hindsight, the focus on computerised data seems entirely sensible, in the period studied here government was keen to restrict the focus of data protection to computers only and to keep their paper records away from any oversight by a data protection regime. Governments were aware of how the bulk of their data was stored and, in this period and for some years beyond, protecting this data primarily meant protecting their paper files from oversight.

None of this however, is to suggest that governments were content to have their computers overseen, they clearly were not. This reluctance to accept oversight of their computerised data is highlighted by the sluggishness of developments following the passing of the 1984 act. Six months after the act became law a meeting of officials noted that the registrar "was not yet very far advanced with his own preparations."[87] Data users were seeking guidance on how to conform to the Data Protection Act, but their enquiries were not being answered and they were thus being thrown back on their own resources. This might have been because at this stage the registrar did not even have an office. Thus, not only did the 1984 legislation do more to buttress government data than to protect the public from the erosion of their traditional "Anglicized" way of life by the creeping standardisation, centralisation and linking of the government's stockpile of files, even the scant safeguarding offered to the public was applied only in the most lackadaisical manner.[88] Thus, the meeting noted, that it was anticipated that the process of registration would be "unlikely to begin before about September 1985" because the registration forms were only likely to be available in July 1985, one year after the act became law or, in other words, fifteen and a half years after the Younger Committee had been announced in Parliament.[89]

Notes

1. TNA, HO 496/49, *Data Protection, Meeting 3 November 1980*, 1.
2. Andrew Gamble, *The Free Economy and the Strong State: The Politics of Thatcherism* (Basingstoke: Macmillan, 1988).
3. TNA, CAB 139/849, *Data Protection, Meeting 12 September 1980*, 3.
4. TNA, HO 411/46, *Briefing for the New Home Secretary, Report of the Data Protection Committee*, 24 April 1979, 1.
5. Ibid.
6. TNA, HO 287/2353, *Summary of Paper on Results of Consultation on the D.P.C. Report*, n.d., ca. December 1979, 3; TNA, HO 287/2353, *Data Protection Proposals and the Police*, n.d., ca. December 1979/January 1980, 1.
7. TNA, HO 287/2353, Andrew to Shuffrey, 4 December 1979, 1.
8. TNA, CAB 139/849, *A Possible Form of Data Control*, 18 September 1980, 1.
9. *Summary of Paper on Results of Consultation on the D.P.C. Report*, 3.
10. TNA, CAB 139/850, *Draft White Paper on Data Protection, Meeting 28 September 1981*, 4.
11. *A Possible Form of Data Control*, 1.
12. Ibid.
13. *Summary of Paper on Results of Consultation on the D.P.C. Report*, 3.
14. TNA, HO 287/2353, Jenkin to Whitelaw, 26 July 1980, 2.

15. Desmond S. King, *The New Right: Politics, Markets and Citizenship* (Basingstoke: Macmillan, 1987).
16. Gamble, *The Free Economy and the Strong State*, 35; Ian Gough, "Thatcherism and the Welfare State," in *The Politics of Thatcherism*, eds. Stuart Hall and Martin Jacques (London: Lawrence and Wishart, 1983), 155.
17. Nikolas Rose and Peter Miller, "Political Power Beyond the State: Problematics of Government," *The British Journal of Sociology* 43 (1992): 191.
18. TNA, HO 287/2353, Cairncross to Fitall, 10 April 1980, 2.
19. TNA, HO 287/2353, Whitelaw to Joseph, 5 July 1980, 1.
20. TNA, PREM 19/2219, Butler to Patten, 10 February 1983, 1.
21. TNA, PREM 19/2219, Butler to Prime Minister, 23 February 1983, 1.
22. Margaret Thatcher, *The Downing Street Years* (London: HarperCollins, 1993), 271.
23. TNA, PREM 19/2219, Butler to Prime Minister, 23 February 1983, 2.
24. TNA, CAB 139/849, *Data Protection, Meeting 3 September 1980*, 3.
25. TNA, HO 496/49, de Deny to Calder, 13 October 1980, 3.
26. TNA, HO 411/47, Whitelaw, *Draft Paper for H Committee*, n.d., ca. January 1982, 1.
27. TNA, CAB 139/852, *Draft White Paper, Data Protection*, n.d., ca. February/March 1982, 7; TNA, HO 411/47, Johnson, *Data Protection, Mr Price's Question*, 14 January 1982, 2.
28. Cairncross to Fittall, 2.
29. TNA, HO 287/2353, Jenkin to Whitelaw, 26 July 1980, 1.
30. Gamble, *The Free Economy and the Strong State*, 31 and 35.
31. *Summary of Paper on Results of Consultation on the D.P.C. Report*, 1.
32. TNA, CAB 139/49, Joseph to Whitelaw, 6 August 1980, 1.
33. Cairncross to Fittall, 1.
34. TNA, CAB 139/849, Carlisle to Whitelaw, 7 August 1980, 1.
35. *Data Protection, Meeting 3 September 1980*, 2.
36. *A Possible Form of Data Control*, 8–9.
37. Ibid., 3.
38. TNA, HO 411/48, Walters to Chief Constable, 10 July 1987, 2.
39. *A Possible Form of Data Control*, 8–9.
40. TNA, CAB 139/850, Stuart to de Deney, 10 September 1981, 2.
41. *Data Protection, Meeting 3 November 1980*, 2.
42. TNA, CAB 139/849, Central Policy Review Staff to Hewins, 29 September 1980, 1.
43. TNA, CAB 139/849, Johnson to Redfern, 20 February 1971, 1; TNA, CAB 139/849, "Computer Privacy Safeguards," *Times*, 11 June, 1981.
44. TNA, CAB 139/849, *Data Protection Legislation*, 27 July 1981, 4.

45. TNA, PREM 19/2219, Hoskyns to Pattison, 4 December 1980, 1.
46. TNA, CAB 139/850, Coates to de Deney, 16 October 1981, 1.
47. TNA, CAB 139/851, *Draft White Paper on Data Protection, Meeting 22 December 1981*, 1.
48. TNA, HO 411/47, *Proposals for Data Protection*, n.d., ca. January/February 1982, 3.
49. Gamble, *The Free Economy and the Strong State*, 35.
50. *Proposals for Data Protection*, 3–4.
51. TNA, CAB 139/852, Coates to Johnson, 22 January 1982, 1.
52. Ibid.
53. TNA, CAB 139/851, *Data Protection, Technical Sub-group, Meeting 2 February 1982*, 5.
54. TNA, CAB 139/852, Coates to Johnson, 22 January 1982, 3.
55. *Data Protection, Technical Sub-group, Meeting 2 February 1982*, 2.
56. TNA, CAB 139/852, *Draft White Paper, Data Protection*, n.d., ca. February/March 1982, 7.
57. TNA, CAB 139/853, *Powers of the Registrar*, 15 June 1982, 3.
58. TNA, CAB 139/850, *Draft Data Protection White Paper*, n.d., ca. September 1981, 3.
59. *Draft White Paper on Data Protection, Meeting 22 December 1981*, 3.
60. TNA, CAB 139/853, *Data Protection Legislation, Powers and Procedures of the Appellate Tribunal*, 15 June 1982.
61. Cairncross to Fittall, 3.
62. *Summary of Paper on Results of Consultation on the D.P.C. Report*, 4.
63. *Draft White Paper on Data Protection, Meeting 28 September 1981*, 2.
64. TNA, HO 411/50, *Data Protection Bill, Registration of Police Data*, n.d., ca. November 1982, 2.
65. TNA, CAB 139/853, *Data Protection, Exemptions for the Purposes of Law Enforcement* etc., 15 June 1982, 6.
66. TNA, CAB 139/853, *Data Protection, Paper 3, Registration Procedures*, 15 June 1982, 1.
67. TNA, CAB 139/854, *Data Protection Policy Group, Meeting 16 July 1982*, 1.
68. *Data Protection, Meeting 3 November 1980*, 2.
69. TNA, CAB 139/852, *Data Protection, Draft White Paper*, n.d., ca. February/March 1982, 1.
70. TNA, CAB 139/849, Hand-Written Note on, Johnson to Redfern, 20 February 1981, 1.
71. TNA, HO 498/29, Association of Chief Police Officers, *Comments on the Proposed Legislation for Data Protection*, 10 September 1982, 1.
72. Ibid.
73. Ibid., 1–2 and 3.

74. TNA, HO 411/50, *Data Protection Bill, Registration of Police Data*, n.d., ca. November 1982, 2.
75. Ibid.
76. Ibid.
77. TNA, HO 411/48, Scoble to Soden, 21 January 1985, 1.
78. TNA, HO 411/48, Scoble to Holmes, 23 January 1985, 3.
79. TNA, HO 325/551, Chesterton to Gilfillan, 23 March 1983, 1.
80. TNA, HO 411/48, Harrington to Pike and Boys Smith, 1 May 1986, 3.
81. TNA, HO 411/48, B. H. Fair, *Data Protection Act: National Security Exemption, Immigration Service Suspect Index*, 27 May 1987, 2.
82. TNA, HO 411/48, Mawer to Fair, 23 June 1987, 1.
83. Andrew Belsey, "The New Right, Social Order and Civil Liberties," in *The Ideology of the New Right*, ed. Ruth Levitas (Cambridge: Polity, 1986), 171.
84. Duncan Campbell and Steve Connor, *On the Record: Surveillance, Computers and Privacy—The Inside Story* (London: Michael Joseph, 1986), 20.
85. Rhodri Jeffreys-Jones, *We Know All About You: The Story of Surveillance in Britain and America* (Oxford: Oxford University Press, 2017), 167.
86. TNA, HO 411/50, Chesterton to Davidson, 11 November 1982, 1; TNA, HO 411/51, Chesterton to Gillespie, 26 November 1982, 1.
87. TNA, HO 223/171, *Home Office Data Protection Working Group, Meeting 8 January 1985*, 2.
88. Michel Foucault, *The Birth of the Clinic* (London: Routledge, 1989), 48.
89. TNA, HO 223/171, *Home Office Data Protection Working Group, Meeting 8 January 1985*, 2.

CHAPTER 10

Conclusion

Unlike any of the other governments studied in this book, Thatcher's Conservatives were faced with the reality of a data oversight body and became obsessed with keeping its costs to the bare minimum. However, this novelty should not obscure the striking degree of continuity in the fundamental attitudes of Labour and Conservative governments to both data gathering and its antithesis: data protection. Thus, under administrations of both parties going back to the mid-1960s, there were moves towards the standardisation, centralisation and linking of government data through the creation of population registers or systems that used common numbering to create de facto registers. Similarly, when in government, both parties sought to limit the scope of any data protection to computerised files only, and even here both vehemently demanded limitations on what could be controlled and the extent to which it should be controlled.

Though these ideas were brought forward before, during and after the war, they really took off when they came from the heart of government with the reforms brought in under Wilson. However, the continuation not only of this drive for data but also of policies, such as population registration and the common numbering of files, that Wilson's government had sought to introduce in order to reap the data harvest, make it all the more necessary to explain how and why this happened. To do this, it is useful to consider the remarkable fact that the wartime system of population registration was abolished and that this was accomplished against the wishes of its creators, who had sought to turn it into

K. Manton, *Population Registers and Privacy in Britain, 1936–1984*,
https://doi.org/10.1007/978-3-030-02753-7_10

a common service instrument of precisely the same design and use that Wilson's government would later seek to introduce. Given the overwhelming hostility of British people towards registration, the post-war abolition of the National Register allowed the Conservative government, elected in October 1951, to position itself alongside Clarence Willcock as the people's champion. But, the reality was that abolition was effected because those who wanted to keep the register could not marshal a set of political imperatives that attracted enough support from across government to justify keeping it in peacetime. The politicians on the Statistical Policy Committee along with officials across many departments, who in the 1960s and 1970s would think up ways to standardise, centralise and link data, along with rouses to conceal what they were up to, were thus a world apart from their forebears in the immediate post-war years who could not see a real peacetime need for the data the National Register could readily provide. Appreciating this throws into sharp relief the desire of successive governments from the mid-1960s onwards to reintroduce some form of registration and begs the question of what had changed by the mid-1960s to promote such a volte-face? In other words, why did governments of all political persuasions from the mid-1960s want the same data that the post-war administrations had been content to abandon?

In examining the motives of governments it is clear, contrary to the view of the wartime registrar general, Sylvanus Vivian, that this data was not a neutral and objective scientific instrument. Rather it was, at all levels, an intensely political technology designed to engineer changes in the lives of ordinary British people by using day-to-day interventions delivered through social policy. Therefore, it can be seen that an extension of what Foucault termed biopolitics, driven through the policies of welfarism, was crucial in forming the mentality of governments. To put it simply, government could not intervene in people's lives if it did not know these lives, and modern government knows the people it rules as statistical data. Moreover, just as the desire for more power to manipulate the peoples' lives led to a need for more knowledge, so the possession of this knowledge alone was not enough. This stockpile had of necessity to be open to manipulation: it had to be standardised, centralised and linked. Thus, an insight into the thinking of governments allows an understanding of why ministers and officials were prepared to go to such lengths to attempt to get more data about the British people.

However, this biopolitical inclination was a mind map, not a route map and so examined alone it cannot explain the precise course of events that played out from the mid-1960s. Thus, it is impossible to read directly off from this biopolitical mode of thought the details of how governments would attempt to reach their goals, or whether these efforts would come to fruition. This understanding can only come from an empirical, historical, examination of the political forces at work in the country in this period with all their complexities, contingencies, variables and twists (not the least of which was the attitude of the population). Consequently, these plans were tested in the heat of political struggles as government was forced to defend its proposals for increased data gathering against the critiques of the countervailing force of the privacy campaign.

One element of this defence was a series of broadsides and asides from officials lambasting the ignorance of the public. Throughout the peacetime years studied here, the British people remained attached to their "looser, Anglicized" way of life and all the signs were that they did not want to become habituated to a life lived in the nets of government data trawls.[1] Government was obliged to pay a lot of attention to this opposition. But, just as the actions of government were conditioned by the political terrain, so too the form and focus of this opposition was, to a considerable extent, reciprocally conditioned by the political plans and ploys of the government. So, in order to understand how this popular opposition came to be focused only on computerised data, it is necessary to remember that this did not occur in a political vacuum, rather it was a product of this British political relationship and thus it is important to examine what the government did. Opposition to government data gathering and opposition to computerisation rightly seem, from the vantage point of the twenty-first century, to be synonymous, but in the period studied here computerisation was the data gatherers' ideal, not their day-to-day reality. The privacy campaign began when opposition to computerisation in the USA spread across the Atlantic in the mid-1960s. But while the Younger Committee's survey clearly showed that hostility to computerisation was prevalent among the British people, it also revealed that this was a symptom of a wider opposition to all centralised databases. All of this was well known in government circles where it was admitted on many occasions that there was no logical reason to treat computerised and paper-based data differently.

So, the privacy campaigners became almost exclusively focused on computers because of two interconnected processes: the government was able to keep its plans to connect its paper files secret, while computers came to the public's attention. The government did not want this attention, far from it, but once this development was in play the government sought to limit the damage to its data by keeping the attention of privacy campaigners focused on computers in order to protect paper files. Indeed, the government went to inordinate lengths to make sure it achieved this strategic goal. First, it hamstrung the privacy inquiry set up under Kenneth Younger in a variety of ways, most importantly by guaranteeing that Younger's report would not advocate a general right of privacy. Second, by framing the committee's remit to exclude all government bodies and agreeing to apply only its findings about computers to government work, thus excluding all its paper-based records from any oversight recommended by Younger. Third, while Younger was meeting and hearing evidence, it set up a committee under Francis Graham-Harrison to coordinate the defence of its predominantly paper-based data and to reduce, as much as possible, the impact of any limitations recommended by Younger on the use of government computers. Through its endeavours, the Graham-Harrison Committee secured a strategic advantage for the government, because, by replacing political disputes with technical arguments about computerised methods, it was able to move the discussion from a focus on ends, to one that examined means. This reformulation of the agenda for data protection assumed legislative form in 1984.

However, the transition from the Graham-Harrison Committee to the 1984 act was not frictionless, far from it, in fact officials and ministers had to twist through a minefield of political complexities and contingencies. Thus, it was necessary to manoeuvre around Heath's comments likening computerised and paper-based data and then to steer data gathering plans through the Sieghart-Lyon proposals under the Wilson government elected in 1974. The tenacity with which officials and ministers maintained a united front while doing this and successfully contrived to achieve their goals speaks volumes for how attached Whitehall had become to data and how determined was their pursuit of more, eventually leading these data trawlers to safe habour under Callaghan and Rees. The emergence, in 1984, of data protection legislation was not at all indicative of a Conservative desire to stand up for the people's privacy. Thatcher's Conservatives did not intend to "set the people free" in the same way that the Conservative government in 1952 had been able to claim. The 1984 Data Protection Act was described at the time as being little more than "a lot of holes stitched together" and, where the defence of the individual citizen's data is concerned, this is indeed a fair description of a piece of legislation that in many ways encapsulated the fundamental attitudes of ministers and officials to the twinned issues of data gathering and privacy from the 1960s onwards.[2]

Nevertheless, looking at the Data Protection Act from another angle, it is possible to see that rather being a lot of holes, it was in fact a solid firewall, for what it achieved was one of its main unwritten purposes: it protected government data. It did this in four ways. First, by offering only the scantiest fig leaf to protect the individual data subject, while second, throwing a blanket over anything the government defined as being connected to national security. Third, and most importantly, the 1984 act protected the government's data by completely shielding the paper-based records that still held the bulk of government data, from any scrutiny whatsoever. Fourth, and commensurate with its exclusion of paper files, the act presented computerisation solely as a technical issue and thus was able to depoliticise data and launder the government's actions. This was the reality of data protection and this, since the arrival of Wilson's schema of "day-to-day interventions" in the 1960s (or more accurately, since the advent of the countervailing force of the privacy campaign), had been the defensive aim of all governments. But as well as defending data from oversight, governments throughout this period also sought to extend the reach of their information about the population by using a variety of systems up to and including common numbering and full-blown population registration.

This book has been a work of history and as such it has attempted to illustrate and explain these defensive and expansionist tendencies and the contingencies that acted upon them in the period 1936–1984. Given the limited extent of computerisation in this period, it might be thought that the events and processes studied here, coming as they do from a quaint era of black and white TV, triplicate carbon copies and a British embrace of Europe, are of historical interest only and have little relevance for a contemporary Britain where the breadth and depth of scandals concerning the abuse of online data seem to grow exponentially. In other words, it might be assumed that the past really is a foreign country. However, though it is obviously true that, as a result of computerisation, the government now harvests, stores and manipulates data to an extent that would have been beyond the wildest dreams of Sylvanus Vivian or Claus Moser, this does not mean that the fundamental issues of data policy have changed. Indeed given how this book has shown that the paper-based files, which dominated government data in this period, were widely regarded as the same thing as computerised files, this continuity might be expected. However, even with this in mind it is still worth highlighting the extent to which the processes of standardisation, centralisation and linking remain, in the twenty-first century, the basis of government drives to increase both the scope and the malleability of the information at its disposal.

On 4 August 2014, *The Daily Telegraph* published a story reporting proposals contained in a discussion document produced by the Cabinet Office Data Sharing Policy Team the previous April. This was "a radical blueprint to link up thousands of state databases used by schools, councils, police and civil servants." If this project were successful, it would mean that for the first time "the personal details of millions, including their financial history, qualifications, energy use and property wealth [and 'even whether they use a bus pass'] … could be shared by Whitehall departments … without their consent."[3] In other words, it seems very much as though contemporary government is keen to develop the type of data matrix that was described by its 1960s and 1970s advocates as a de facto population register.

In addition to this overall similarity, there are five aspects of this reported plan that clearly echo the events studied in this book although the first of these would seem to suggest that the 2014 report amplified rather than echoed the tendencies studied here. For while, under Wilson and Heath, the Statistical Policy Committee set the pace for discussions on population registration and common numbering it also undertook other work. But the 2014 report speaks of a cabinet office team whose dedicated purpose seems to be broadening and deepening the cross-departmental linkage of data.

Second, while, in the period covered by this book, British governments felt embarrassed by their lack of progress towards population registration or data linking and compared themselves unfavourably to other states, to medical researchers or to local government so, in 2014, government clearly felt that it was similarly lagging behind the trend. The only difference being that this time, the trendsetters (whose "sophisticated customer analysis techniques" were viewed covetously by government) were the retail giants Amazon and Tesco.[4]

The third way that this twenty-first century scheme revisited earlier plans was that, according to the press report, the government justified its manoeuvrings by arguing that they would lead to "a significantly more 'intelligent', 'nimble' and cheaper state." Thus, it was reported that the government would be able to "save up to £37 billion a year in error and fraud if they were able to harmonise thousands of databases."[5] Though the amount that the government claimed this 2014 scheme would save was considerably inflated when compared to the claims made by the advocates of earlier plans, the fact remains that the process was justified in a similar way: by claims that its enhanced panoptic view of the British, along with its imposition of increased fidelity techniques across the state, would usher in a new golden age of efficiency, probity and prudence.

Fourth, there is the attitude of those formulating this scheme towards the subjects of this data: the British people. According to this press report, "ministers are 'acutely sensitive' to public concerns about privacy. … However, it is understood they are split as to when the public should be consulted, and fear the project could be derailed if there was a damaging showdown with privacy campaigners." This fear of a public backlash in defence of "a much looser, Anglicized system,"[6] which clearly echoes the concerns of politicians and officials since the time of Wilson's premiership, probably goes at least some way towards explaining why the report later stated, in terms that would surely meet the approval of Vivian and Moser, that "people may have no choice over whether their private data is shared. The proposals merely say it is an 'option' to discuss 'how best to ensure that consent is used where appropriate.'"[7]

Fifth, and most importantly, there is the fundamental motivation for this scheme. This plan was not, as might be imagined in the increasingly strained political circumstances of the second decade of the twenty-first century, driven by the perceived need to bolster national security, control people trafficking or prevent cyber crime, but rather to push welfare-driven biopolitical policies. Thus, "ministers believe that the ability to aggregate and 'mine citizens' data under a new legal framework will allow them to monitor population movements better, identify troubled families and elderly people in need of support."[8] The accent in this reported announcement stresses new parts of the government's lexicon: "troubled families" and the "elderly," but the language would be understood by Peter Shore and Harold Wilson since in 2014 the government still clearly articulated a desire to intervene in the day-to-day lives of ordinary British people.

Any government must, of course, govern the people. But as this study of their relations shows, when the government views the people as a population and targets policy at improving them, then the relation between the government and its data intensifies. Thus, achieving the heightened goals of day-to-day intervention requires yet more knowledge: knowledge that is standardised, centralised and linked through a population register and this increased knowledge is reciprocally connected to an increase in power. It has been shown here that this power-knowledge complex weighed heavily on the scales against the countervailing power of the people's desire for privacy in the period 1936–1984. Moreover, the presence of this biopolitical drift, along with the other points made in this press report of the 2014 cabinet document, clearly shows that though Whitehall may have replaced its metal filing cabinets with computer drives, the political attitudes and policies that gained traction within government in the 1960s are still very much part of the governing mind. Thus, the words of the veteran privacy campaigner Leslie Huckfield in the 1972 debate about the Younger report still ring true: "knowledge is power."[9]

Notes

1. Michel Foucault, *The Birth of the Clinic* (London: Routledge, 1989), 48.
2. Duncan Campbell and Steve Connor, "The Battle Against Privacy," *New Statesman*, 9 May 1986, 15.
3. Matthew Holehouse, "Whitehall Wants to Share All Our Financial Secrets," *The Daily Telegraph*, 4 August 2014, 1.
4. Ibid.
5. Ibid., 1–2.
6. Foucault, *The Birth of the Clinic*, 48. OWN.
7. Holehouse, "Whitehall Wants to Share All Our Financial Secrets," 2.
8. Ibid., 1.
9. *Parliamentary Debates*, Commons, 13 July 1973, Vol. 859, col. 2023.

Index

K. Manton, *Population Registers and Privacy in Britain, 1936–1984*,
https://doi.org/10.1007/978-3-030-02753-7